THE COATS BOOK OF

SOFT FURNISHINGS

THE COATS BOOK OF

SOFT FURNISHINGS

ELAINE BRUMSTEAD

DORLING KINDERSLEY LONDON

DK

First published in Great Britain in 1987
by Dorling Kindersley Limited
9 Henrietta Street, London WC2
Second impression 1987

British Library Cataloguing in
Publication Data

Brumstead, Elaine
The Coats Book of Soft Furnishings
1. Drapery 2. Slip covers 3. Bedding
4. Upholstery
I. Title
646.2′1 TT387
ISBN 0-86318-176-7

Manufactured in Hong Kong

The Coats Book of
SOFT FURNISHINGS
was produced by Nigel Osborne
38 Welbeck Street, London W1

Managing Editor Amy Carroll
Art Director Nigel Osborne
Editors Judy Martin & Chris Jefferys
Projects Jan Eaton
Artwork Fraser Newman
Photography Steve Tanner & Mark French

· HOW TO USE THE BOOK ·

The book, which covers all aspects of making sewn items for the home, begins with a general chapter on choosing and using fabric and equipment. Each of the main areas of soft furnishings has its own individual section. Here, you will find information and advice to help you choose the right design and fabric to create your desired effect, as well as complete instructions illustrated by practical step by step photographs showing you how to make each item. At the back of the book there is a chapter packed with decorative ideas for the more ambitious, and an illustrated reference section showing in detail the basic techniques used in the projects. Words printed in bold in the project instructions cross-refer to this technique section.

Boxed features
Additional information, tips and techniques appear throughout the book in special sections. Sometimes the information may be purely practical showing the various types of fittings and haberdashery that are available, and where and how they could be used to best effect. Or the box may explain a technique in more detail, or give tips which will help produce a more professional finish. Others contain design ideas showing decorative trims which could be added to the project, or the different effects achieved by choice of design.

Diagrams show the various design options and how different combinations will affect the shape and mood of a room setting.

General techniques needed to make the specific item are clearly set out at the beginning of each section.

Introductory text: At the beginning of each chapter, the different items covered within that section are described as to effect and use.

Fabric amounts and supplies: Each project contains detailed information on calculating fabric amounts, and other items needed.

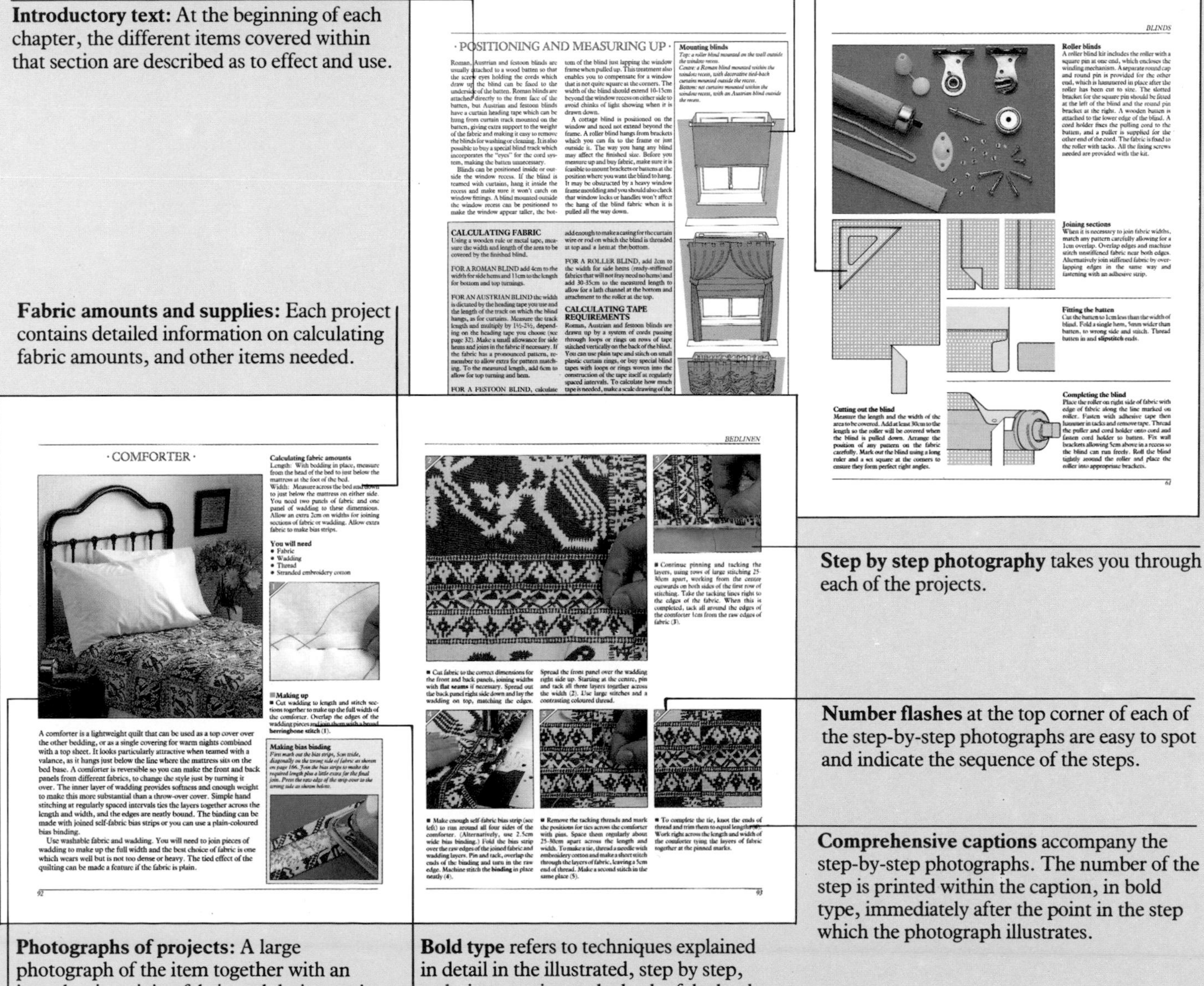

Step by step photography takes you through each of the projects.

Number flashes at the top corner of each of the step-by-step photographs are easy to spot and indicate the sequence of the steps.

Comprehensive captions accompany the step-by-step photographs. The number of the step is printed within the caption, in bold type, immediately after the point in the step which the photograph illustrates.

Photographs of projects: A large photograph of the item together with an introduction giving fabric and design options enables you to see the finished effect.

Bold type refers to techniques explained in detail in the illustrated, step by step, technique section at the back of the book.

· CONTENTS ·

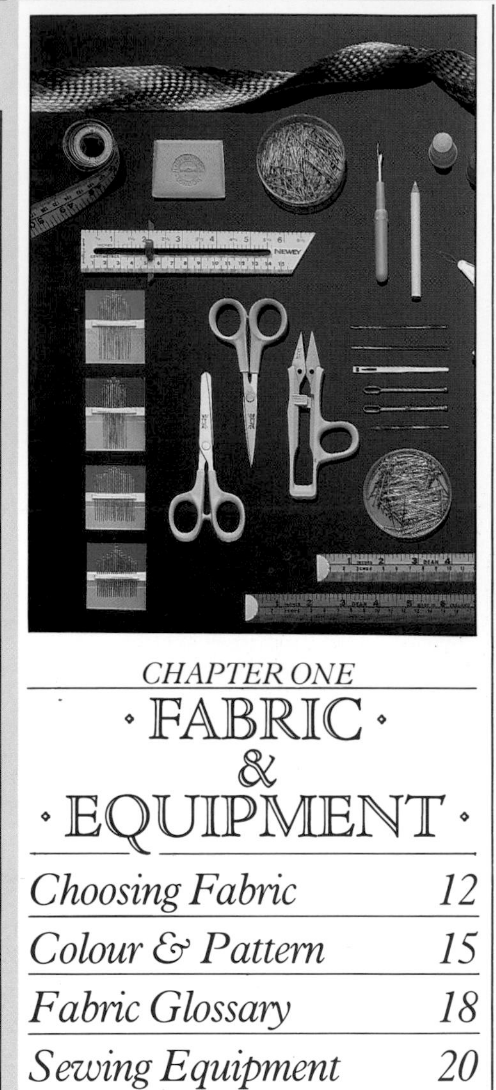

CHAPTER ONE

· FABRIC · & · EQUIPMENT ·

CHAPTER TWO

· CURTAINS ·

CHAPTER THREE

· BLINDS ·

CHAPTER FOUR

· BED LINEN ·

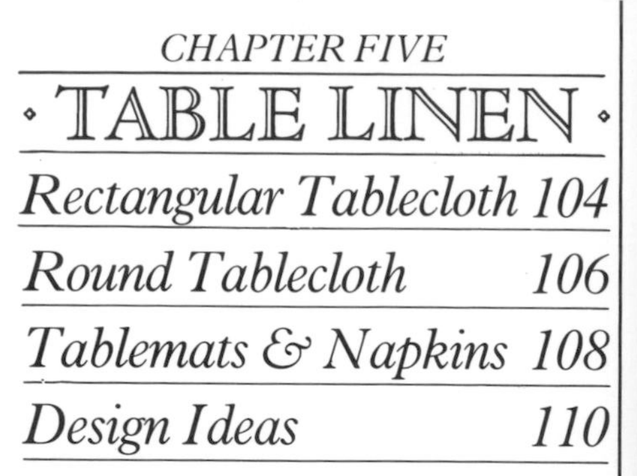

CHAPTER FIVE

· TABLE LINEN ·

CHAPTER SIX

· CUSHIONS ·

CHAPTER SEVEN

· LOOSE COVERS ·

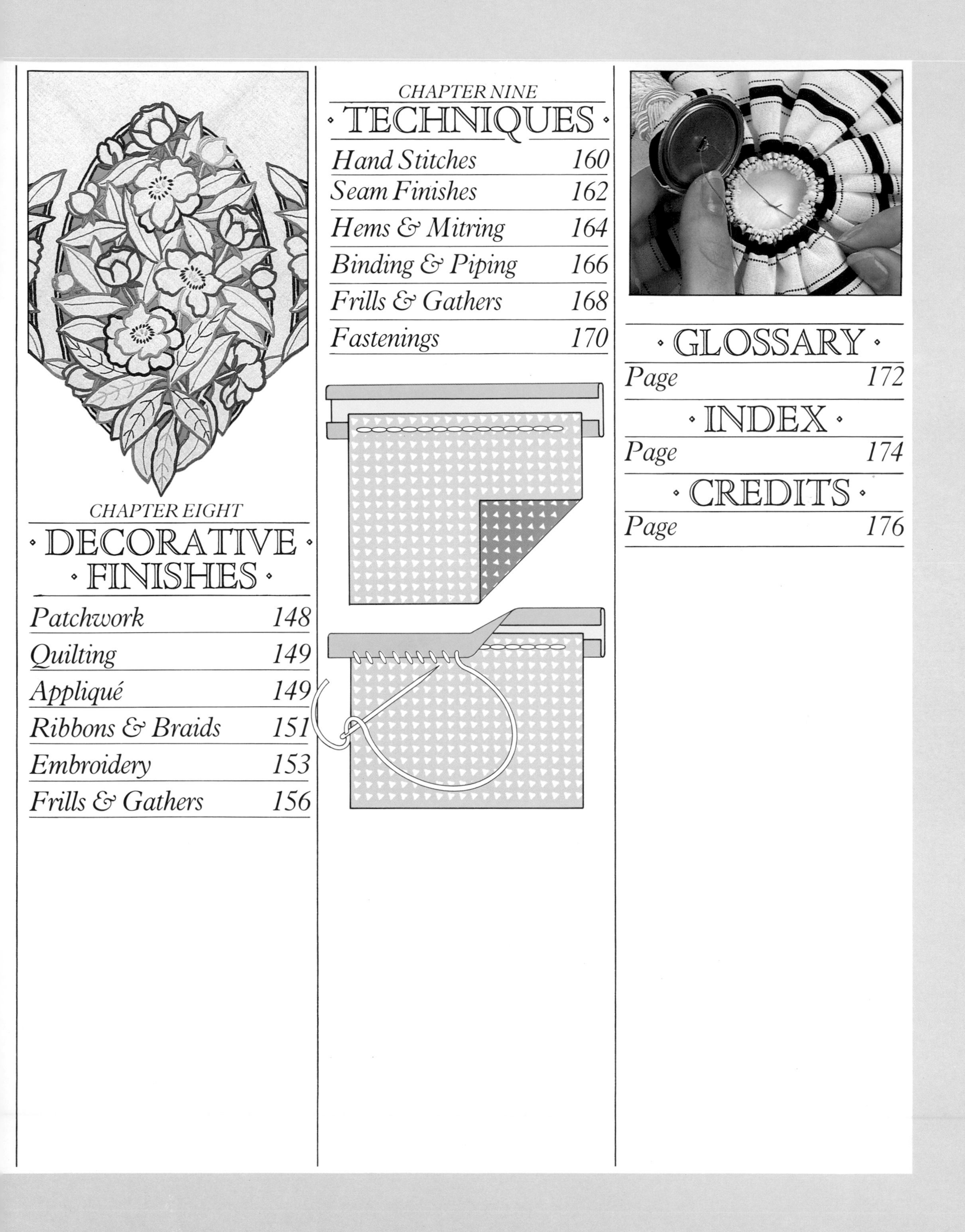

CHAPTER EIGHT

DECORATIVE FINISHES

CHAPTER NINE

TECHNIQUES

GLOSSARY

INDEX

CREDITS

CHAPTER ONE

FABRIC & EQUIPMENT

The choice of suitable fabric and use of efficient equipment will produce beautiful furnishings with a professional finish.

· CHOOSING FABRICS ·

Fabrics are made from different fibres, come in a range of weights and textures, and are found in hundreds of different colours and patterns. This vast wealth provides the greatest opportunity to transform the appearance of a room, but also makes the individual choices all the more difficult. This brief introduction covers the practical considerations you need to take into account and explains the basic elements of composition, construction and weight – factors that should be considered along with choice of colour and pattern.

PRACTICAL CONSIDERATIONS

The fabric you choose should be appropriate in its use as much as in appearance. Many stores now helpfully indicate suitable uses for the various materials, and sales staff should be able to give sound advice. Always read the label on a roll of fabric, to check its fibre content and any special properties. Be sure of instructions for care and cleaning; whether or not a fabric is washable may be the most important thing you need to know about it.

Check that fabrics are fade-resistant, especially those for curtains, blinds and curtain linings. Material for loose covers may also be vulnerable to sunlight if your chair or sofa stands near the window. Stain-resistance is another important property; some fabrics are treated with a stain-resistant finish; alternatively, you can apply such a finish to a made-up article using a special aerosol spray.

Don't try to save on the amount of fabric in order to afford your most expensive choice; it is a false economy and you will get a better effect from being generous with a less expensive material. But do go for good quality, whatever the price range: it is not worth spending time and effort on making up an item which soon appears worn and lifeless. If your budget, or the effect you want, seems to dictate a choice of inexpensive light or medium-weight fabric, rub it between your hands to see if any dressing comes out, leaving the cloth itself rather limp. Check for flaws in the weave or pattern; these should be indicated by a contrast thread marker at the selvedge. Be sure to buy sufficient length to complete what you intend to make; it may be difficult to colour-match fabric from a different roll.

Some fabrics have a shrink-resistant finish. If not, shrinkage must be generously allowed for as it can make a considerable difference to calculation of the amount needed: there may be 6 per cent or more shrinkage on untreated cottons. Certain synthetics require this allowance, too, particularly loose-weave types.

Patterned fabrics are usually more practical than plain, since they do not show soiling so readily, but remember to buy enough fabric to allow for matching of patterns. If you are unused to measuring up, ask the sales assistant to go over your calculations and make sure that the pattern matches are easily made without too much wastage. Fabric pieces left over can be used to make cushion covers and small items.

FABRIC COMPOSITION

Fabrics are composed of fibres which may be natural, from animal and vegetable sources; manmade, manufactured from vegetable raw materials which are put through various chemical processes; or completely synthetic, manufactured entirely from chemicals.

Natural fibres

COTTON A vegetable fibre from the cotton plant. Cotton fabric is strong and durable, even stronger when wet. Weight and texture can be varied to create light voiles or corduroy, chintz or cotton satin. Glazing may be added to enhance the appearance and resist surface soiling. The fibres take dye well and good quality cotton fabrics should be colourfast; they may be given various finishes – minimum-iron, crease-, stain- or shrink-resistant.

LINEN The vegetable fibre of the flax plant. Linen fabric is strong, hardwearing and stronger when wet, but subject to mildew if kept in damp conditions. Crease-resistant finishes are now generally added to overcome a strong tendency to crease easily.

SILK Animal fibres from the cocoons of silkworm larvae. Silk fabrics are strong, resilient and resistant to creasing, but can be weakened by sunlight. Their lustre is unsurpassed and shows subtle or vibrant colours clearly and well. Colours may not be fast and dry-cleaning is often specified.

WOOL Animal fibre from the coats of sheep or goats. Wool fabric is a good

insulator and absorbent, but may shrink and is susceptible to attack by moths. To reduce these tendencies it may be preshrunk or treated for shrink-resistance, and can also be made mothproof and stain-resistant.

Manmade and synthetic fibres

ACETATE Cellulose fibre with wood pulp as the chief raw material. The fabrics are heat-sensitive, absorbent, weaker when wet and may shrink. On its own, acetate is not very hardwearing but it provides good draping qualities and is used in making satins and brocades. It can be given flame-resistant treatment.

ACRYLICS Basic substances include one or more of oil, coal, petroleum, natural gas, water, limestone. Acrylic fabrics have the softness and warmth of wool but little stretch, so they retain their shape. They are hardwearing and mothproof, but sensitive to heat.

CUPRO A cellulose fibre similar to viscose, but stronger and capable of being formed into finer yarns. It is used mainly in mixtures and blends, particularly for good quality lining fabrics.

MODACRYLICS Fibres made by further processing of acrylics, used with natural or other manmade fibres to produce mixed and blended yarns.

MODAL Cellulose fibre made from cotton waste or wood, used in mixtures and blends to modify the properties of natural and synthetic fibres.

NYLON Fibre synthesized from petroleum, used in a range of fabric types. Nylon fabrics are crease-resistant and strong, of low absorbency, heat-sensitive and liable to fade or discolour in sunlight. A number of useful fabrics are derived from fibre-mixes containing nylon.

POLYESTER Made by chemical processing of petroleum derivatives. Polyester fabric will not stretch, has low absorbency and is quick-drying. These, and its considerable strength, are the qualities which make polyester/cotton mix ideal for sheeting and other lightweight print or plain fabrics for furnishings.

RAYON The first manmade cellulose fibres were given this name, which is now less commonly used as it is usual to specify different fibre percentages in fabric under particular names, for example, modal, acetate or viscose.

TRIACETATE A cellulose fibre which is resilient and non-absorbent, commonly used in mixtures and blends with natural or other manmade fibres.

VISCOSE Regenerated vegetable fibre made by chemical treatment and processing of wood pulp. The fabrics are not very strong or hardwearing, but are mothproof and non-static. Generally, they have a good drape and can be made with the appearance of silk, but they also have a tendency to fray and to shrink. Treatments include crease-, shrink-, stain- and flame-resistance. The fibres are sometimes referred to as viscose rayon.

Natural, manmade and synthetic fibres may be blended together in various combinations before spinning to achieve different qualities of appearance and surface finish in the woven fabric. A polyester/cotton mix gains lightness, strength and crease-resistance from the synthetic fibres; the natural cotton provides pleasant softness. Many manmade and synthetic fibres are now made to imitate natural fibres; their processing can provide similar qualities, possibly at reduced cost. Modified rayon, for example, looks very like cotton and has almost equal properties. This is also known as Modal.

FABRIC CONSTRUCTION

The majority of fabrics used in home furnishings are plain weaves, with the pattern, if there is one, printed on the surface. However, fabrics are also woven to produce textured surface effects, self-coloured pattern motifs and pattern weaves of two or more colours.

Weave

Most furnishing fabrics feature weaves that it is possible to construct on a basic loom with no special attachments. These provide a surprising range of textures.

PLAIN WEAVE The simplest woven structure; it may be made in one or more colours and with various types and thicknesses of yarn. When different colours are used for warp and weft, the result is described as "shot" fabric.

SATIN WEAVE More warp thread is exposed on the surface of the fabric than in plain weave, resulting in a smooth, unbroken and luxuriously shiny surface appearance.

TWILL WEAVE A diagonal, ridged pattern of varying effects according to yarn weight and direction of ridging. Traditional herringbone is a variation on twill weave; diagonal ridging is reversed at regular intervals to create a zig-zag pattern.

PILE FABRICS The most common examples are corduroy and velvet. Pile is produced by use of two warp threads: one forms the base fabric while the other is pulled upwards and cut to produce the pile. A furnishing item should be made up with the pile running in the same direction on every section, otherwise a distinct colour difference may show.

• Fancy weaves are produced by special attachments on the looms.

LENO WEAVE A lacy, open weave which may be combined with other weaves, this is produced by twisting warp yarns around each other in figures-of-eight as the weft passes between. This gives stability to widely-spaced yarns forming cellular type holes.

DOBBY WEAVE A more complicated loom is used for this weave, to develop intricate texture, such as small geometric motifs woven in at regular intervals.

JACQUARD FABRICS Produced on a special type of loom invented in 1801 by Joseph Jacquard for the weaving of figured fabrics. Self-coloured or designs of two-or-more colours can be woven. In damask, flat figuring is created by a contrast of satin and matt finishes; in brocade the pattern is raised from a different-coloured background area.

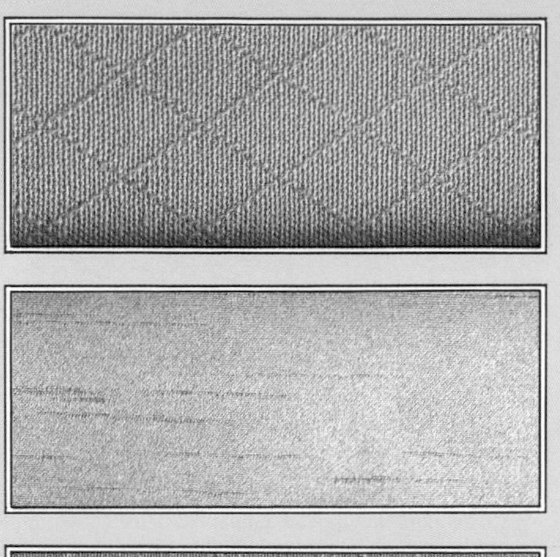

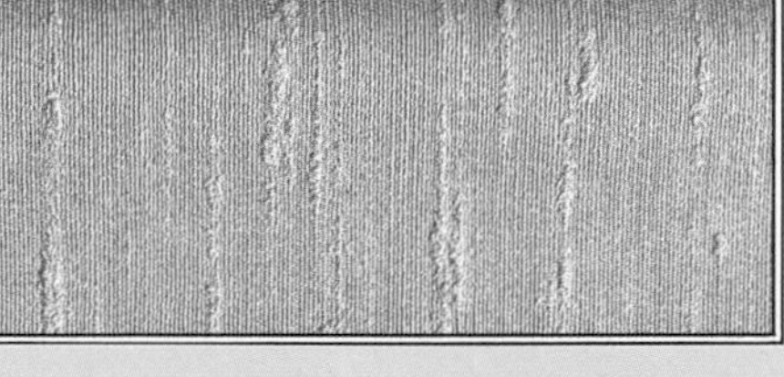

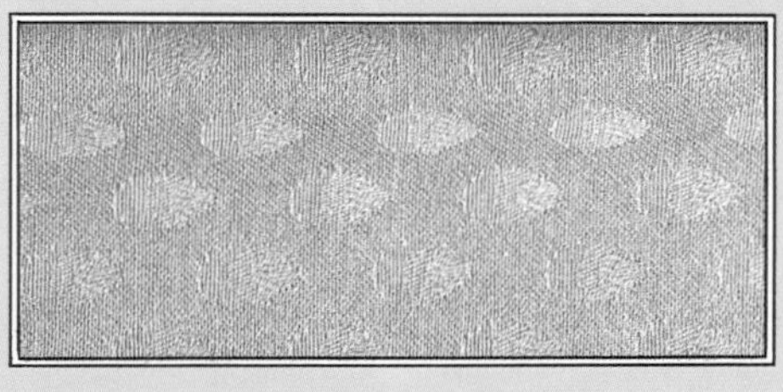

Texture

The texture of a fabric derives from the fibres and the method of construction. Textural variations are applied to the complete range of fabrics, from the finest sheers to the heaviest of natural-fibre materials. Their visual and tactile surface qualities create the atmosphere of a room design scheme.

SMOOTH, SHINY SURFACES give a cool look appropriate to sophisticated schemes. Depending upon the weight of the fabric, this can be designed to complement sleek hi-tech styling, or a formal, traditional style of decor.

ROUGH OR SOFT TEXTURES – matt, fluffy, slubbed, loosely woven – create a warmer atmosphere which may be formal or luxurious, with a rich pile fabric such as velvet, for example, or casual and informal as with a coarsely woven material such as hessian or a heavily slubbed weave.

DISCREET TEXTURES such as fine ribs and inlaid pattern motifs can be used in any type of decor as a balancing factor. The introduction of textural interest is especially important where plain colours are favoured rather than a patterned fabric scheme.

FABRIC WEIGHTS

Versatile treatments of natural, manmade and synthetic fibres result in different fabric weights. It is important to match the fabric weight to the purpose it is to serve and the appearance you require – from a smart, crisp look to a gentle fall of loose folds. Fabrics range from flimsy, delicate materials to heavy drapes, but they are almost all easy to care for and durable if used appropriately.

In general, a good drape in light to heavy fabric weights is needed for curtains; washable medium-weights are suitable for tablecloths and bedlinen; a firm, closely woven fabric of medium to heavy weight is the proper choice for loose covers. Interfacing should be used to stiffen fabrics where a particular shape or firm edge is required. Work out what you want to do with the fabric and identify the important properties. If you use two or more fabrics to make up a single article, they should be of similar weight, otherwise the stronger fabric tugs on and distorts the weaker, or the joining seam may tend to pull apart.

Lightweights

Lightweight fabrics often have a pleasantly translucent quality which lends itself to illusionistic effects. Sheers, particularly those in sunny colours – yellow or apricot, for example – create a welcome warm glow in a living room or bedroom. Fine fabrics of various types show to good effect with the light falling on, as well as through, them. They have a good gathering quality that makes them suitable for festoon blinds and billowing curtains. Beginners in sewing may find lightweight fabrics difficult to handle. It can help to place tissue paper under or between the fabric pieces to help them feed evenly through the sewing machine.

Medium-weights

This range of fabrics is generally the easiest to work with and they are adaptable to different purposes. A medium-weight curtain fabric with insulating lining can provide better insulation than a single layer of thick, heavy fabric. Medium-weight, easy-care fabrics are highly practical for bedcovers and table-linen that require frequent laundering. Offcuts are useful for cushion covers, patchwork and furnishing accessories.

Heavy-weights

Heavy curtains can look positively regal and a plain fabric can be given striking detail with a bold, interesting trim. Tweedy heavy-weights create a warm, comfortable look. A thick, matt fabric used for loose covers will disguise and fill in unwanted lumps and dents in a favourite comfortable sofa, where a medium-weight or shiny fabric will only draw attention to the irregularities. Before deciding on a heavy fabric, think about the work involved in handling and shaping it – machining at bulky seam joins, pleating or gathering on curtain headings. Consider whether the finished effect will work visually and in practical terms.

Fabrics checklist

- *Fabric should be appropriate for its use – robust for loose covers; with good drape for curtains; firm but comfortable for cushion covers.*
- *Always use washable, easy-care fabrics for articles which need regular cleaning, particularly tablelinen and bedlinen.*
- *When budgeting for fabric, choose to buy a generous quantity of inexpensive material rather than risk a skimped effect with a more expensive type of fabric.*
- *If using two or more fabrics to make up a single item, select similar weights and check that they are compatible for washing or cleaning.*
- *Allow for shrinkage if the fabric has no shrink-resistant finish and is not pre-shrunk.*
- *Check fabrics for flaws before purchasing.*
- *Try to get the full length you need taken from one fabric roll. If two rolls are used, check that the colours match perfectly.*
- *Test inexpensive fabrics for large amounts of dressing which will wash out at the first laundering, leaving the fabric limp and lifeless.*
- *Make sure your fabric choice has the finishes – easy-care, shrink-, stain-, fade- and flame-resistance – required for its purpose.*
- *Don't use dress fabrics for main furnishing items, except as trimming or decoration. They are not constructed to stand up to this type of prolonged use.*

· COLOUR & PATTERN ·

Design on fabric goes a long way towards setting the style of a room. It's a message about your personality and way of life, so your instincts and natural preferences are important when it comes to choosing colours and patterns. Fabric choices should suit not only the shape of the room and its furniture, but also the function of the room and the way you occupy the space.

Colour creates impact and many people find it difficult to visualize colour effects on a relatively large scale. This often leads to a choice of "safe" or neutral colours for basic decor, with small areas of contrast or bold focus. A scheme devised in this way can be highly effective, but consider also the richness of a jumble of strong colours confidently thrown together. Vivid and dark colours tend to create a centralized, enclosed effect, but can cloak imperfections of shape and proportion. Light colours open out a room but also emphasize existing qualities of surface and contour – which may be for better or worse.

Although colour may be the strongest feature of a design, it is never an independent factor. Two colours together are mutually affecting; the proportion of one to another dictates the apparent changes they undergo. This principle holds true

whether you are dealing with large areas of plain colour, flat colour with contrasting detail, or multi-coloured patterns. The way two colours react when used, say, for a bare wall and floor-to-ceiling curtains is not the same as their reaction within a small, busy pattern on fabric. So place blocks of colour together when choosing.

If you intend to use patterned fabrics, your thoughts on colour become further complicated by the style and scale of the pattern design. If you decide on blue, for example, as the theme colour, you have a wide and wonderful choice of blue flowers, checks, stripes, geometrics, floral motif miniprints or boldly painted abstracts, not to mention a glorious range of shades from the mauve section of the spectrum through true blues to turquoise and blue-green.

Co-ordinated fabrics may solve the problem, but it can be more exciting, and a far more personal choice, to mix and match from the full range available. Think about the many possibilities – mixing large and small patterns; using the same fabric in reversed colourways; opting for a monochromatic or harmonious scheme, or a riot of paintbox colours.

Combining prints

When mixing patterns, choose a key element such as shape, colour, scale or direction to make a link between different designs, but don't make too many rules beforehand. Look at plenty of samples and allow the fabrics themselves to suggest an individual scheme.

Pattern and texture checklist

- *Patterned fabrics are more practical than plain, as they don't show soiling so readily.*
- *Texture affects the "seen" value of colour, and this varies with change of light.*
- *Viewed from a distance, subtle colouring can merge and pattern detail may disappear.*
- *Light colours suggest an expansive effect, whereas dark shades tend towards intimacy.*
- *Fabric patterns should be printed on the straight grain of the fabric, to give the correct effect at seams and hems.*
- *A large pattern repeat will mean that more fabric is required overall.*
- *When different patterns are combined to make up a single article, the fabrics should have equal weight and "give".*
- *The mutual enhancement or contrast of colours may be visible between schemes in adjoining rooms, as well as within a single room.*

PATTERNED FABRICS may be woven or printed on fabric and you should see the effect of a drawn-out length from the roll, preferably draped or hung if you are intending to use it for curtains. Remember, too, that the effect may be seen with the light falling on or through the fabric, and under natural and artificial light. Check out the pattern repeat and the wastage likely to be involved in matching the pattern if you are intending to make up a large item, such as curtains or loose covers.

MINIPRINTS come in abstract, floral or geometric designs, printed as a small, all-over pattern. The majority are light or medium-weight cottons or cotton/synthetic mixes, though some heavier weights are often available.

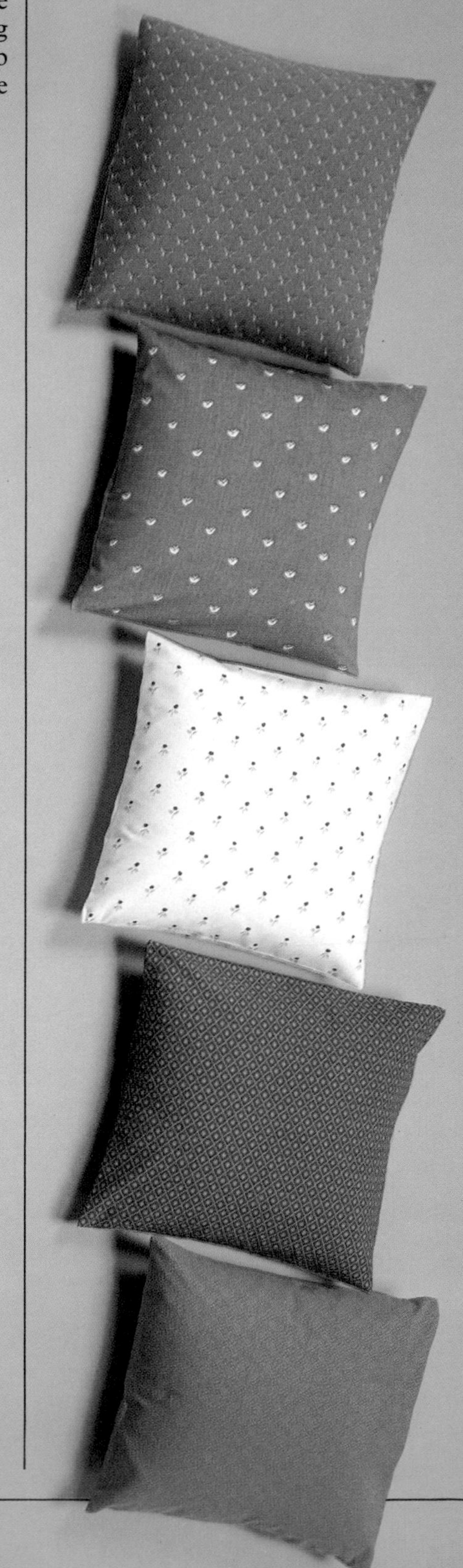

GEOMETRICS range through circles, squares, diagonals and purely linear patterns. A close or fine-lined pattern may lose its identity at a distance and merge into a single shade, whereas bold, large-scale geometrics are likely to have a dramatic effect. These designs are available in all fabric weights and may be printed or woven, in single-fibre or fibre-mix fabrics.

TRADITIONAL PATTERNS are often developed from historical sources, commonly chintzy florals, oriental influences and Art Nouveau patterns of serpentine foliage. Medium-weight glazed and unglazed cottons, heavier cottons or sturdy linen union are available, with designs on a large or small scale.

CONTEMPORARY STYLE is a term which covers a multitude of design ideas – completely abstract, splashy patterns or improvisations on traditional themes. Some of these will in time become classics in their own right, but when making your choice remember that this year's fashion may look depressingly out of place in two years' time. You will find contemporary designs in light and medium weights, in cotton, pure silk or synthetics.

BARKWEAVE A self-coloured fabric with a texture imitating the roughness of tree bark, generally made from cotton.

BROCADE Heavy woven fabric with a relief pattern, monochrome or with pattern and background of different colours. The raised motifs commonly have a silky texture set against a matt base. Fibres may be a combination of natural and manmade.

BRODERIE ANGLAISE A lightweight cotton fabric, usually white or a pale pastel colour, with a lacy embroidered pattern and cut out detail. It is available from the roll, but also in the form of narrow frills or edge trimmings.

BUCKRAM A coarse, woven cotton, heavily sized, used for stiffening pelmets and tie-backs. Washing the fabric removes some of the stiffening.

BUMP A lightweight, thick, soft fabric made from cotton waste, used as interlining in curtains. It acts as a wadding to add weight and body, particularly useful with loose-weave fabrics, and also provides a degree of insulation.

CALICO Plain cotton fabric, firm and strong but rather coarse, sold in bleached or unbleached form. It is used for inner covers or hidden sections of main loose covers and bed valances.

CAMBRIC A fine, plain-woven cotton or linen fabric. It may have a glaze on the right side which adds a little stiffening. Down-proof cotton cambric is used as a permanent inner cover for quilts, pillows and cushion pads.

CANVAS A firm, heavy and robust woven fabric usually made from cotton, flax or jute. It is an informal and hardwearing fabric.

CASEMENT CLOTH A general term for open-weave, sometimes sheer fabrics.

CHAMBRAY Cotton or cotton/synthetic mix fabric made with coloured warp yarns and white weft yarns. Pattern variations include checks, stripes, figuring and dobby-weave designs.

CHENILLE A heavily textured pile fabric made from cotton and/or manmade fibres. Fuzzy yarns in the weft give a decorative pile.

CHINTZ A plain-weave cotton, printed and glazed. Designs are usually traditional, incorporating flower and bird motifs. The fabric wears well, but is not heavy duty. The glaze may wash out.

CORDUROY Fabric with cut-pile ribs (cords) running down the length: the width of cords and distance between can vary, from fat elephant cord to narrow needlecord. It is hardwearing, usually of cotton but manmade fibre may also be used sometimes.

CRETONNE A printed cotton fabric, heavier than chintz, and available with a plain or twill finish.

DAMASK Fabric made on a jacquard loom in such a way that the threads form an unraised design, usually floral or geometric, against a satin-weave ground. It may be a single colour, or another colour may be added in the weft.

DENIM Hardwearing twill-weave fabric, usually of cotton or cotton/synthetic mix fibres, made with coloured warp yarns and white weft yarns.

DOMETTE An open-weave fabric with a soft, fairly long nap on the surface, used as a padded interlining.

DRILL A medium-weight, twill-weave cotton fabric.

DUPION Originally, a fabric woven from an irregular thickness, double cocoon of silk, but it may now be produced from various fibres. Characteristically, it is medium-weight and firm with a slubbed surface texture.

FOLKWEAVE A fairly coarse, loose-weave fabric, usually of cotton fibres, often printed with a stripe or check.

GEORGETTE Fine, sheer fabric with a crepe texture, available in various fibres ranging from silk or wool to synthetics. It has good draping quality.

GINGHAM This fairly lightweight, washable cotton fabric, is typically woven in a combination of white and coloured yarns to form a pattern of checks or stripes.

HESSIAN A strong, coarse and loosely woven fabric usually made from jute. It is hardwearing and informal, but the weave may sag when draped.

INTERLININGS Woven or non-woven fabrics used to add strength and body to a main fabric. Non-woven, bonded interlinings are widely used; they have no grain and may be sewn into the fabric or ironed on by means of an adhesive backing. Woven interlinings have a grain which should be matched to the fabric grain.

LACE All-over lace is a fine, openwork mesh fabric with an applied pattern, which may be made from cotton or synthetic fibres. A wide range of lace trimmings is also available.

LAWN A fine, lightweight fabric usually of cotton and in plain weave, although some may have woven-in satin stripes.

LININGS A wide variety of fabrics can be used for linings. They protect the face fabric, add body and improve drape and should be chosen to suit the weight and type of the main fabric and the use – for example, both fabrics should be either washable or for dry-cleaning only. Cotton sateen is widely used as a lining for curtains. Insulated fabric treated with aluminium is available for curtain lining; the metallized side is placed to the wrong side of the curtain fabric.

MOIRÉ A special "watered" effect which may be applied to cotton, silk or synthetics. Moiré fabrics usually need to be dry-cleaned and there is a tendency for the watering to disappear gradually with successive cleanings.

MUSLIN A plain-weave fabric of cotton or cotton/synthetic mix. It may be pliable or slightly stiffened. Swiss muslin is a type with decorative embroidered detail.

NET A lightweight open-mesh fabric, usually of synthetic fibres but also available in cotton.

NINON A lightweight voile-like fabric, but more closely woven, originally of silk but now usually made from synthetics.

ORGANDIE A sheer, lightweight fabric, originally of cotton but now sometimes made with manmade fibres. It has a slightly stiff finish.

OTTOMAN A heavy fabric with a crosswise ribbed effect. It may be made from various fibres, including cotton, silk and manmades. The rib is formed by a thick filling yarn overlaid by the warp yarns.

PERCALE A good quality, fine, plain woven cotton. It is available with printed designs and a glazed or unglazed finish.

PIQUÉ Light to medium-weight cotton fabric with an embossed pattern effect on one side and a textured weave on the reverse side.

PVC COATED FABRICS Woven or knitted fabrics used as a backing for a topcoat of polyvinyl chloride, a tough, non-porous finish. The coating can be wiped clean.

REPP A strong, fairly heavy, closely-woven fabric with a prominent horizontal rib, made from cotton, worsted or sometimes synthetic fibres.

SATEEN Cotton fabric with a satinized finish, widely used as curtain lining and available in an excellent range of colours as well as neutral and white.

SATIN The term refers to a type of weave and a silk, cotton or manmade-fibre fabric constructed with this type of weave. The right side is smooth and shiny, the reverse side matt. It is available in different weights and sheens.

SEERSUCKER A cotton or manmade-fibre fabric with a puckered texture, often embossed in stripes. A printed pattern may also be imposed. The fabric is washable but should not be ironed, unless it has a glazed finish when dry cleaning only is probably recommended.

SHANTUNG A medium-weight slubbed fabric, originally of silk but now usually of synthetic fibres.

SHEETING Plain-weave linen, cotton or more commonly polyester/cotton mix fabric of a weight suitable for sheets and other bedlinen. For this purpose it is available in a larger-than-standard width and in a range of colours and printed patterns including co-ordinating prints and plains.

TAFFETA A crisp, close-weave fabric with a slight weft-direction rib, originally of silk but now commonly made with synthetic fibres.

TICKING A closely woven cotton fabric with plain or twill finish, which may be a single colour or striped. Traditionally used for the inner covers of cushions and pillows, the informal effect can be attractive for simple, hardwearing furnishings in a functional scheme.

TWILL A form of weave which creates diagonal lines within a fabric. This adds slightly to the thickness and gives a firm surface texture.

UNION A name given to fabrics which consist of mixed fibres in the yarn or cloth. Cotton and linen unions are robust and hard-wearing fabrics.

VELOUR A warm, heavy fabric with a thick pile, made of cotton, wool or synthetic fibres.

VELVET A cut-pile fabric made from silk, cotton or synthetic fibres, available in medium or heavy furnishing weights which are usually for dry-cleaning only. A "with nap" fabric.

VOILE A crisp but lightweight, open-textured fabric, made from cotton, synthetic or wool fibres.

WADDING A bonded-fibre filling, commonly of polyester which provides the most versatile, easy-care qualities. Wadding is available in various thicknesses, usually defined by weight, and creates a padded effect in interlining and quilting.

WORSTED A combed wool yarn or woollen fabric. The fabric is hardwearing with a smooth surface texture.

· SEWING EQUIPMENT ·

The first requirement is a good workspace in which to cut out and sew. If you intend to do a lot of sewing, especially for home furnishings projects which may involve large sections of fabric being cut and long seams matched, a sewing area set apart for the task saves time and effort. Ideally, reserve part or all of a spare room in the house. Install open shelving or a shelved cupboard where you can store all your items of sewing equipment together, so they can be kept in good condition ready for use as required. If you cannot allow space for a permanent sewing area, at least keep all your sewing equipment stored in one place near a table and area of floor which you can clear quickly when you want to start work.

Choose a sewing area with good natural light, if possible, and have suitable artificial lighting available. Fluorescent tubes shed a strong, even light: if you prefer lamps, arrange them to illuminate the workspace clearly, casting the minimum of shadow. The area must have convenient electrical sockets to supply lamps, sewing machine and iron. Adaptors and extension leads are useful if sockets are limited, but take care that you cannot accidentally cut or trip over the flexes – and don't overload a single socket.

As well as a permanent storage area for equipment, keep a portable sewing box handy for close work or fitting of the item *in situ*. Do a regular stock check of items in continual use to make sure you have everything to hand.

CUTTING EQUIPMENT

Cutting out fabric with poor scissors is hard work and leads to inaccuracies which will ultimately show up in the hang or fit of the finished item. Have two pairs of good scissors – one used only for cutting out fabric and the other for close cutting when making up. Keep these separate from household scissors so the blades do not become blunted by general use.

When choosing scissors, take along fabric pieces of different weights and ask if it is possible to test before buying. If scissors are sold in sealed packaging, a sample pair may be available for testing. Check that they not only perform the task of cutting efficiently, but also are well-contoured and feel comfortable in your hand, for straight cutting, curves and corners.

DRESSMAKER'S (SIDEBENT) SCISSORS are large and suitably weighted for cutting out fabric. Sidebent means that the lower blade is designed to lie flat on the work surface while the upper blade moves to cut the fabric. They are usually made of stainless steel which will not rust. They should be strongly made but not too heavy, cutting with precision along the whole length, including the point, with a firm but easy movement; 20 to 25cm is a suitable length. Lefthanded and "ambidextrous" models are now widely available.

NEEDLEWORK (EMBROIDERY) SCISSORS are small, about 12 to 14cm long. They are sharp at the point and cut with a clean, quick action for trimming or clipping threads and seams, for cutting into confined areas or following intricate shaping. The blades are of stainless steel but many types have a brightly coloured plastic coating on the handles, comfortable to manage and easy to identify among other items in your sewing kit.

ELECTRIC SCISSORS are either mains or battery operated; you may find the cordless type more easily manipulable. They have short blades set in a smooth, bulb-shaped handle which fits neatly into the hand. Test them before buying, as some types are not useful for fine or bulky fabrics, though they deal efficiently with the range of medium-weight materials.

PINKING SHEARS are more useful in dressmaking than for soft furnishings but can be used on small items, to trim seam allowances on non-fraying fabric as an alternative to overcasting. The shears should be used for neatening seams after sewing, not for initial cutting out.

A SEAM RIPPER is indispensible for quick unpicking of seams, a small, sharply curved blade with a long and short point, fixed in a narrow plastic handle. It is provided with a slot-on plastic cover which should be used to protect the tool when it is not in use.

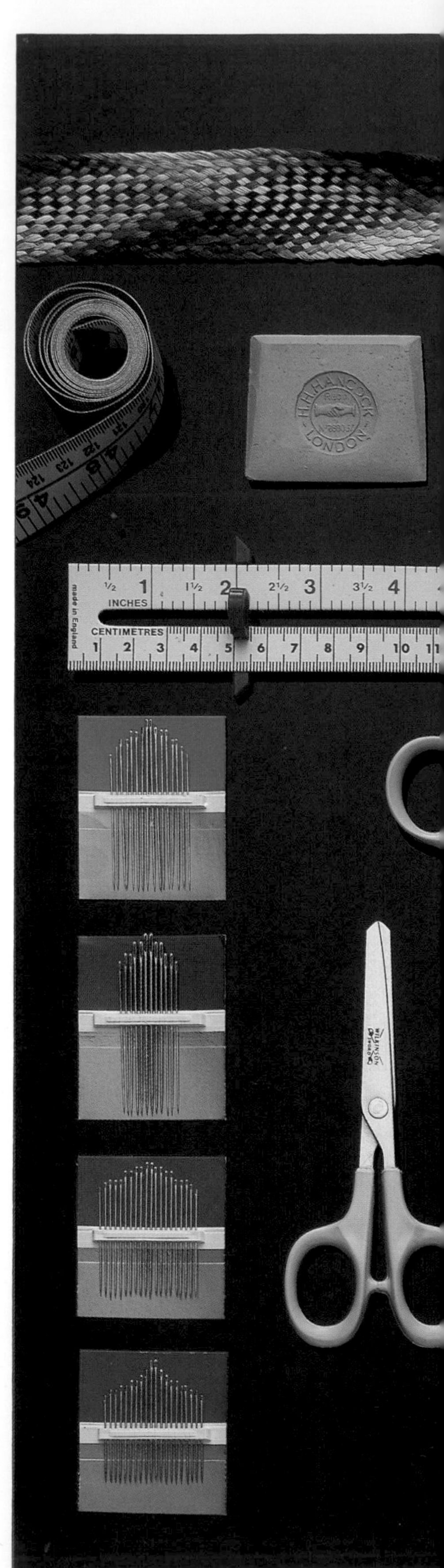

WILKINSON SWORD
WILKINSON SWORD
WILKINSON SWORD
NEWEY
INCHES DEAN MADE IN ENGLAND HOME SEWING AID ONLY
CMS
INCHES DEAN MADE IN ENGLAND HOME SEWING AID ONLY
CMS

MEASURING AND MARKING EQUIPMENT

These items are also essential for accurate cutting: faulty measuring may lead to wastage of fabric and a pair of curtains, for example, has a distinctly "home-made" look if hems and headings are not equal.

METRE STICK Use this long rule to get accurate measurements when marking out fabric for curtains; it's easier to handle than a tape measure and cannot stretch.

TAPE MEASURE A fibreglass or linen measure is best. A flexible measuring tape gives easy movement around corners and curves and either of these types will stretch only minimally, whereas a plastic tape may stretch enough to distort the measurements after a lot of use.

RETRACTIBLE STEEL MEASURE This has enough flexibility to allow accurate checking of measurements for chair or bed covers and a good length for double-checking markings on large fabric pieces.

TRANSPARENT RULER A useful measure for short seams, its transparency is an advantage in accurate positioning and pattern matching.

SET SQUARE You will find this a valuable addition to basic equipment when making loose covers or curtains. The right angle allows you to check corners and folds on or across the straight grain of the fabric.

SEWING GAUGE This specialist item is a rule with a sliding marker, used to fix measurements for pleats, scallops, and trimmings.

GRAPH PAPER If you need to draw up a pattern, squared paper makes the task more simple and accurate.

TAILOR'S CHALK This is sold in flat pieces or in pencil form. The pencil type usually has a small brush fitted at the top for removing chalk marks if you make an error. Chalk is sold in several colours and it is useful to keep at least two, to show up on dark and light fabrics.

WATER-SOLUBLE MARKER An alternative to tailor's chalk is a fabric marker with colouring designed to rinse out easily in water.

SEWING AIDS

THREADER If you find it difficult to thread fine needles, this little gadget is a useful, inexpensive investment. A fine metal, looped filament passes through the needle eye; the thread is slotted into the loop and drawn back through the needle.

THIMBLE A useful but often ignored sewing aid, it is invaluable when you are dealing with a tough fabric or with several heavy layers.

PINS You can choose the plain stainless steel type, or larger glass-headed pins, which are easily identifiable. Ballpoint pins are available for use with knit fabrics. Don't use pins on leather or suede; keep the edges together with small pieces of adhesive tape on the wrong side.

Make sure you have sufficient pins when starting a big project. Keep them together in a box and don't use any that are rusted or bent. Don't leave them too long in the fabric as they may cause marking. A pincushion makes them more accessible while you are working; a magnet is a handy device for picking up spilled pins.

BASTING ADHESIVE Special fabric adhesive, usually sold in stick form, is a quick and easy way to turn up a hem on lightweight fabric before you finally stitch it in place.

NEEDLES

Although the hard work of seaming and stitching heading tapes is best done by machine, various stages of making up involve careful hand sewing. Keep a good range of needles for tacking, finishing and adding decorative detail; a clumsy needle will wreck a fine fabric, while a small, sharp needle is difficult to manipulate through heavyweight fabric.

Hand sewing needles are classified according to length, point and eye-shape. Thicknesses vary from 1 (thickest) to 12 (finest), depending on type.

SHARPS Long and oval-eyed, for general domestic sewing.

BETWEENS Similar to sharps but shorter, used for quilting and other hand-stitching on medium and heavier weight fabrics.

STRAW/MILLINER'S NEEDLES Similar to sharps but longer, used for tacking and other stitching where extra length is an advantage.

CREWEL/EMBROIDERY NEEDLES The same length as sharps, but with a longer eye to simplify threading with stranded embroidery threads.

DARNERS Longer than crewels, easily threaded with wool or cotton yarns.

BODKIN A blunt, long-eyed, thick needle, used to thread cord, ribbon, elastic or tape through a casing.

UPHOLSTERY, MATTRESS AND LAMPSHADE NEEDLES Curved needles designed to cope with specific tasks; each type features an extra-long eye.

BALLPOINT NEEDLES Specially designed for use with knit fabrics, these push apart the fibres and do not damage the texture of the fabric.

GLOVERS Essential for sewing suede, leather or PVC, the triangular, three-edged point penetrates a dense, resistant fabric with ease.

TAPESTRY NEEDLES Thick, large-eyed, blunt needles designed for tapestry and needlepoint embroidery, but can also be used for counted-thread cross stitch and threading ribbon or elastic.

PRESSING EQUIPMENT

Pressing is an important part of home-sewing projects – to flatten and smooth out seams and hems as you go along and to give a crisp, professional look to the finished item. Equip yourself with a steam or steam-and-spray iron; it's not the weight of the iron but the heat and moisture which take out the creases. Ask for pressing instructions as well as washing and cleaning advice when you purchase fabric. Match any symbol markings on the fabric label to the settings on your iron. A non-stick coating on the soleplate of the iron gives easy movement over the fabric; take care not to press any pinned areas as the pins could damage the coating.

Choose an ironing board or table of suitable height and width – a pull-out sheet rail, available on some models, is very handy for pressing large items, keeping them flat and clear of the floor.

A muslin or soft cotton cloth, slightly dampened, protects the surface of the fabric while it is pressed, although some steam irons can be used without a pressing cloth. A piece of light, firm woollen cloth, again made lightly damp, prevents the flattening of woollen fabric. Wash out the cloth before use to remove any dressing. It can be kept damp during pressing by sprinkling with water – a plant-mister spray is an inexpensive but invaluable accessory for this purpose. When pressing pleats, use brown paper under the folds to prevent depressions pressing into the fabric underneath.

If the soleplate of the iron picks up a deposit from dressing in fabric, periodic use of a proprietary brand cleaner, usually sold in stick form, helps to restore "slide" to an iron that has developed a tendency to drag on the fabric.

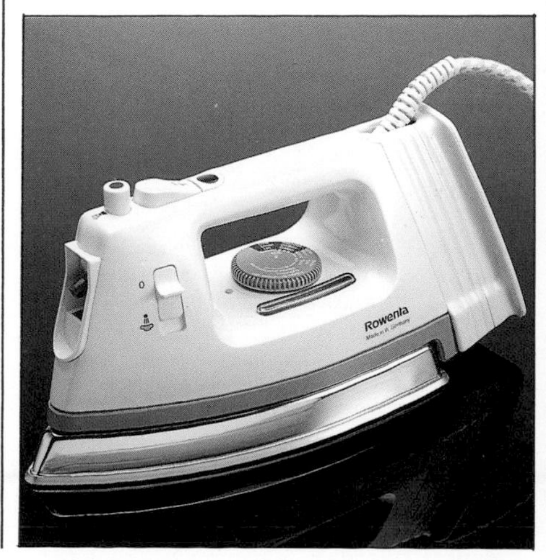

THREADS

Thread should be chosen individually for each project to suit the weight and type of fabric. Use cotton thread for natural fabrics – cotton, linen and wool. Synthetic threads are made for use with manmade and synthetic fabrics – acrylic, polyester, nylon. Silks and fine fabrics should be stitched with silk thread or a fine cotton filament. Special tacking threads are available, or you can use up left-over reels for tacking, but don't make do with what you've got for finished stitching: an unsuitable thread is likely to break or cause puckering.

If you cannot get a precise colour match between thread and fabric, choose a slightly darker shade, which will blend in more evenly than a lighter colour. Secure loose ends on the reels after sewing and keep reels together in a box or on a board fitted with wooden or metal spikes.

SEWING MACHINES

Small items can be made without a sewing machine, but it is impractical to think of attempting large projects by hand sewing. An electric machine with straight-stitch and zigzag settings is efficient and adequate for work on home furnishings. A reverse stitching facility is useful for securely finishing off the end of a seam. A machine with these relatively limited functions is called a zigzag or swing-needle model.

A semi-automatic machine is rather more sophisticated, including facilities for blind-hemming, buttonholing and a few simple embroidery stitches. A fully automatic model has all the above and a stretch-stitch capacity which is ideal for knit fabrics. This offers additional embroidery stitches and a more efficient method of working buttonholes. Some models have the extra stitch facilities built in; others are equipped for fancy stitching by the use of drop-in cams – devices for controlling the stitch pattern.

Electronic machines have exceptionally easy, push-button or touch-control selection for a wide range of stitches, often with a "mirror" facility which allows any pattern to be worked in reverse, so the pattern direction can be alternated. Other functions include an automatic technical adjustment which allows equal needle penetration at all speeds on all types of fabric. There may also be stitch-by-stitch control for accuracy in areas of intricate work, and a memory which stores a selection of stitches and repeats them as required at the touch of a switch. It's also possible to work lettering and border motif repeats. A machine with this range of functions is an expensive but worthwhile investment if sewing is your main interest and you do dressmaking as well as making up soft furnishings, but you will not need this range of facilities if you are working only on home-sewing projects.

When considering which sewing machine to buy, arrange to have a demonstration and see the machine at work on different weights and types of fabrics. When you have bought your chosen model, read the instruction book carefully, to make sure you're using the machine correctly and are aware of all its capabilities.

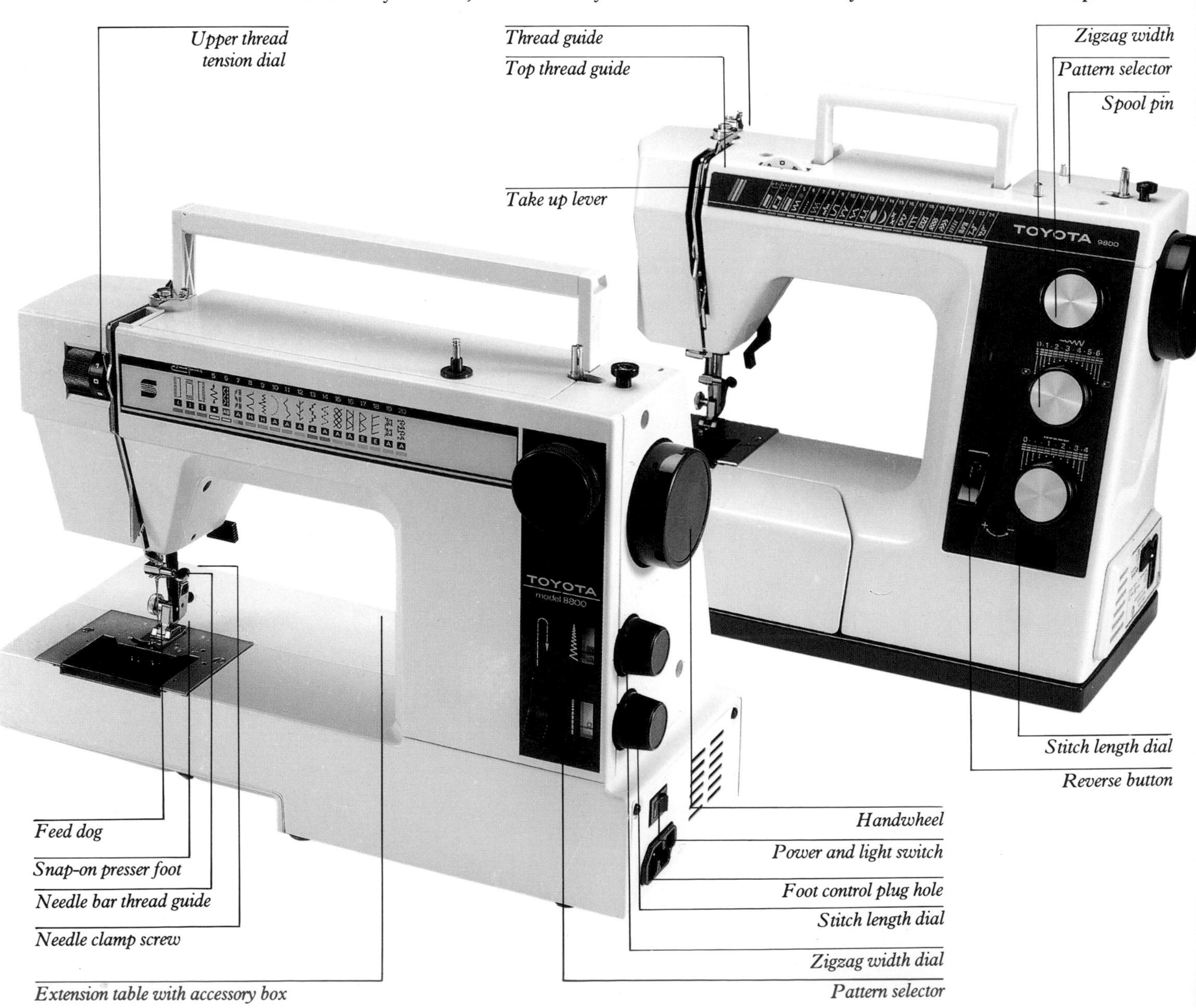

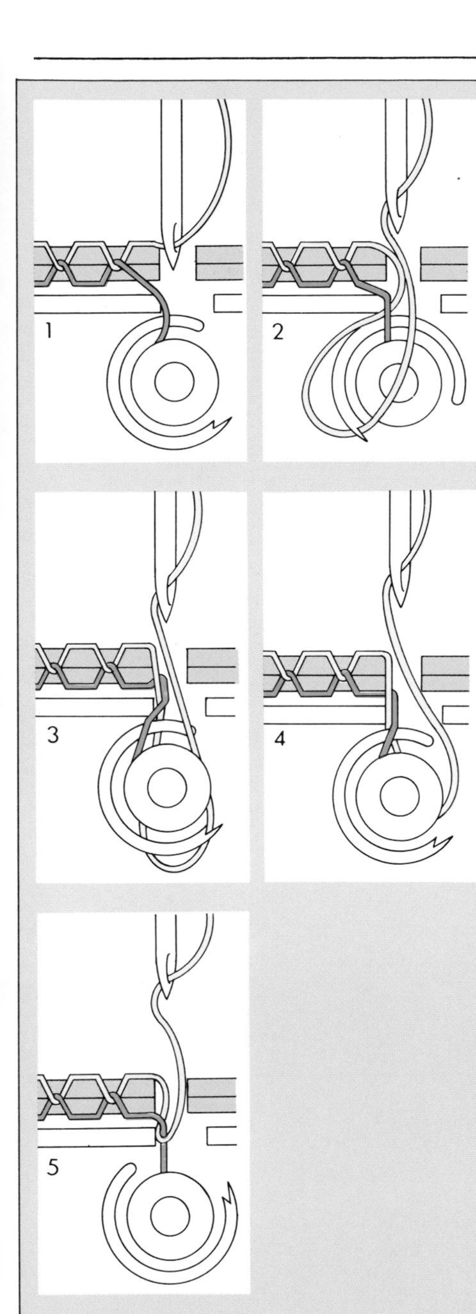

Sequence of stitch formation

*The needle passes down through the feed plate to bring the top thread down into the bobbin area of the machine (**1**).*

*As the needle goes back up, a loop of thread is left which is caught by the shuttle hook (**2**).*

*The shuttle hook then carries the loop around under the bobbin and bobbin case (**3**).*

*As the needle continues upwards, the loop slips off the front end of the shuttle hook as the hook reverses its motion (**4**).*

*The thread loop is now around the bobbin thread and, as the needle continues upwards, the loop is pulled up into the fabric to form the stitch (**5**).*

Threading the machine

Machine stitching is formed by the interlocking of an upper and lower thread; the upper thread comes from a bought reel slotted on to the machine, the lower from a bobbin loaded with thread and positioned under the needle plate. Most machines are threaded in a similar way – the upper thread is taken across from the reel, down into the tension discs, up through the take-up lever, down again and through the needle. Thread the machine with the take-up lever and presser foot raised: the instruction booklet will explain this and how to wind thread on to the bobbin and insert it below the needle.

In straight stitch the needle creates a single line of stitching. In zigzag and decorative stitching the needle swings from side-to-side as well as moving forward. Stretch stitches include a backward movement which allows "give", so that stitches don't break as the fabric itself – jersey or knit fabric – gives in use. Some of the stretch stitches provide useful extra strength in stitching heavy fabrics. A wide range of machines also have the facility for twin-needle work which creates a double line of stitching.

The presser foot of a machine controls the feed-through of the fabric. There are usually several types supplied with the machine and one of the most useful is the zipper foot. This allows you to stitch very close to the teeth of an inserted zip and works equally well for seaming alongside a bulky piping cord.

Sewing-machine needles

These are available in all points as for hand-sewing needles – sharp for woven fabrics, ballpoint for knits, wedge-shaped for leather, suede and vinyl. They are sold in English sizing from 10 to 18 (finest to thickest) and continental sizing from 70 to 110. Correct size is important; the wrong needle puts strain on the thread and if it is too thick it can leave ugly holes in the fabric or split the seams of fine fabrics such as voile and organdie. Be guided by the sewing-machine manufacturer's instruction manual.

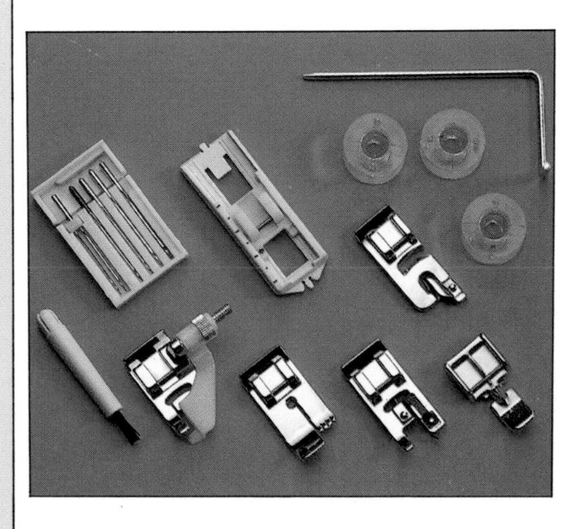

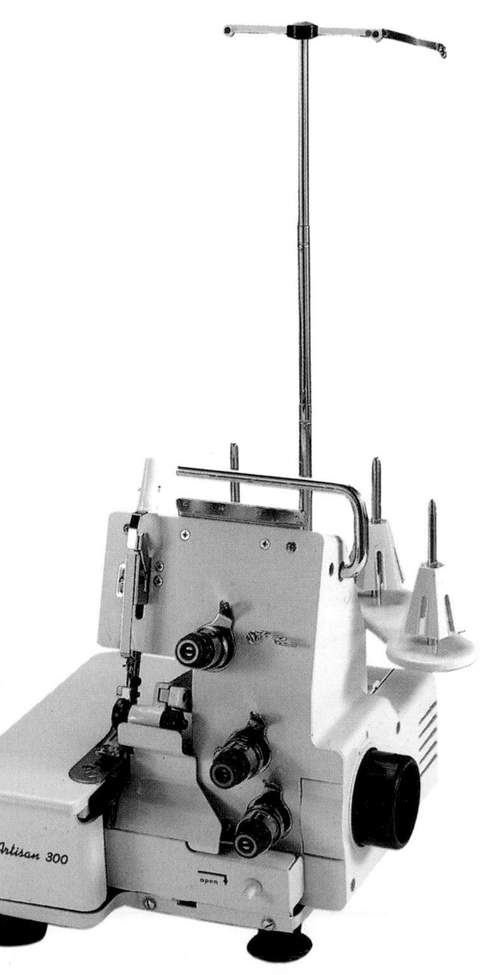

Accessories and overlocker

Shown above, sewing machine accessories; left to right top row: needles including a twin needle, buttonhole foot, roll hemming foot, bobbins, quilting guide bar; bottom row: cleaning brush with bobin extractor, blind hemming foot, straight stitch foot, zigzag stitching foot, zipper foot.

Shown right, an overlocking machine, a worthwhile investment for semi-professional sewers.

CHAPTER TWO

CURTAINS

There are methods and styles to suit every room, from large traditional drapes to soft sheer nets.

· CURTAINS ·

Few things affect the look of a room more than its window dressing, so it is worth taking time and trouble to choose a really effective scheme. You may already have a firm idea of the effect you want and how to achieve it; or you may have no particular plan except to suit the style to existing furniture and fittings in the room.

Alternatively, you may be starting from scratch, with *carte blanche* to do anything you like. There are now literally hundreds of ways to dress up – or dress down – a window, from simple roller blinds to elaborately frilled curtains complete with tie-backs and valance. Different methods of making and styling curtains are explored in this chapter; blinds are covered in the next one. However, don't forget that a combination of blinds and curtains at the same window provides the answer to many practical problems while making quite a visual impact.

Books and magazines on interior design provide plenty of inspiration for creating impressive window treatments, but it is important to be aware of the functional aspects of curtains at the planning stage. Medium and heavy curtain weights provide both privacy and insulation, keeping out the light, keeping in the warmth of the room, and reducing noise and draughts from outside. Sheer curtains ensure daytime privacy while letting in light, and can also be designed to soften an unattractive view or hide unpleasant features.

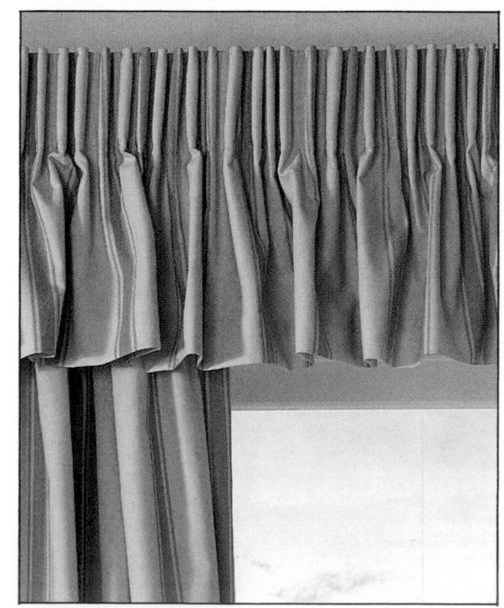

The style and shape of curtains will form an important part of a room setting and the curtain detail will add to the overall impression. In a formal setting, tie-backs, made from matching fabric or cord and tassles, add an elegant draped effect to full curtains. A wooden curtain pole and rings gives a less formal finish and a country atmosphere. A gathered valance is a simple but effective alternative to a pelmet and has a more cottagey feel. Half nets diffuse the light softly and will hide an unpleasant view, while cafe curtains give a cosy atmosphere and provide privacy in an overlooked room.

VISUAL EFFECTS

It is also possible to use fabric to alter the appearance of less-than-perfect windows, to make them seem larger or smaller, of better proportions or simply more interesting or unusual.

To block a dreary view, hang full-length, pretty nets or sheers that transmit enough light for permanent daytime use.

To preserve your privacy without cutting out all the light, place cafe curtains over the lower half of the window. This also draws attention away from aging or unpleasantly designed window frames.

■ An illusion of width comes from extending the curtain rail at either side of the window, so that the curtains, when drawn back, cover only the edge of the window. As well as improving the proportions of a narrow window, this does not cut out any of the light entering the room.

■ To make a large window look smaller, or to make the shape more interesting, fix curtains to meet at the top of the window but loop them up at the sides with tie-backs. The tie-backs could be made from stiffened fabric, cord or ribbon.

■ To avoid covering a radiator beneath the window, hang long "dress" curtains but keep them permanently drawn back, and pull down a blind over the window glass when required.

To lower the height of a tall window, fix a deep pelmet or valance across the top. Conversely, to make a window appear taller, place a deep pelmet slightly above the window area, so that the bottom edge just laps over the top of the window frame.

PLANNING YOUR CURTAINS

There are various elements to be considered when you select the styling and shape for your curtains:

- length
- fabric
- the lining, if any
- the heading – how the top of the curtain is gathered or pleated
- the track or pole – the device used to hang the curtains and the fixings which attach them.

These factors, explained in detail in the following pages, are affected by practical considerations – for example, if it is important that bedroom curtains cut out all the light, then they should be lined with a lightproof fabric – but the overall decorative effect is paramount.

Additionally, you can run a rigid pelmet or loosely falling valance across the top of the curtains, tie them back in any of a number of attractive ways, or add trimmings, borders or frills to the lower hems.

Pelmet shapes

Choose a design to match the style of the curtains and complement the fabric. A pelmet with a scalloped edge will suit a pretty room and floral fabric. Elegant curves are more traditional for a formal room setting, while a pelmet with angular corners would enhance a geometric print.

· CURTAIN FABRICS ·

The choice of fabric is the most important element determining the look of your window treatments, and it's as well not to rush into making a decision. Take with you offcuts or colour samples of existing furnishings, wallpaper or paint colour in the room – it's sometimes possible to have quite the wrong impression about colours and patterns that you live with every day, so don't take the chance of guessing that the fabric you have your eye on is exactly the right shade to match the sofa covering. Ask to borrow a large sample of the chosen design – it may be worth buying a short length of the fabric – as the lighting in the room and the other things around it will alter the effect of the colour or pattern when it is in place.

Curtain fabrics are available in an almost endless variety of colours, textures and patterns, also ranging from lightweight sheers to heavy-weight velvets and figured weaves. There isn't any particular restriction on the type of fabric you could use – as long as it suits your purpose and is reasonably practical from the point of view of cleaning and rehanging. Loose-weave and open-textured fabrics can be a problem, tending to sag dismally soon after hanging, but you can get round this by supporting them with a firm, medium-weight lining. Of course, as the fabric must hang permanently in the window, you want a type that does not fade or discolour in the sun.

LIGHTWEIGHTS Sheers, voiles, laces and nets are primarily used to gain some privacy while allowing light to come into the room, so they are often hung under heavier curtains. These fabrics are usually sold in light colours – white, cream, beige and pale pastels – although some stores stock deep-coloured laces which create an unusually dramatic effect. If you are given to browsing round second-hand shops and markets, you may be lucky enough to come upon an undamaged length of old lace which will enhance a period decor or disguise a stained table.

MEDIUM WEIGHTS Available in a variety of fibres and with a wide range of patterns and finishes, these are the most popular and versatile curtaining fabrics. Medium weights can be used almost anywhere and are particularly useful if you want the loose covers and cushions in the room to be made to match.

HEAVY WEIGHTS Brocade, linen union and velvet fall into this category, which really includes the traditional and formal styles of curtaining. It is usual to line heavy fabrics and they give excellent draping qualities for floor-length curtains, hanging evenly by their own weight. They also have a good insulating effect, though medium weights can be given insulating linings which are just as effective.

LININGS

Most medium-weight and heavy curtains benefit from being lined. The additional layer of fabric improves the hang of the curtains and provides more effective insulation. It also protects the main fabric from sunlight, dirt, or condensation at the windows. Cotton sateen is the most popular, and very practical, fabric for curtain linings, available in a wide range of colours and some simple patterns. It is often advisable to choose a colour which matches or closely tones with the main fabric, but for deliberate contrast you can use lining of a quite different, but complementary, colour, or use another printed furnishing fabric as lining – more expensive but extremely stylish when curtains are draped back showing the underside.

Linings are made in different ways – tube-lining involves seaming the curtain and lining fabrics; locked-in linings are sewn to the curtain vertically at intervals across the width; detachable linings hang by a special heading tape from the same hooks used to hang the curtain, but are not actually stitched to the curtain fabric.

Interlining can be inserted between the two layers to provide extra body and insulation. Thermal lining fabrics designed to improve insulation are available in neutral colours and can be used for sewn-in or detachable linings.

USING PATTERNED FABRICS

You may need to join widths of fabric to make the full window-width of curtaining, so keep this in mind if you favour large or directional patterns as you will need to allow quite a bit extra for pattern matching. Lengthwise and horizontal stripes are crafty disguises for short or narrow windows, but you must match the pattern perfectly at seam joins and work to the straight grain of the fabric, getting the folds for hems and headings absolutely even. Stripes and checks are available in printed or woven-in patterns. All-over miniprints are easy to manage, a good choice if you haven't handled anything as large as curtains before. There is also a wide range of textured and figured fabrics which create excellent effects from roughly practical to elegantly formal. If you do decide to play it safe and choose a plain, single-coloured fabric, consider using hem trimmings or decorative tie-backs to add individual styling and link with other furnishings in the room.

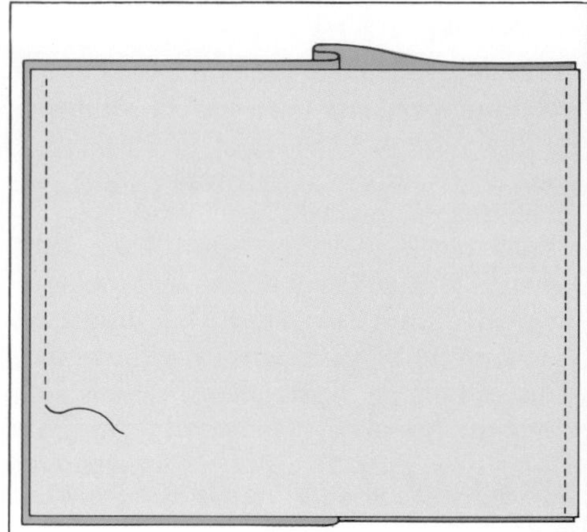

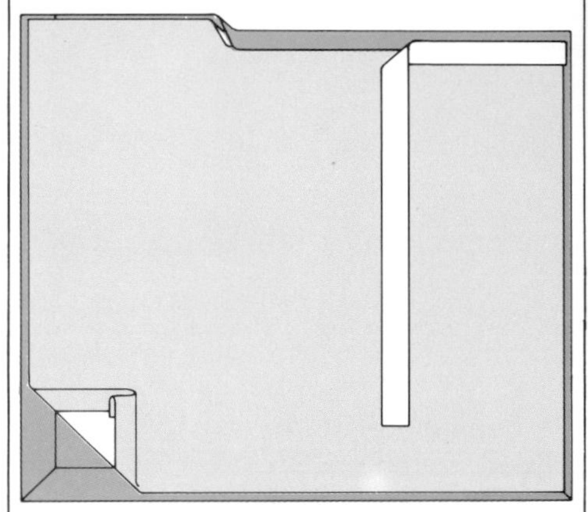

Tube lined curtains

The lining fabric should be 5cm narrower than the curtain fabric. With right sides facing and edges level, stitch the lining to fabric down the side edges finishing the stitching about 25cm up from the lower edge. Turn the curtain right side out and press the side edges so 2.5cm of curtain fabric folds over to the lining side. Make separate hems at the lower edges, then complete stitching the side edges of lining by hand. Fold top hem over and stitch on the heading tape.

HEADING TAPES

The important thing about your curtains is how they look to you. They can set the style of the whole room, and although they must have the necessary practical qualities, easy-care properties won't compensate for a mistake in styling that you have to live with day-in, day-out. Once you have an idea of the type of fabric you may choose, the next important decision is the heading tape, which can dictate informal or formal styling, the fullness, width and overall effect of this focal point in the room.

There is a remarkable range of heading tapes now available, in different materials to suit different fabrics – special tapes for nets and sheers, for example – and with a good variety of interesting design effects. The tape gathers or pleats the top of the curtain by means of cords threaded along the length, which draw up the fabric to a specific style – simple gathers, smocked gathers, narrow pencil pleats, clustered triple pleats. The tape also has lines of pockets where the curtain hooks are inserted and can be narrow or deep, with one row of pockets or three. Deep tapes allow you to position the curtain hooks to bring the top of the heading level with the track or standing slightly above it. If you are using a decorative pole to hang the curtains, the hooks can be placed on a line which leaves the curtain heading clear of the pole while concealing the hooks and base rings.

The design of the heading tape is the key to the amount of fabric you need to buy to make up the curtains. Gathering tapes require fabric of 1½-2 times the track width, while pencil pleats or box pleats take 2½ times the track width to draw up the fabric into the correct effect.

Hint

Check care instructions for the heading tape as well as the fabric when it comes to washing and ironing your curtains – some tapes should be ironed at a lower heat than that used to iron the main fabric.

Standard tape

This is a narrow heading tape, about 2.5cm wide, which forms gathers. It is used mainly on small informal curtains and valances, and where the curtain heading will be hidden behind a valance or pelmet. It requires 1½-2 times curtain fullness. Standard tape has only one row of hook suspension pockets, so the tape should be positioned so it will hide the track.

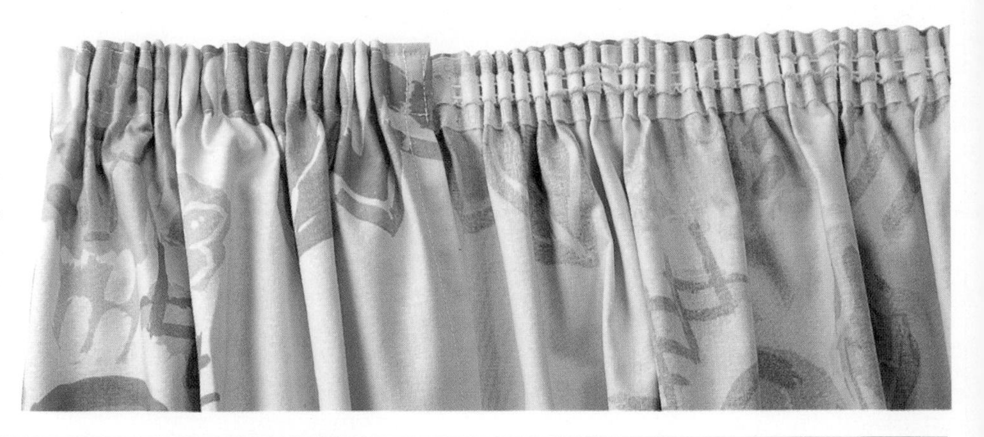

Lightweight pencil pleat

This type of heading tape is specially designed for use on lighter-weight fabrics, sheer fabrics and nets. It normally takes 2¼-2½ times curtain fullness, but on static nets, which will not be drawn back, 3 times fullness looks more attractive. This type of tape also has two rows of suspension pockets making it suitable for any type of track or pole.

Triple pinch pleat

An elegant heading tape with groups of three pleats spaced apart. The pleats are pinched in close together at the lower edge of tape and fan out at the top. This tape requires 2 times curtain fullness. The tape has two alternative rows of suspension pockets making it suitable for any type of curtain track or pole. Special curtain hooks are needed.

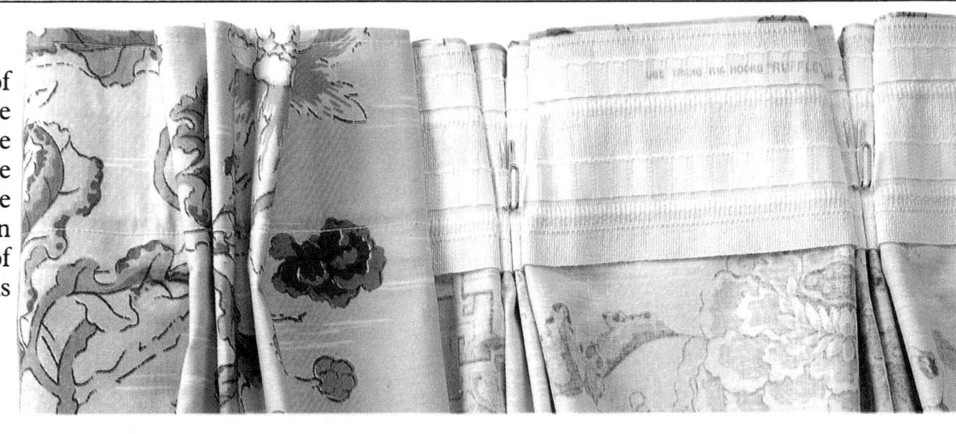

Pencil pleat

Classic pencil pleat heading tape forms crisp, even, upright pleats. The type shown has a special monofilament thread woven in, which keeps the heading upright. This tape requires 2¼-2½ times curtain fullness. It has two alternative rows of suspension pockets so it can be used with any type of curtain track or with a decorative curtain pole.

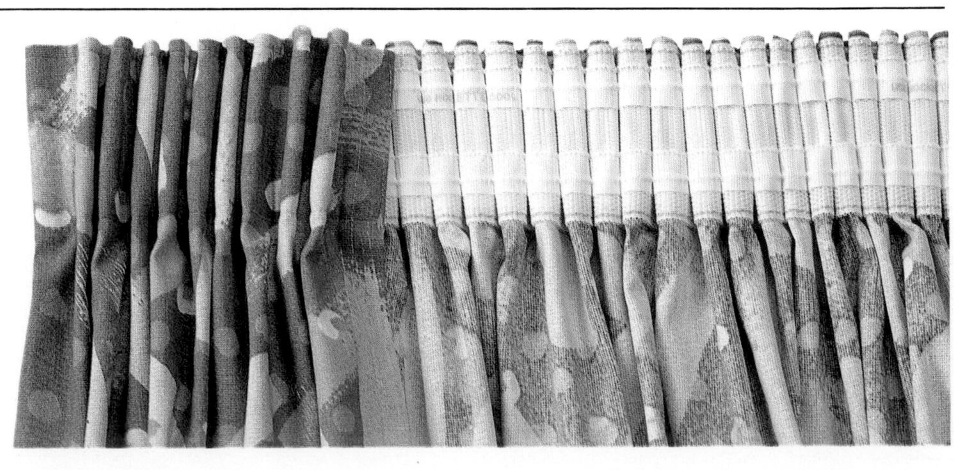

POLES AND TRACKS

Basic track

This inexpensive track supports the curtains directly; the hooks attaching the heading tape function as both hook and runner and are threaded over the track. If they are attached to the lower pockets of a deep heading tape, the heading will cover the track completely.

Traditional track

This is designed to have runners or gliders hanging from the track. Hooks are inserted in the curtain heading and then attached to the runners. Any standard or decorative heading tape can be used. Tracks are usually supplied with their own small wall-brackets and the necessary fixing screws.

Decorative poles

A metal or wooden pole can be of any thickness you wish, providing it will support the curtains adequately and you can find rings large enough to thread over the pole. Large curtain rings are fitted with a smaller ring at the base to which the curtain hooks are attached. The pole is fixed on brackets screwed into the wall or the ceiling.

Expandible rods

Expandible or sprung-tension rods are ideal for nets or sheers. They are fitted between flat facing walls, in a narrow bay or across the window inset. Net tapes incorporate loops to be threaded over the curtain rod; alternatively, you can attach rings to the top of the curtain.

Fine rods and curtain wire

Either of these can support a lightweight curtain directly through a cased heading on the curtain which threads over the rod or wire. Narrow metal and plastic rods are available. Curtain wire is a coiled length in a plastic sheath, slightly expandible and fixed by means of eyelets screwed into the wire at either end which can be attached to simple cup-hooks or similar fixings.

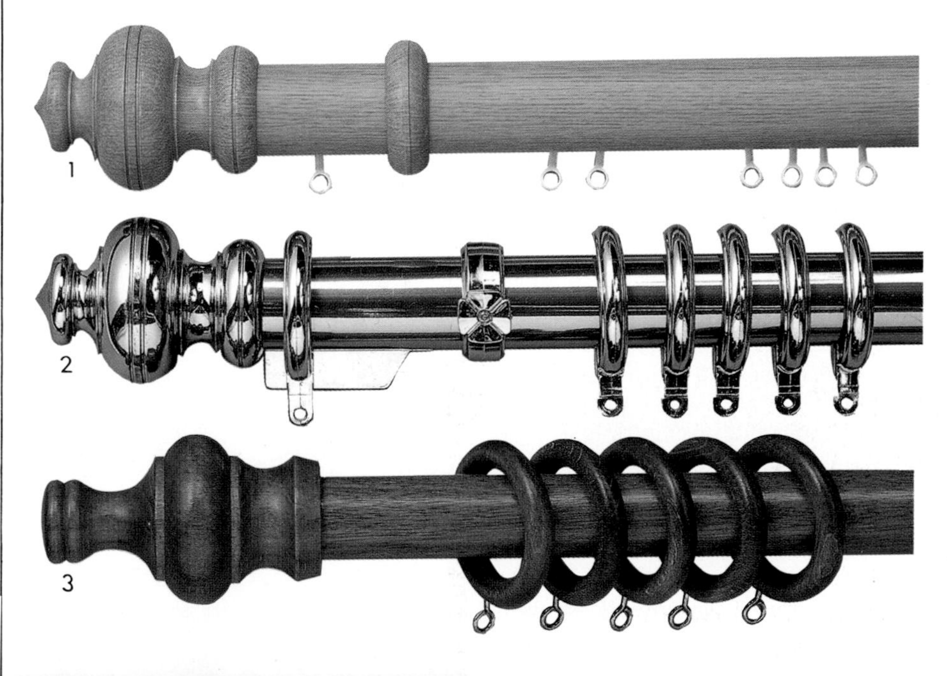

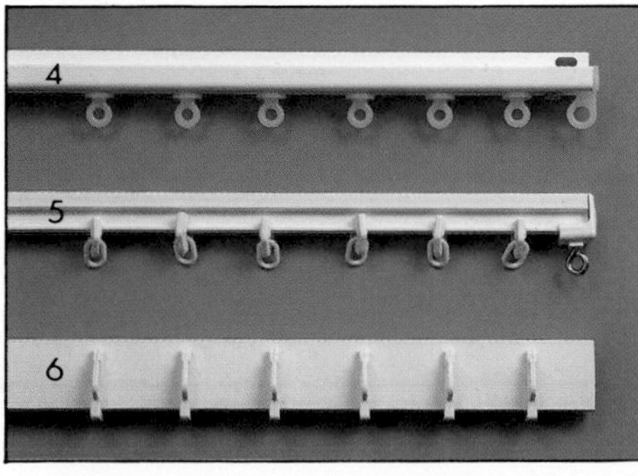

Poles and tracks

Curtain tracks were traditionally hidden by a pelmet or curtain valance, but the modern streamlined tracks are unobtrusive when curtains are drawn back and poles are a decorative feature.

1 *Light wooden pole with concealed runners.*
2 *Metallic-finished pole with rings.*
3 *Polished wooden pole with rings.*
4 *Track with concealed runners.*
5 *Track with exposed runners.*
6 *Basic track with combined hooks and runners.*

HANGING METHODS

The method you choose for hanging curtains may affect the way they should be made, so you must consider the type of track, pole or rod that can be used at the same time as deciding on a suitable heading tape for the styling you have in mind.

The simplest way of suspending curtains is to make a cased or channelled heading and thread this directly on to plastic-coated curtain wire, an expanding rod or lightweight cafe-curtain pole. No tapes or hooks are required with this method, but it is only suitable for light to medium-weight fabrics and curtains designed to hang permanently over the window without being drawn back – cafe curtains, nets and sheers. Threading the casing on to wire or a narrow rod gives a simple gathered heading: a wider, flat rod is also available which creates a deep shirred-effect heading, ideal for a valance or pretty gauzy sheers.

Most curtains are designed to be drawn back and forth and for these, choose a sturdy track or pole. Metal or plastic tracks are available in a wide variety of lengths, strengths and styles, with accessories such as overlaps. Tracks are generally more versatile than poles as they can be fitted to a wall or ceiling, turned around a window bay or angled into a corner. There are special types for hanging a double layer of curtains – sheers under heavy curtains, for example – and some types have a cording system for drawing the curtains. Tracks are usually designed to be concealed by the curtains when they are drawn.

A pole provides a very decorative way to hang curtains – a carved wooden pole or heavy brass fitting. The curtains hang just below the pole, leaving it visible.

Whichever you choose, it is important that the fittings are fixed securely in position, particularly if the window is quite large and the curtains made of a heavy fabric. To let in as much daylight as possible, extend the track or pole beyond the window frame by 15-45cm, depending on the curtain width and fabric weight.

· CALCULATING FABRIC AMOUNTS ·

The measurement of fabric width is based on the length of the curtain track or pole, not the width of the window frame, and also depends on the type of heading tape you intend to use. You should first decide how far the curtains extend beyond the window area: if you are having heavy, luxurious floor-length curtains, you may wish to allow the full width to be drawn back clear of the window glass, and this will take up quite a bit of space as the heading will not bunch up tightly due to the thickness of the fabric. Then, if you have also selected a pencil-pleat heading, this requires a width of fabric 2½ times the track measurement (see page 32) to draw up the pleats. On the other hand, your choice may be a lightweight cotton fabric – for gathered kitchen curtains, say – which will not need much extra width beyond the window frame; and a standard gathered heading can be made with fabric only 1½ times the track width.

It is essential that you calculate the fabric amounts accurately – guesswork inevitably results in too much or too little, either way an expensive mistake. It is preferable to buy all the fabric at one time – if you try to match lengths later you may get a different bolt of fabric with a slight variation of colour which will be quite noticeable when the curtains are hung.

MEASURING UP

When you have decided on the full width, fix the track or pole in position. Measure with a wooden rule or steel tape to arrive at the width of the finished curtains after the heading is drawn up. To arrive at the finished length, you must decide whether the curtains are to end at the windowsill or fall just clear of a radiator below, or are to sweep down to the floor, in which case they may end at the floor or have a little extra length for a generously draped effect. Floor-length curtains always look more formal than the sill-length version.

Fabric width

The measured width of the track is the basis of your calculation. Remember to allow a little extra if you are having an overlap at the centre. Multiply this measurement by 1½, 2 or 2½, depending on the heading tape you have chosen. It will probably be necessary to join widths of fabric to make up this full measurement.

Fabric length

As well as deciding on the finished drop of the curtains, allow for the heading to cover or stand slightly above the curtain track. If you are hanging the curtains from a decorative pole, they will hang just clear of the pole so it is visible. Measure from the point where you estimate the top of the curtain should be, to the point representing the finished length.

To this measurement, you need to add allowances for the top turning and lower hem. The top turning allowance is generally 4 cm when a heading tape or facing is to be attached, but allow more if you are making a gathered heading with a frill standing above the tape. Extra length is required for a cased heading (see page 48). The lower hem allowance is usually 15cm for unlined curtains – more if shrinkage is likely – and 10-15cm for lined curtains. The finished length with these extra allowances shows how much fabric needs to be cut for each drop, whether the curtain is made from a single width or joined widths of fabric.

Total fabric allowance

To work out how many drops are needed, divide the total width of both curtains by the width of your chosen fabric. Round up the final amount to the next whole number, which will create an allowance for seams and side hems. Divide the figure in two to find out the number of full-length fabric pieces in each curtain. This will also tell you whether a half-width is needed on either side.

The number of drops multiplied by the cut length is the total amount of fabric you need to buy. Add extra for pattern matching if necessary – if you find this difficult to calculate, an experienced sales assistant in a furnishing fabrics department will be able to help if you can provide the basic measurements.

LINING FABRIC

A useful rule-of-thumb for calculating lining is that it should be cut to the size of the finished curtain. Allow for joining widths, but less for hems, as turning in hems ensures the lining is slightly smaller than the curtain and doesn't show from the right side. Lining fabrics are usually plain, so there's no need to allow for pattern matching.

Measuring cross-over drapes

The outer edge of each curtain should equal the window drop. To find the length of the inner edge, drape a tape measure across the window and down to the sill (**1**).

Cut both curtains to longer length. Mark off shorter length down one side. Lay the curtains right sides together and cut across the bottom from the marked shorter length (**2**).

Lay one curtain on top of the other right sides upwards. Tack top edges together and treat as one curtain. Hang the curtains, catching them back at the sides with tie-backs (**3**).

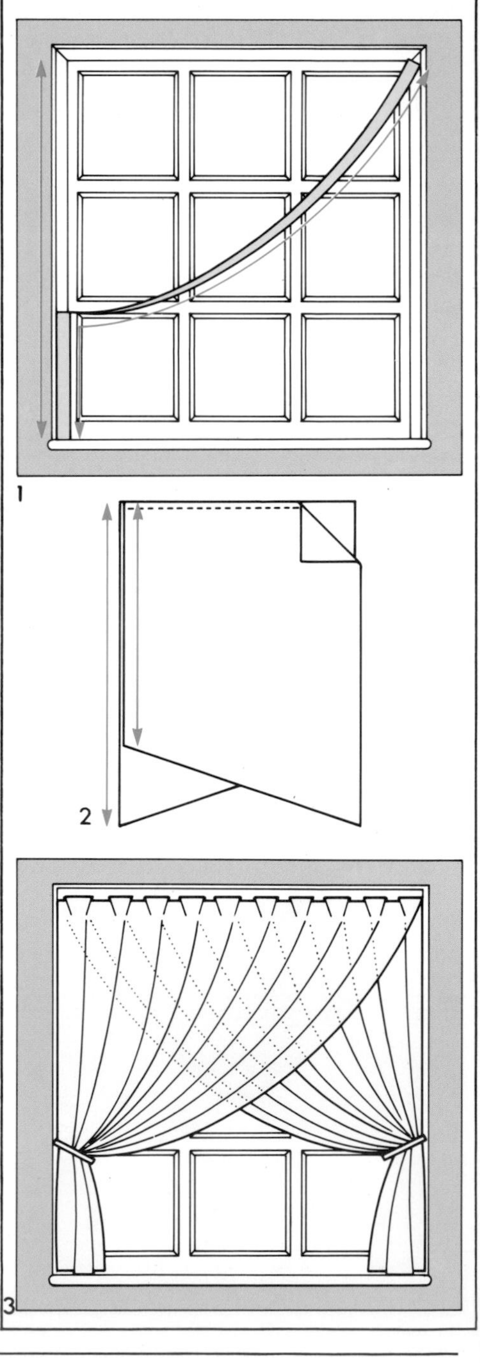

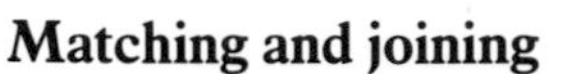

Matching and joining

Fabric with a strong repeating pattern must be cut and joined very carefully. Try to centralise the pattern on each curtain and if you have to join widths make sure the pattern aligns once seamed.

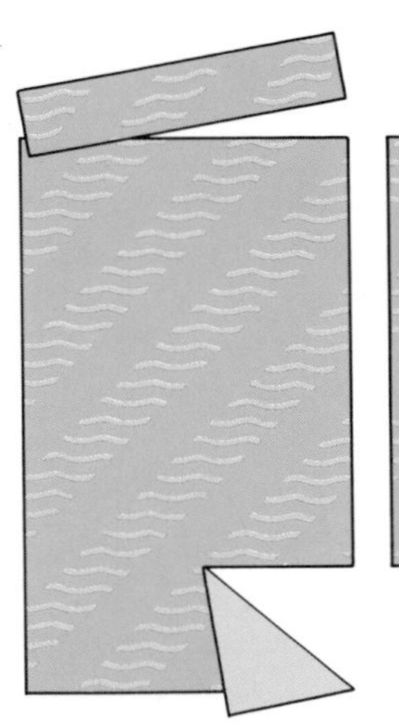

Matching horizontal patterns

Ideally, fabric with a strong horizontal pattern should be cut so that there is a complete motif at both the top and bottom of the curtain. In fact, the pattern should be centralised vertically and horizontally, if possible. Once you have cut the fabric for the first curtain align the rest of the fabric and cut the second curtain so that it matches exactly.

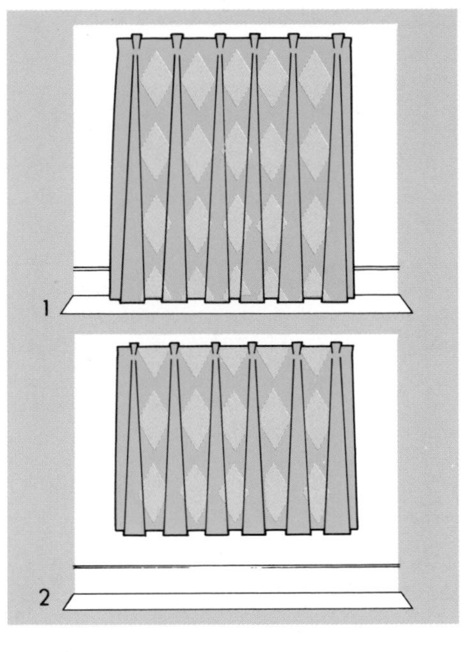

Partial repeats

If you cannot avoid cutting through a horizontal motif then it is best to position the partial repeat at the bottom of a floor-length curtain, where it will not be noticed (**1**). Make sure there is a whole motif at the top of such a curtain.

For a shorter length curtain, place the cut-off repeat at the top and a full motif at the bottom, where it will be in direct line of vision of those seated in the room (**2**).

Joining Panels

An **overlock** seam is ideal for joining fabric widths as it encloses raw edges and no stitching is visible. With the right sides of fabric facing, stitch a flat seam (**1**). Trim one seam allowance to 3mm (**2**). Press 3mm under along the edge of the other seam allowance (**3**). Fold this pressed edge over to meet the seam stitching and hand-stitch in place as close as possible to the seam stitching (**4**).

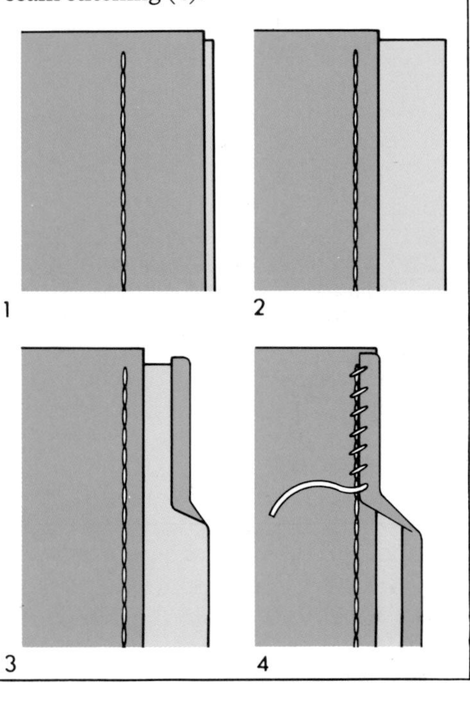

CUTTING OUT

The most comfortable way to cut out is to lay the fabric on a large rectangular table with a selvedge placed to the table edge; this enables you to check the straight grain of the fabric. Otherwise, spread the fabric on the floor. Plain fabric should be cut along the straight grain; patterned fabric on the line of the pattern, even if it is not printed straight according to the grain. Use a set square, long rule and tailor's chalk to make accurate guidelines for cutting along.

Mark out the first length and place pins along the lines where the top turning and hem allowance will be folded in. Double-check your measurements before cutting. Mark and cut the other lengths in the same way. As lengths are cut, mark the top end of each one with a contrasting thread, so that you seam them the right way up when it comes to joining widths. This is particularly important if you are using velvet or other cut-pile fabric, as the pile should run in the same direction on every length.

PATTERNED FABRICS

If you use patterned fabric, an allowance must be made for matching the pattern at seams and across both curtains. One extra pattern repeat should be allowed for each drop of fabric after the first (so add two pattern repeats if your curtain has three drops, and so on). In a pair of curtains, the pattern repeats should occur in the same place on each length for both curtains. If the pattern is large and distinct, the lower edge of the curtains should preferably finish with a complete motif; the heading tends to obscure an awkward break in the pattern at the top.

An easy method for matching the pattern in different lengths is to place a cut length over the next section of the fabric, aligning pattern details and marking them with pins. There will probably be some excess material to cut away between the end of one curtain length and the start of the next; these offcuts come in handy for tie-backs, a valance or pelmet, or cushions to match the curtains.

Checklist

- *Measure the width of track or pole. Multiply by 1½, 2 or 2½ (according to choice of heading tape) for finished width of curtains. Round up to nearest whole figure for number of drops required.*
- *Measure the required length of finished curtains. Add allowances for top turnings and hems to find cut length for each drop of fabric.*
- *Multiply the total number of drops by cut length to find total amount of fabric required.*

· UNLINED CURTAINS ·

Quick and simple to make, inexpensive but attractive and practical, unlined curtains are ideal for the kitchen or bathroom, or other working area where they may be exposed to dirt and need frequent washing. Printed cottons are definitely the best choice and offer a range of lovely colours and patterns, from quaintly traditional florals to bright, bold abstracts.

Curtain widths can be joined using ordinary flat seams, but a flat fell seam makes a neater finish on the reverse side of the curtains. A gathered heading suits the simple styling, but you can use a more elaborate pleated or smocked effect if you prefer; look at the range of available heading tapes and decide on the style when you choose the fabric, so you know how much to buy. With a gathered heading, you can allow for a small frill standing above the heading tape, turning over 4cm at the top edge of the curtain and stitching the tape 2.5cm below.

Calculating fabric amounts

Width: Multiply width of track by amount of fullness required for heading. Add 3.5cm for each side hem. Divide total by width of fabric rounding up to the next full width, allow 3cm for each join.

Length: Measure the length of the area you are curtaining; add 4cm for top heading hem and 15cm for bottom hem. Multiply the length by the number of widths needed to give fabric amount.

You will need
- Curtain fabric
- Matching sewing thread
- Heading tape

Making up

■ Along each side of the curtain, turn a 1.5cm hem to the wrong side. Press in place. At the bottom of the fabric, turn 7.5cm of the hem allowance to the wrong side and press (**1**). Remove pins.

■ To make neat, less bulky corners at the bottom of the curtain, measure a further 7.5cm from the raw edge of the turned-under hem towards the top of the fabric. Fold over the side hems from this point and press in place (**2**).

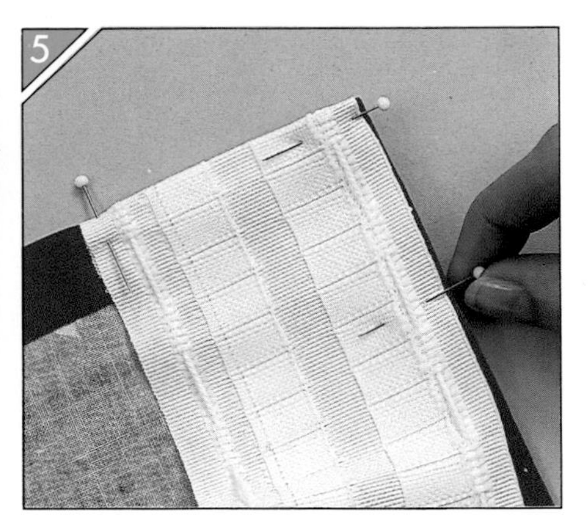

■ From the point of the raw edge of the bottom hem, turn the remainder of the side hem allowance to the wrong side. Pin and press firmly in place to provide a steep diagonal edge at the bottom (**3**). This forms half a mitred corner. Repeat at the other side.

■ Fold over the other half of the bottom hem, aligning the two diagonal edges of each mitred corner. Pin and press in place. **Slipstitch** down the diagonal joins to secure the corners. Neatly **sliphem** side hems and bottom hem in place (**4**).

■ Turn a 4cm hem to the wrong side at the top of the curtain and press in place. Cut a length of heading tape to the finished width of the curtain plus 2cm. Place the heading tape on the wrong side of the top of the curtain, just below the top edge. Tuck under raw ends of tape level with side edges of curtain. Pin and tack the tape in place (**5**).

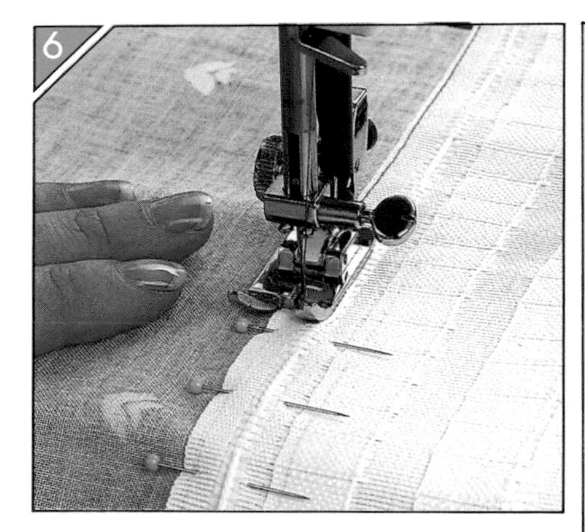

■ Machine stitch the heading tape to the curtain. Stitch one short edge first, then one long edge and other short edge. Repeat stitching the other long edge, so the short ends are stitched twice to secure the ends of tape cord (**6**). It is a good idea to stitch the long edges in the same direction to make sure the tape does not pucker.

Gently gather up the fabric by pulling the tape cords from the centre. Hold the cords together with one hand and ease the tape into pleats with the other. Finally loosely knot the cords at the centre.

Seaming fabric widths

You will probably need to join several fabric widths in order to make up the total width required for each curtain. If you have to cut a half width as well as full widths, place the half width at the outer edge of the curtain.

*You can join the panels with a simple **flat seam**, but a **flat fell seam** is preferable as it conceals the raw edges of the seam and yet lies flat when finished.*

*Alternatively, if your fabric is strongly patterned, **sliphem** the flat seam in place from the right side (left). This enables you to match the motifs accurately.*

*To make a **flat fell seam**, place fabric right sides together and pin and stitch a **flat seam**. Turn the fabric over and press the seam open. Trim one seam allowance to 3mm and turn under 5mm on the other seam allowance. Press. Fold the larger seam allowance over the trimmed one to enclose the raw edge. Press to the main fabric. Pin and stitch through all the fabric layers close to the edge of the fold (below left).*

Only one line of stitching will show on the right side of the fabric.

· TUBE-LINED CURTAINS ·

It is often assumed that, because curtains are large items and tend to be dominant in a room scheme, they are difficult to make, especially if lined. Tube-lining requires no more sewing skill than making unlined curtains; the lining is simply machine-stitched to the main fabric at the side seams only – forming a "tube" of fabric, hence the name. The proper finish is achieved by cutting the lining slightly narrower than the full curtain, so that when the tube is turned out to the right side and pressed flat, the main fabric laps round on to the back of the curtain, forming a neatly finished edge at both sides with the seams and lining completely invisible from the right side.

With this construction, the raw edges of any seams joining fabric widths on curtain or lining are concealed within the tube. However, as the lining is not attached to the curtain at any point within the width, it can move independently of the main fabric and tend to separate as the curtains are pulled back, effectively forming two draped layers. This is not necessarily a disadvantage, depending on the curtain width and type of fabric, but if you want absolutely smooth draping, turn to the locked-in lining method shown over the page.

Calculating fabric amounts
Curtain fabric: Calculate the width and length as for an unlined curtain (page 36). Lining: Width should be 5cm less than the finished width of the curtain; length should be the same as the finished curtain minus the hem allowance at the top.

You will need
- Curtain fabric
- Matching sewing thread
- Lining fabric
- Heading tape

Making up

■ Right sides together, place the lining on the curtain fabric, aligning the bottom edges. With tailor's chalk, mark the centre point of the curtain width on both the curtain and lining fabrics (**1**).

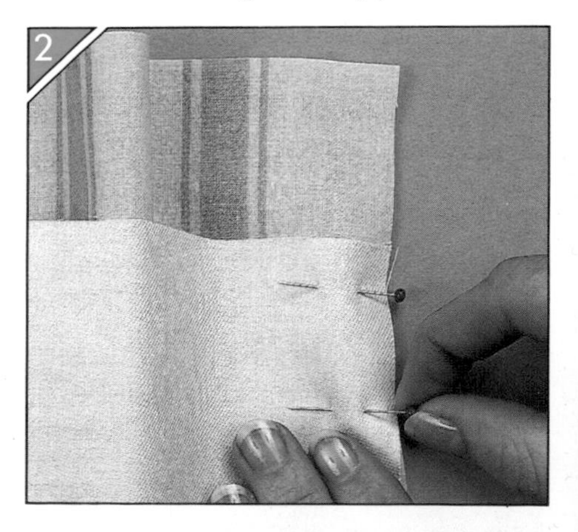

■ Pin and tack the side edges of the lining and curtain fabric together (**2**). As the curtain fabric is slightly wider than the lining, allow the curtain fabric to form undulating folds beneath the lining while you tack it in place. Make sure that the lining and curtain fabric still align at the bottom of the curtain.

■ Mark the finished length of the curtain, together with the hem sewing line on the lining with tailor's chalk; allow for a 15cm hem. Turn, pin and stitch 1cm side seams from the top of the lining to within 10cm of the hem sewing line (**3**).

■ Turn right-side out. The curtain fabric should pull over to the lining side at the side edges by 2.5cm. Press the curtain and lining (**4**).

Match the centre marked points on the lining and curtain fabric at the top. Fold over the curtain fabric at the top edge of the lining and press in place.

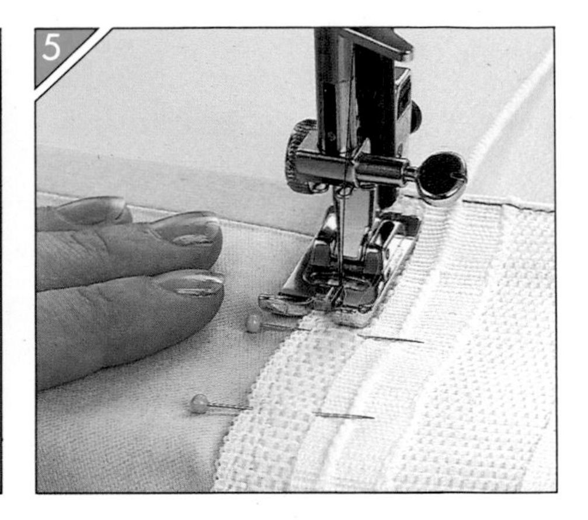

■ Position the heading tape just below the top of the curtain fabric tucking under raw ends to neaten. Pin and tack in place. Machine stitch one short side first. Then stitch each long side in the same direction to avoid puckering (**5**).

Do not pull the cords up yet.

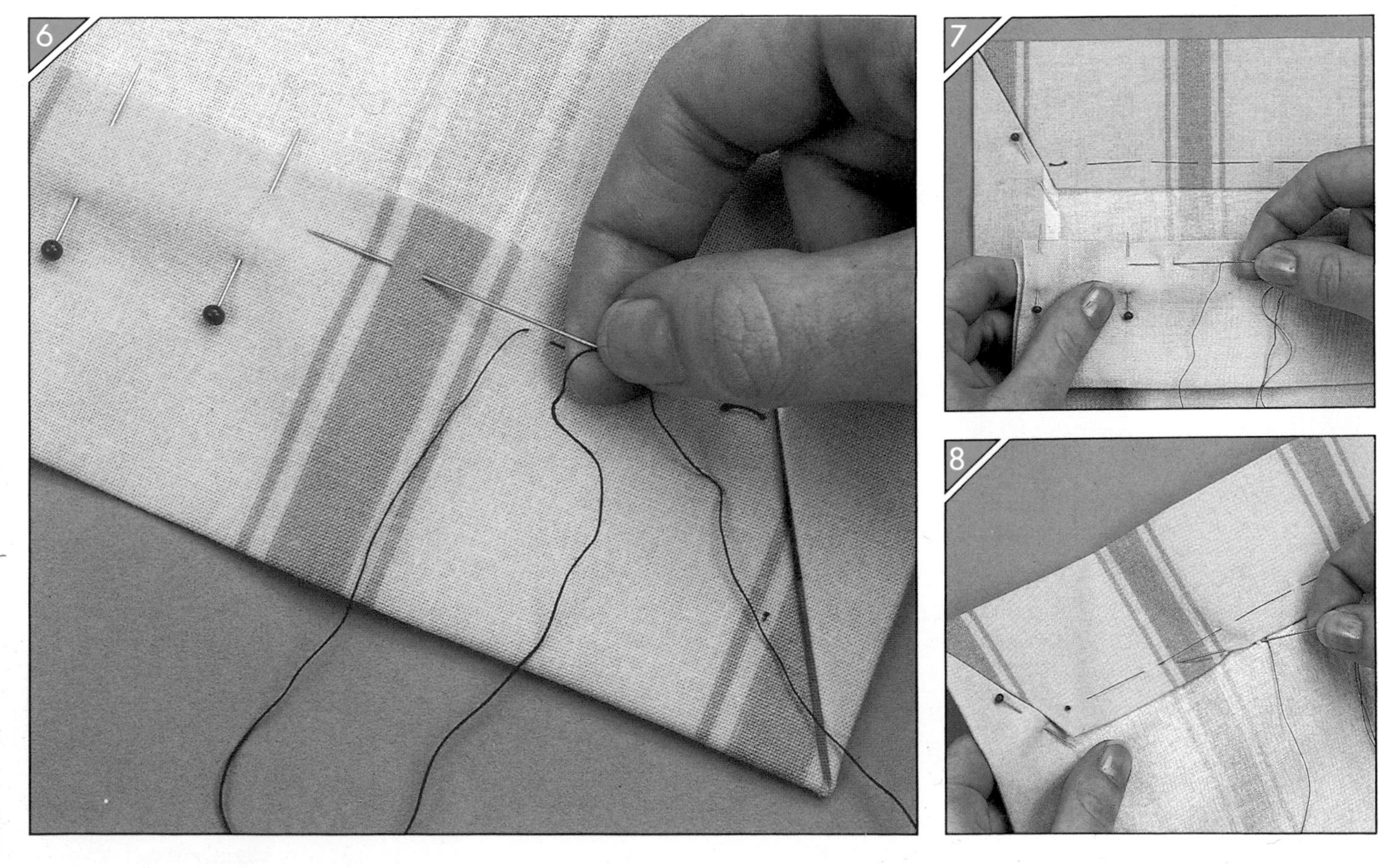

■ At the bottom of the curtain fabric, turn under a double 7.5cm hem and press in place. Mitre the corners to minimize bulk in same way as unlined curtain. Tack hem in place to secure (**6**).

Turn up a double hem to the wrong side of the lining fabric. The lining should hang about 2cm above the hem level of the curtain fabric. Trim any surplus lining. Tack hem of lining in place (**7**).

■ Pull up curtain heading tape. Hang the curtain for several days to allow the fabric to drop. **Sliphem** the hems and the lining to curtain down rest of sides (**8**).

· LOCKED-IN LININGS ·

A locked-in lining is the most professional finish for lined curtains, especially good for wide and deep curtain styles where fabric widths are joined to make up the full finished width of the curtain. The lockstitching must be done by hand, but the stitching method is surprisingly quick. The lining is lightly sewn to the curtain fabric at regular intervals right down the length, so the fabric layers move as one and the lining cannot bunch up behind the drawn curtain, to spoil the smoothness of the drape. If you are using a dense, heavy fabric the lining adds thickness and improves insulation, as well as making the curtains look well-finished from the reverse side; with a looser weave or textured curtaining material, the locked-in construction prevents the main fabric from sagging when hung.

For the main fabric, choose the traditional formality of velvet, brocade or heavy chintz and team it with a richly coloured sateen lining, or a slightly slubbed and sheeny synthetic. For less formal styling, consider a roughly textured, heavyweight fabric such as hessian or a tweedy weave. As the main fabric and lining are locked across the whole construction of the curtain, it is vital that you check the care instructions for both to ensure they can be cleaned in the same way and if washable, do not shrink at different rates.

Calculating fabric amounts

Curtain fabric: Calculate the width and length as for an unlined curtain (page 36) but allowing only 10cm for the bottom hem of curtain.

Lining fabric: Width should be the same as the unmade curtain width; length should be the same as the required finished curtain length.

You will need

- Curtain fabric
- Matching sewing thread
- Lining fabric
- Heading tape

Weighting the curtain

To help the curtain hang well it is a good idea to insert weights in the bottom hem and corners of the curtain fabric.

Individual circular weights, such as coins or metal buttons, can be sewn into the hem at each corner while mitring the corners, so that they are completely concealed.

Alternatively, you can slot a chain of small weights encased in fabric into the hem when it is turned. The string of weights will lie at the very bottom of the curtain.

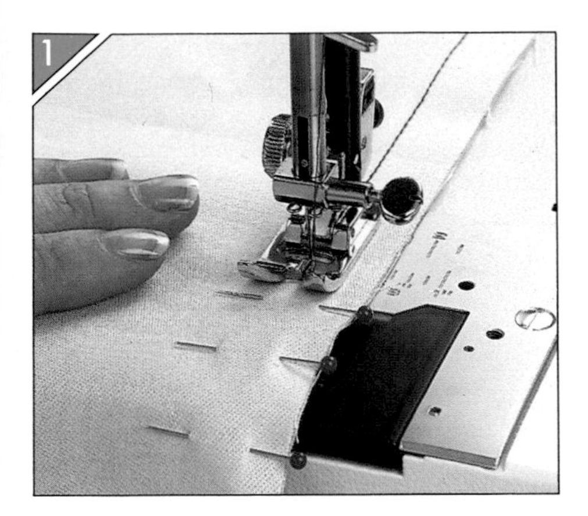

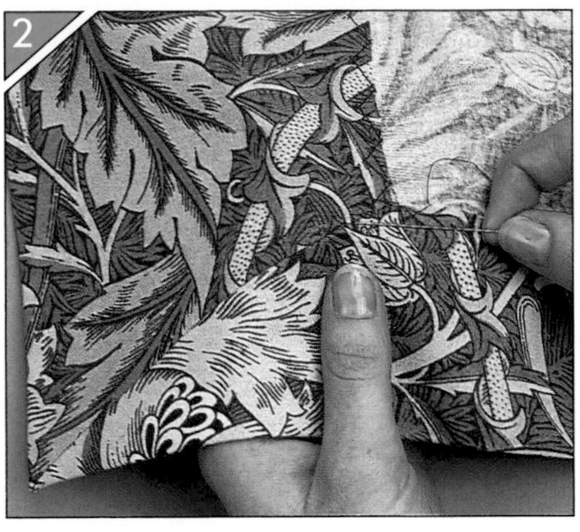

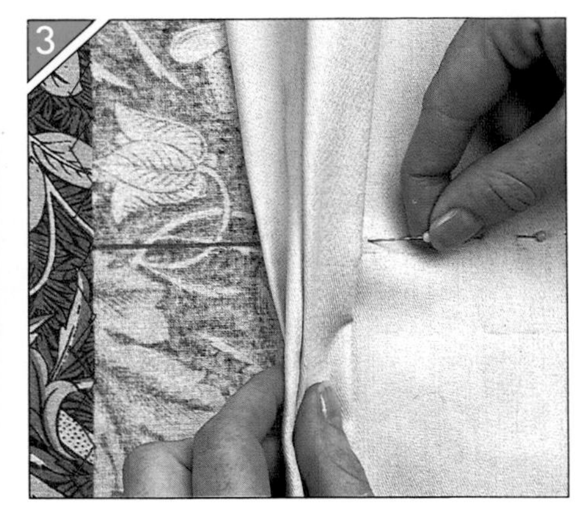

Making up

■ Stitch curtain fabric widths together with flat seams to make the full curtain width. Press seams open. Pin and stitch lining widths together in the same way (**1**). Press seams open. Trim 4cm from side edges of lining.

Turn and press a 2cm hem down the sides of the lining, and a 1.5cm hem along the bottom of the lining. Turn an additional 3.5cm under along the bottom. Press, pin and stitch lower hem in place.

■ Press a 4cm turning down each side of the curtain fabric to the wrong side. Turn up a 10cm hem at the bottom of the curtain fabric, **mitring** the corners. **Slipstitch** the mitred corner seams.

Using a large **herringbone** stitch sew the side and bottom hems in place (**2**). Pick up just a thread of the flat fabric so that the stitching will not show on the right side.

■ At approximately 30cm intervals, mark vertical lines on wrong side of curtain material with tailor's chalk.

Place lining on fabric with wrong sides together so side edges of lining are 2cm in and lower edge is 5cm up from curtain edge. Trim top of lining level with curtain fabric.

Pin then tack the lining and curtain fabrics together, following the first vertical line beginning 15cm down from the top of the curtain fabric (**3**).

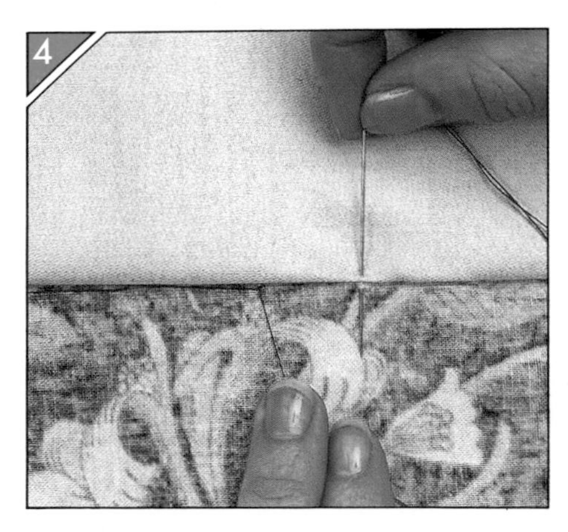

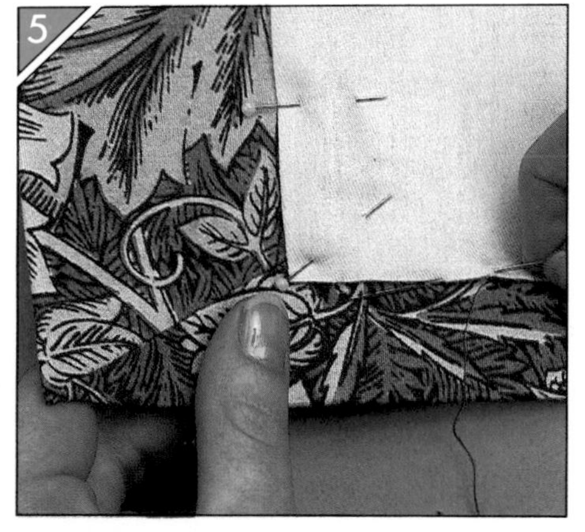

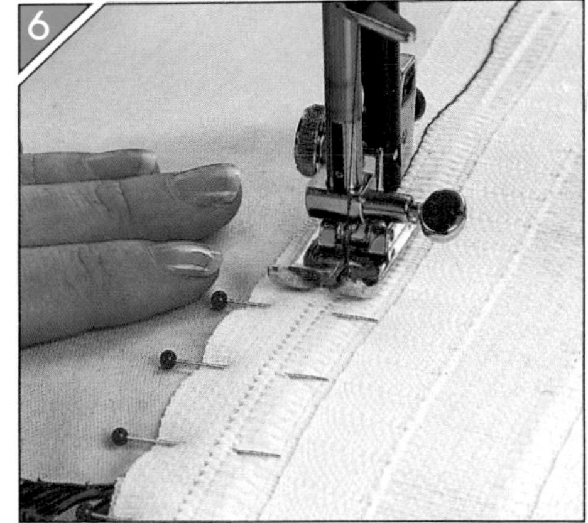

■ Fold back the lining material along the tacked line. Lock stitch the curtain fabric to the lining fabric, beginning 15cm from top of curtain fabric (**4**).

Pick up only a thread of the curtain fabric at a time so that the stitching will not show on the right side of the curtain fabric. To avoid puckering the fabric, do not pull the stitches tight and space them wide apart. Remove the tacking stitches.

■ Tack and lockstitch the fabrics together along the next vertical line, and so on until the lining is lockstitched in place across the width of the curtain.

Pin and tack the sides and bottom edge of the lining in place. **Sliphem** the folded-in sides of the lining to the folded-in edges of the curtain fabric (**5**). **Sliphem** the bottom hem of the lining to the bottom hem of the curtain fabric. Remove the tacking.

■ Turn hem to wrong side at the top of the curtain and lining. Press. Cut heading tape to fit top edge allowing extra to turn under at each end.

■ Position the length of heading tape just below the top edge of the curtain turning the raw ends of tape under. Pin and tack in place. Stitch along short end and then along both long sides in same direction to avoid puckering (**6**).

· DETACHABLE LININGS ·

A detachable lining doesn't follow the folds of the curtain fabric in the same way as a sewn-in lining, so it does not affect the hang of the main curtaining. It does, however, protect the fabric as much as any other type of lining and there are various advantages in its construction. Because it is separate, the lining does not have to be as fully gathered as the curtain, so you save on the amount of fabric – 1½ times the track width is usually ample for the lining width. The lining can be taken off for washing separately if the main fabric is dry-clean only, and it's an economical way of lining curtains intended for a short life – if you are putting up temporary furnishings until you are fully settled in a new home, or if the room needs a facelift but you're planning to move in the near future.

A final advantage is that you can add a detachable lining to an existing curtain without fully remaking, or transfer the lining to a new curtain when you are revising a room scheme to give a new look with different patterns and colours.

Calculating fabric amounts

Curtain fabric: Calculate the width and length of the curtain material in the same way as for unlined curtains (see page 36).

Lining fabric: Calculate the width and length of the lining fabric in the same way as the curtain fabric.

You will need

- Curtain fabric
- Matching sewing thread
- Lining fabric
- Curtain heading tape
- Lining heading tape

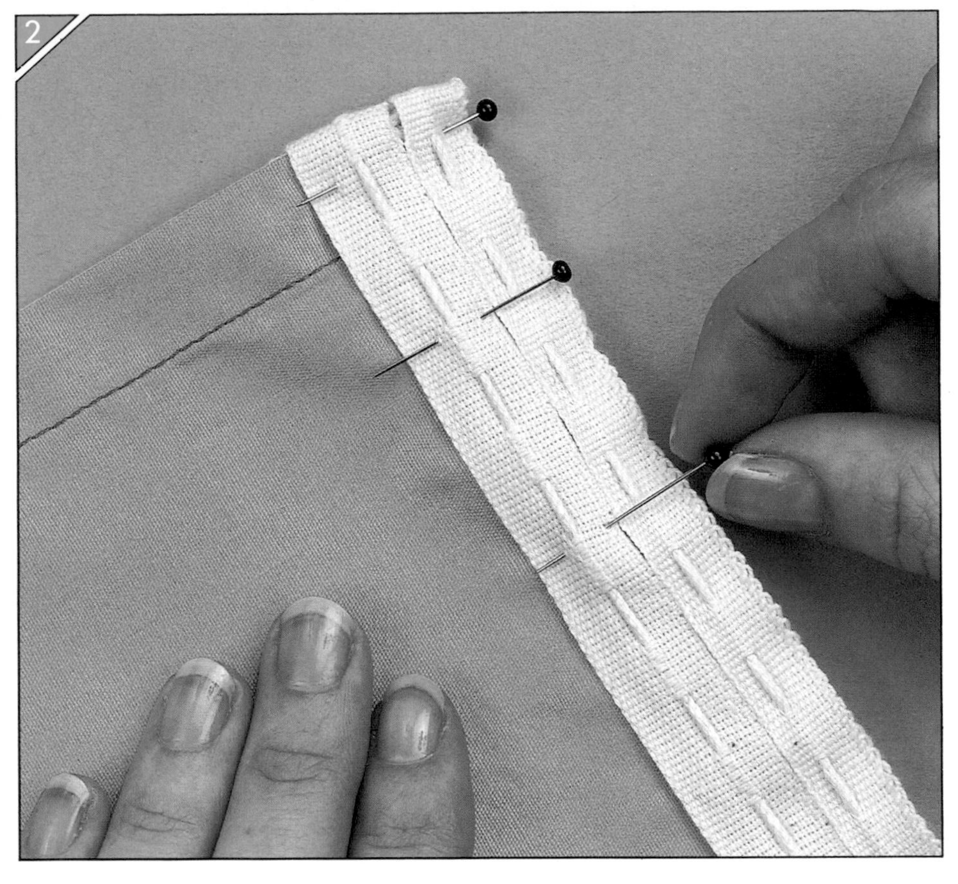

Making up

■ Make up the curtain in the same way as an unlined curtain (see page 36). Attach heading tape to curtain in the usual way.

Hem the sides and bottom of the lining fabric in the same way as the curtain fabric, but leave the top edge unhemmed. Trim top edge so the lining is a little shorter than the finished curtain.

Lining tape has two skirts and is fitted so that one skirt falls to each side of the lining fabric. Cut the lining tape the width of the curtain plus 10cm. Knot the two cords together at the end that will be over the inner edge of the curtain. With the lining tape right side up and the lining fabric right side up, ease the lining fabric between the skirts (**1**). The knotted end of the lining tape should overhang the centre edge of the lining fabric by 1cm.

■ Turn a 5mm hem on the knotted end of the lining tape. Turn a further 5mm hem to the wrong side of the lining fabric, so that the tape is flush with the edge of the lining. Pin the lining tape in place (**2**).

Make sure the top raw edge of the fabric is slotted right into the tape for as far as possible. This will prevent the fabric pulling out if the raw edge frays when the curtain is being cleaned.

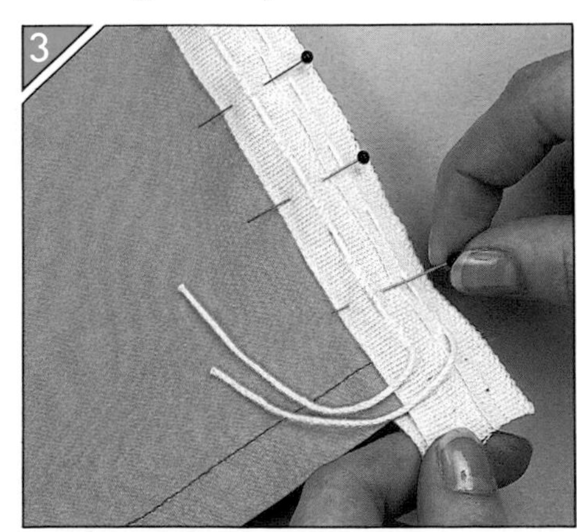

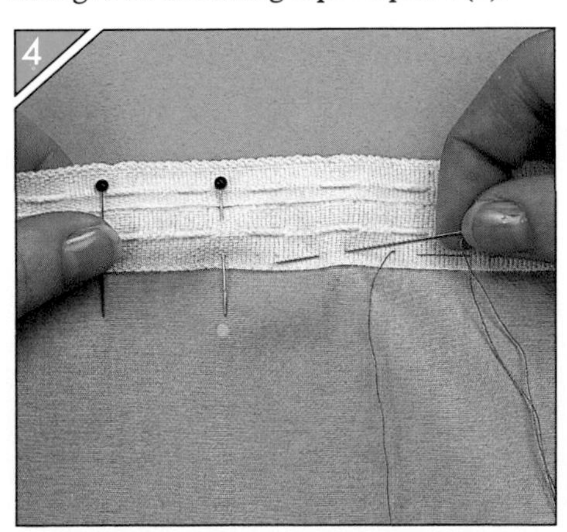

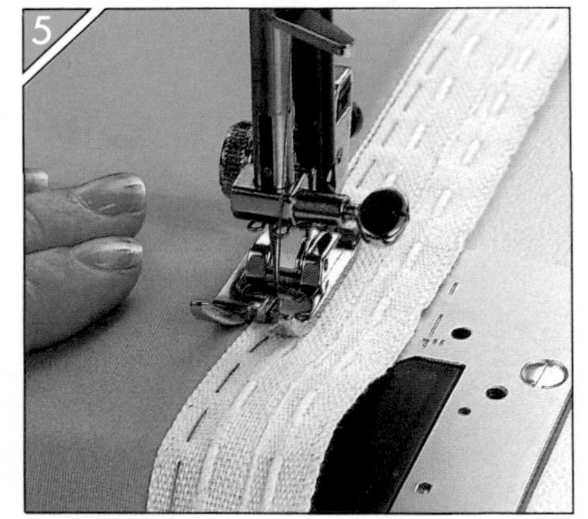

■ At the other end of the lining tape, pull the cords free, so that 4cm of each cord hangs down. Trim the surplus lining tape, so that only 1cm overhangs the outer edge. Turn a double 5mm hem to the wrong side of the lining fabric, as for the end of the lining tape at the inner edge (**3**).

■ Leaving the loose cords free for gathering up the lining, tack the lining tape in place taking care to stitch right through the two sandwiching layers of tape (**4**).

■ Close to the bottom and side edges, stitch the lining tape in place (**5**). Remove the tacking.

Gently pull the two loose cord ends, easing the lining fabric along at the same time. Even out the gathers until the width of the lining matches the width of the curtain, then knot the cords.

· DESIGN IDEAS ·

Curtains are often a major feature of the room, and it is as well to consider the overall effect carefully before applying any decorative detail; if you overdo the trimming it may appear fussy or out of keeping with the rest of the decor once the curtains are in place.

Discreet edgings, such as contrast fabric borders and braid trims, are excellent for large expanses of medium-weight or heavy curtaining. For bright rooms with modern styling, a combination of fabric patterns can have a cleverly eye-catching effect. Traditional styles, such as dense floor-length curtains in velvet or an elegantly satinized finish can benefit from furnishing weight braid trims, fringe or tassels, which look especially effective when applied to a matching valance.

Practical sill-length cotton curtains are enlivened by border patterns such as patchwork strips or ribbon appliqué. Choose colours and designs which pick up detail from the main fabric and enhance the overall impression.

Borders for curtains
An attractive deep border for a curtain can be made by reversing the method for tube-lined curtains. Cut the lining fabric wider than the main fabric and turn the excess evenly on to the right side of the curtain, mitring the corners neatly.

Trims and edgings
Tassels and fringes make a luxurious finish for heavy, traditional style curtains in fabrics such as velvet, chintz or damask. Many different styles are available in ready-made trims: silky textures or chunkier cotton trims; thick short tassels or long and elegant fringes; elaborate braid edgings and narrow banded trims in plain colours or beautifully graduated hues. These can be used on their own to make attractive tie-backs, or for edging on a wide self-fabric tie-back. They also make a sculptured edging for valances or pelmets. Stiff pelmets can alternatively be decoratively finished with a neat wallpaper border.

· SHEER CURTAINS ·

Fine, translucent fabrics create a light, sunny effect perfect for summer. They mask the window subtly and cut down strong sunlight, but transmit enough light during the day. Sheers can be hung as the only form of curtaining or combined with heavier curtains which can be drawn to block the light completely. A finely woven heading tape is available, specially designed for use with sheers and netted fabrics, and if two types of curtain are combined you can hang them on a double curtain track which automatically holds them at the same level and leaves sufficient space between the layers for both curtains to draw easily and separately.

Sheers is not a precise term and it covers a range of fabrics made from natural and synthetic fibres. It is unusual to find strong colours, but lightweight, gauzy cottons may be printed with a small all-over pattern or coloured border; otherwise you will generally find pastels.

Sheer fabric samples
These fabrics are very lightweight and semi-transparent so they diffuse the light softly. They may be plain such as voile, printed with a spaced pattern or decorated with flock dots.

Calculating fabric amounts

Width: Multiply the width of your track or pole by 2 to 3, depending on the fullness required. Add 2cm for each side hem. Divide the total by the width of the fabric, rounding up to the next full width and allowing for seam allowances for each width join. Divide the total by the number of curtains needed.

Length: Measure the length of the window area. Add 4cm for the top heading and 5cm for the bottom hem.

You will need

- Curtain fabric
- Matching sewing thread
- Heading tape

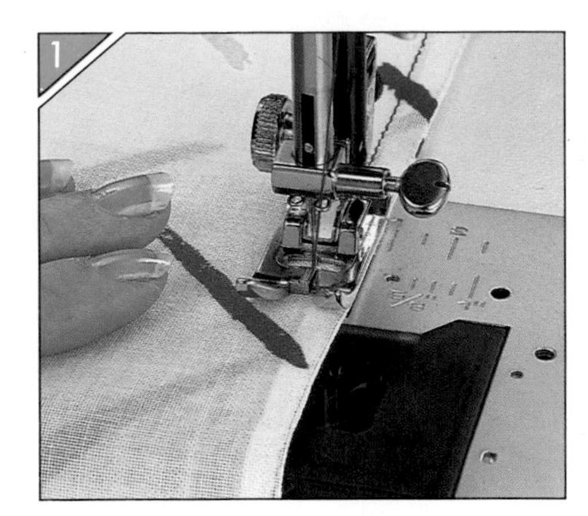

Making up

■ If necessary join fabric widths with **French seams**. Wrong sides together, stitch a flat seam of 5mm and trim to 3mm. Turn so that right sides are facing. Pin and tack two layers together. Machine stitch 1cm in from the first seam (**1**). The raw edges are completely enclosed in the seam and to the back of the fabric; in addition, no stitching line is showing.

■ Double hems are essential when using sheer fabrics, so that raw edges are concealed in the fold of the hem edge.

Turn a 1cm hem to the wrong side along the side edges and press. Turn over again by the same amount. Press and pin in place. Machine stitch through all the layers (**2**).

■ Turn a 2.5cm hem to the wrong side at the bottom of the sheer curtain fabric. Turn over again by the same amount to make a double bottom hem. Press. Pin and stitch hem in place (**3**). When the curtain is hanging, no raw or uneven edge will be visible through the fabric.

■ Turn 4cm to the wrong side at the top of the curtain and press in place. Position translucent, lightweight, net tape wrong-side down just below the top of the curtain. Pin in place. Turn under ends to align with curtain edges and stitch the tape in place (**4**).

This tape allows you to draw the sheer fabric into neat pencil pleats. You can then either thread the bars fixed to it on to a narrow rod or elasticated wire, like nets, or hang it like an ordinary curtain by fixing curtain hooks at regular intervals to the pockets, which are also provided.

· NET CURTAIN ·

Nets serve the same purpose as sheers, protecting privacy while letting in some light, but the term is specific, referring to fabrics with a construction in which the strands of yarn are interlocked to form a pattern of fine or large holes in the fabric. Nets can be very fine or positively chunky, depending on the fibres, thickness of yarn and pattern construction. Some are closely constructed to give a sheer, translucent effect; others have a relatively complex pattern repeated regularly throughout which may give a very open style with a loose, stringy texture.

Like sheers, nets are available in pale colours and natural or synthetic fibres. As they are often styled to cover only half the window area, they are available in a range of standard depths, and the amount you buy relates to the width of the window and the degree of fullness you want in the final effect. Because they are so lightweight, net curtains can hang from a curtain wire threaded through a simple casing.

Calculating fabric amounts
Width: Measure the width of the window area and multiply by 2-3, depending on the fullness required. Add 2.5cm for each side hem.
Length: Measure the height of the window area. Add 6.5cm for the top hem and 6.5cm for the bottom hem.

You will need
- Net curtain fabric
- Matching sewing thread
- Curtain wire

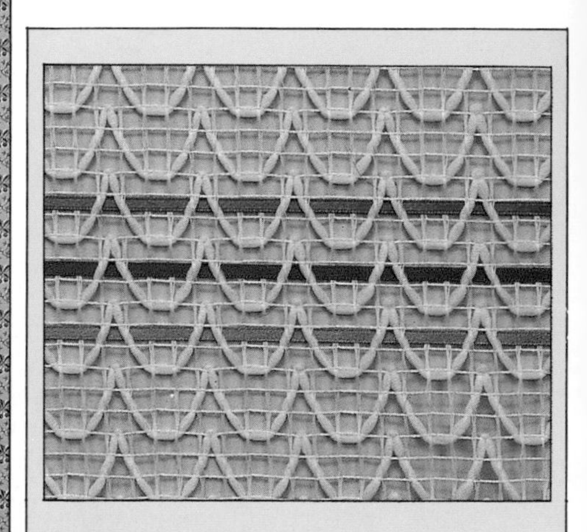

Finishing touches
Ribbons can provide the finishing touch to a loosely woven net curtain. Thread parallel lines of different coloured ribbon across the width of the fabric for a stylish, unfussy finish that here contrasts with the scalloped pattern.

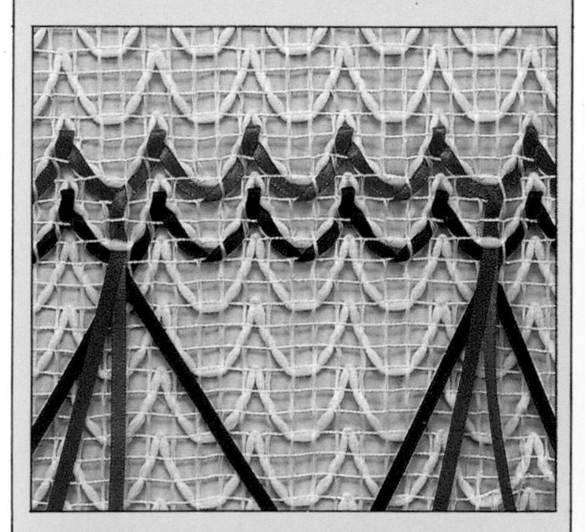

Alternatively, you could emphasize the scallop shape by threading ribbon along the undulating pattern. Add trailing ribbons for an extra flourish.

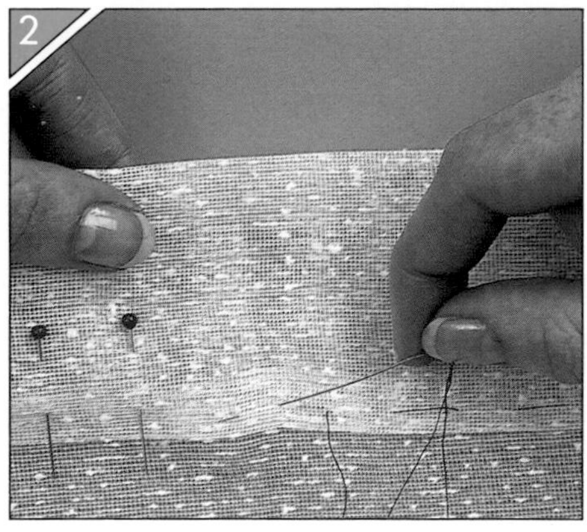

Making up

■ Cut fabric to required size. Avoid joining fabric; rather make separate curtains. If the side edges of the fabric are raw cut edges, turn a double 1cm hem to the wrong side along both edges. Pin and stitch in place (**1**). If selvedges form the side edges of the net fabric, turn under the selvedge and pin and stitch in place.

■ Along the top raw edge of the fabric, turn under 1cm to the wrong side and press. Turn under a further 5.5cm and pin and tack in place (**2**).

Turn under 1cm and a further 5.5cm hem along the bottom raw edge. Pin and tack in place.

■ Measure 3cm in from the outer fold at the top of the net fabric. Machine stitch parallel to the top folded edge at this point keeping stitching level (**3**).

Machine stitch 3cm from the bottom folded edge of the net curtain fabric in the same way.

■ Machine stitch parallel to the tacking stitches 5mm from the inner fold at the top hem. (**4**). Machine stitch 5mm from the inner fold along the bottom hem.

This completes the top and bottom casings. The curtain wire will thread through between the two rows of stitching so a self frill is formed at the top and the bottom of the net.

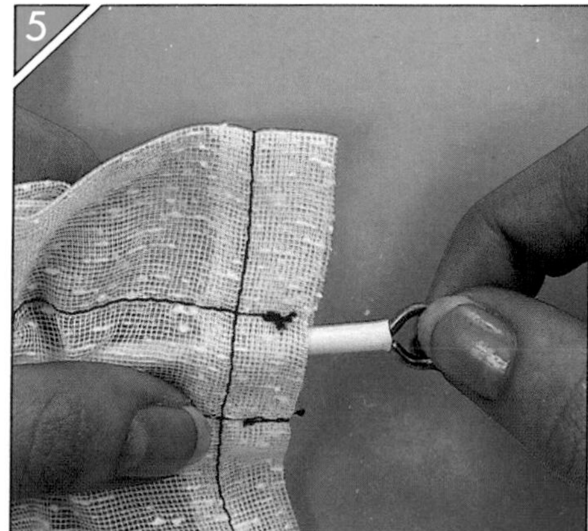

■ Thread a piece of curtain wire through the top casing and another piece through the bottom casing (**5**). The hooks at either end hook on to screw eyes inserted at either side of the window.

Curtain wire is ideal for small net curtains or sheers but curtain rods are usually a better idea for hanging larger net curtains, as rods will not sag. Rods thread through the casing in the same way as curtain wire, although you may need to make up a deeper casing to contain a rod. If so measure the depth of the rod before stitching the casing in step 3. Then in step 3 add 1cm to the rod depth and work the first row of stitching this distance from the inner fold of the hem. Complete the second row of stitching as shown in step 4. This will allow 5mm ease for threading the rod through.

• CAFE CURTAIN •

A pretty alternative to full length curtains, cafe curtains cover only half the window and can be made to remain permanently in place or draw back if hung in pairs. They are both decorative and practical, useful for a kitchen or bathroom window or similarly in any utility area where you need some light but may wish to screen the view from inside or prevent people looking in.

Cafe curtains can be made with a faced, scalloped heading and hung from decorative rings which are threaded onto a curtain pole. An alternative and popular style is a scalloped heading forming loops which can be slotted over a pole or rod. The scallop loops can be plain or pinch-pleated. Otherwise, you can make plain curtains with heading tape and use a pole and rings for hanging. If you choose a pencil pleat or clustered pleat heading, the curtains should be of a good depth to show off the effect.

Any type of suitable curtain fabric can be used, depending on the styling of the surroundings and the practicality of removing the curtains for cleaning. Bright printed cottons are a good choice for the kitchen, being easily washable, informal, and available in patterns and colours to match any style of furnishing, from cottage kitchen to hi-tech. Cafe curtains of this type do not need to be lined, but if you choose more formal styling – for a hallway or landing window bay, for example – a lining protects the main fabric from dirt and exposure to light and helps the curtain to hang elegantly.

Calculating fabric amounts

Curtain: Measure the width of the window. Add 10cm so that the curtain is not absolutely taut. Add 3cm seam allowances. Measure the length of the area to be curtained. Add 6cm for the hems.

Facing: The width of the curtain times 20cm deep.

You will need

- Curtain fabric
- Matching sewing thread
- Pattern paper
- Facing material
- Curtain rings

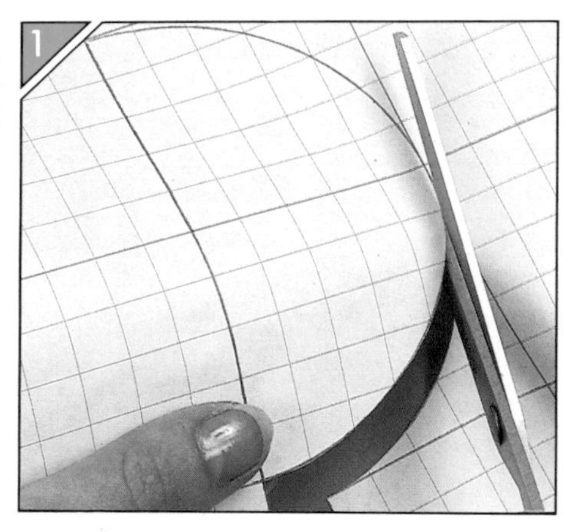

Making up

■ Decide on the size of the scallops at the top of the curtain. Add 1cm to inner curve for seam turnings. Using a pair of compasses or a suitable size plate or bowl, make a semi-circular template.

Cut a strip of paper the width of the finished curtain and draw on a line to represent the top of curtain, add on 1cm for seam turnings. Fold paper in half widthways; crease and unfold. Place the template on the centre of the strip with the straight edge of the semi-circle, aligning with the top line. Draw round the template. Continue along the strip of paper. Work outwards from the centre, leaving regular gaps between each semi-circle of no less than 4cm and finish about 4cm from each edge.

Cut the semi-circles from the paper pattern (**1**).

■ Cut out the curtain fabric to the required size. Pin the paper pattern along the top of the curtain fabric on the wrong side. Cut out scallops and remove paper pattern. (**2**).

Cut out the facing. Pin paper pattern to the top edge of the facing and cut out the scallops, making sure that they match those at the top of the curtain.

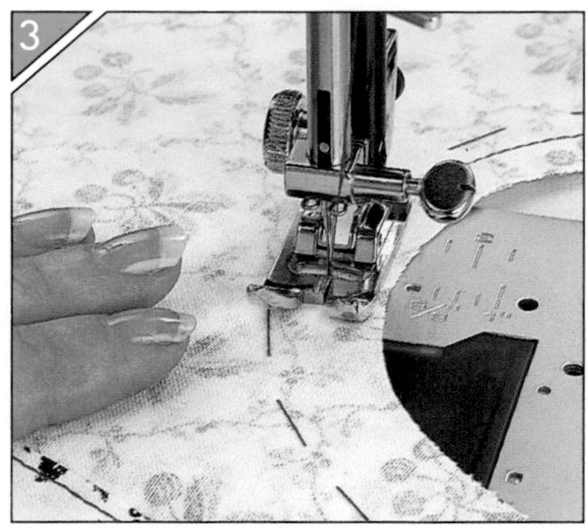

■ Turn a double 1cm hem along the unscalloped long edge of the facing. Pin and stitch in place.

Turn a double 1cm hem along the side edges of the curtain fabric. Pin and stitch in place (**3**).

Turn a double 2.5cm hem along the lower edge of the curtain. Pin and stitch the hem in place.

■ Right sides together and raw edges matching, pin the scalloped edge of the curtain fabric to the scalloped edge of the facing. Tack along the scalloped edge. Machine stitch scallops together, 1cm from raw edges (**4**). Remove tacking.

The raw edges of the facing at the sides will overlap the hemmed edges of the curtain fabric at the sides.

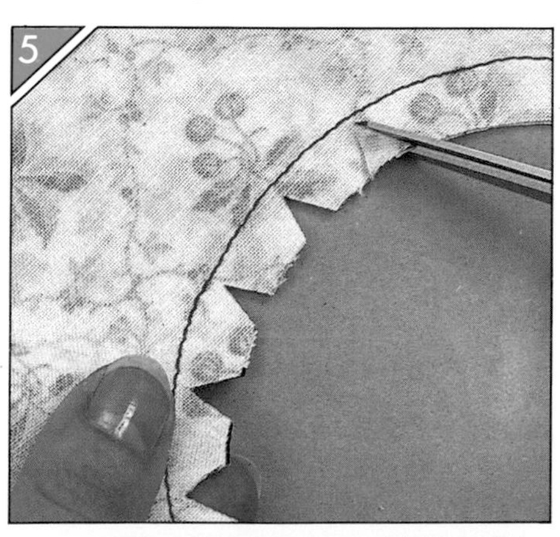

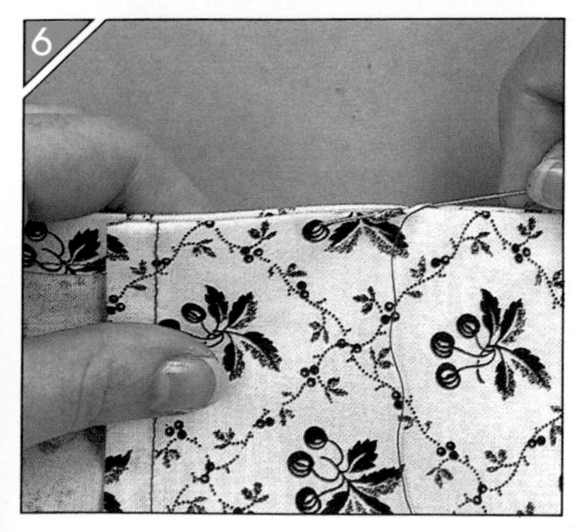

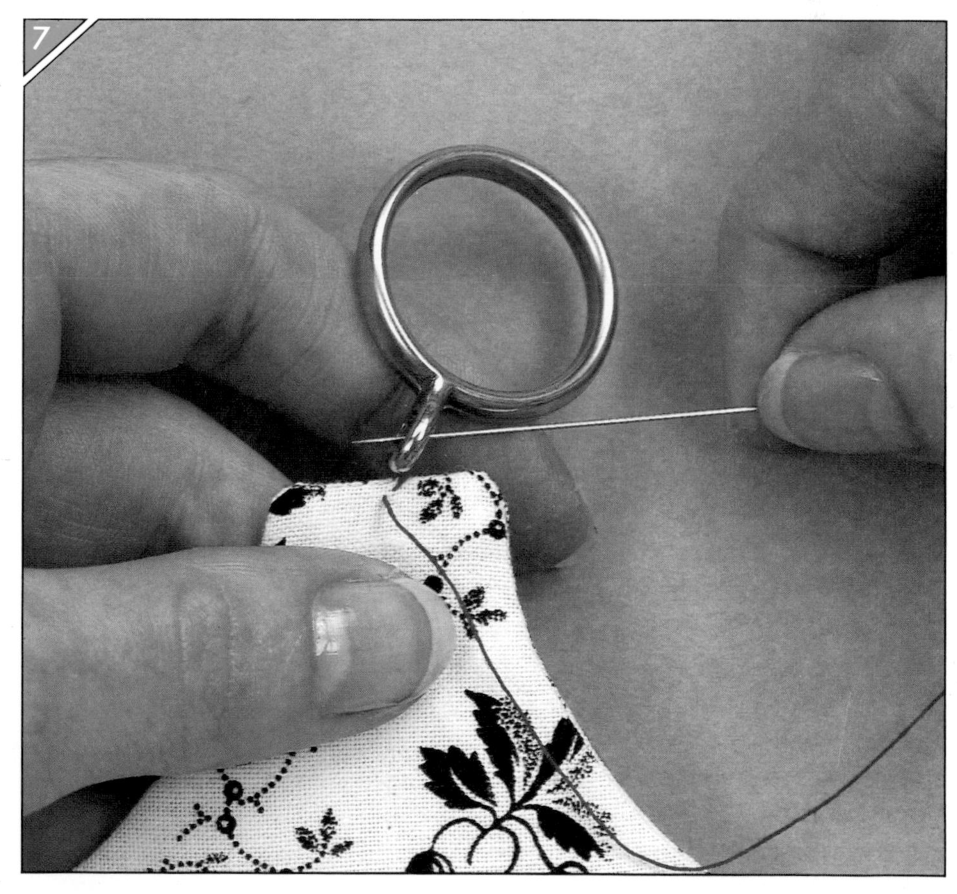

■ To reduce bulk, clip around each curve and across the corners of the scallops (**5**). Turn right side out and press carefully.

■ Turn under raw side edges of facing and press. **Slipstitch** turned-under edges to hemmed edges of curtain (**6**). Press.

■ Oversew a curtain ring at the centre of the space between two scallops to the wrong side of the curtain (**7**). Finish the ends securely.

· CURTAIN VALANCE ·

A deep frill of fabric gives a finished look to the top of a window, framing the proportions of window and curtaining and providing the final disguise for the curtain track. As with the main curtains, the valance can be hung on a track, rod or pole, depending on the weight of fabric, and the fixings can be mounted on a narrow shelf-like projection fitted above the window frame to fall cleanly and loosely over the curtain heading.

To create a stylish effect the valance should be of the same fabric as the curtains – a contrast or co-ordinate will look odd unless well linked to other furnishings in the room, but the valance provides an opportunity to apply neat trimmings if you wish to elaborate plain curtain styling – a braid, ribbon or narrow frilled trim at the bottom of the valance can make a bold or pretty addition to the overall scheme. Decide on the depth and decorative treatment of the valance after the main curtains are hung. You can use a gathered or pleated heading tape and the depth of the valance can be arranged to adjust the window proportions if necessary.

Calculating fabric amounts
Width: Measure the width of the window area and multiply by 1½ to 3 times, depending on the fullness required. Add 2.5cm for each side hem.
Depth: Divide the curtain drop by six; add 2.5cm for the lower hem allowance and 4cm for the top hem allowance.
Lining: Width and depth of the valance fabric, minus hem allowance.

You will need
- Valance fabric
- Matching sewing thread
- Curtain heading tape
- Lining fabric

Hand-pleated valance
A hand-pleated valance can look very attractive if you wish to use a stiff, heavy fabric. It is made in the same way as a lined valance, but before attaching the heading tape, fold and press pleats into equal divisions across the valance, see the section on pleats on page 168. Tack in place, and cover the raw edge with plain tape. Stitch hooks to the tape at regular intervals. Alternatively a curtain heading tape could be used, but not gathered up, to provide pockets for the hooks to be slotted into.

■ Making up
■ Cut out fabric to required size. Press under 2.5cm hems at sides and lower edge. Unfold hems and fold corners diagonally with right sides together. Stitch at right angles to fold from corner crease to 1cm from edge (**1**).

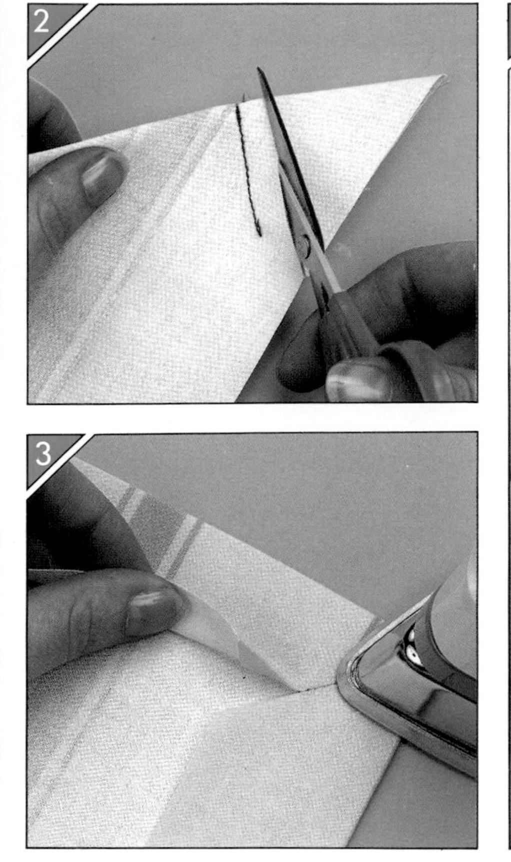

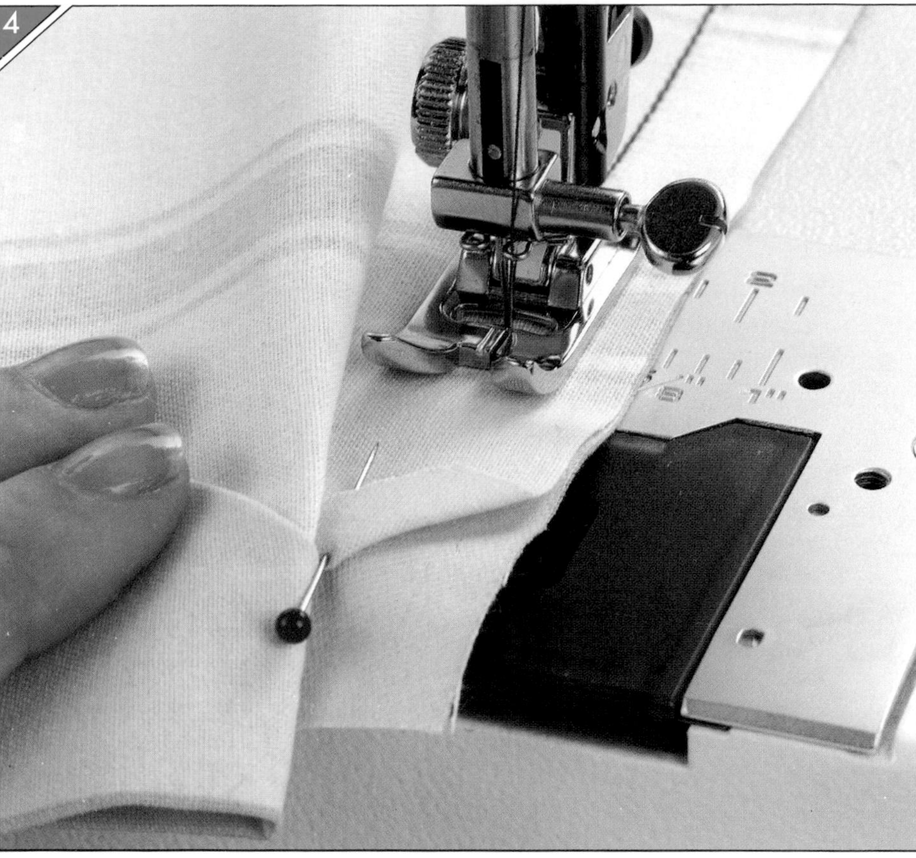

■ Cut off the corner 1cm away from the stitching (**2**). Turn right side out and poke out new corner. Press seam flat (**3**). Repeat for other bottom corner. Re-press side and bottom hems.

■ Trim 5mm from side and lower edges of lining for a sewn-in lining, place valance fabric and lining right sides together. Align side raw edges of lining fabric with side raw edge of valance hem. Pin together. The lining fabric will overlap the valance fabric at the corners. Machine stitch down both sides, 1cm in from the raw edges (**4**).

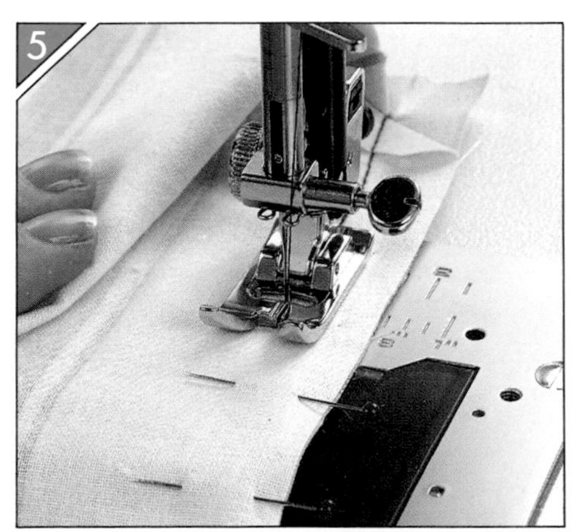

■ Stitch the bottom edge of lining to valance hem, 1cm away from the raw edges in same way as side edges (**5**).

Snip off the two bottom corners of the lining diagonally to reduce bulk. Turn right side out and press seams.

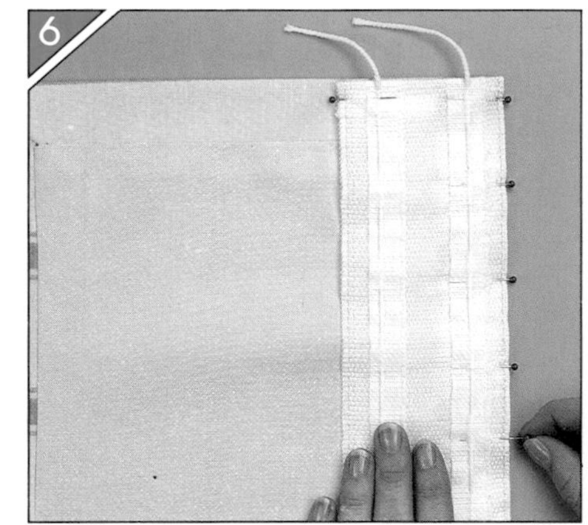

■ Turn top of valance fabric 4cm to the wrong side. It should fold at the top edge of the lining. Press, pin and sew in place.

Wrong sides together, pin heading tape to the top of the valance (**6**). Turn under the side edges of the heading tape to align with the fabric.

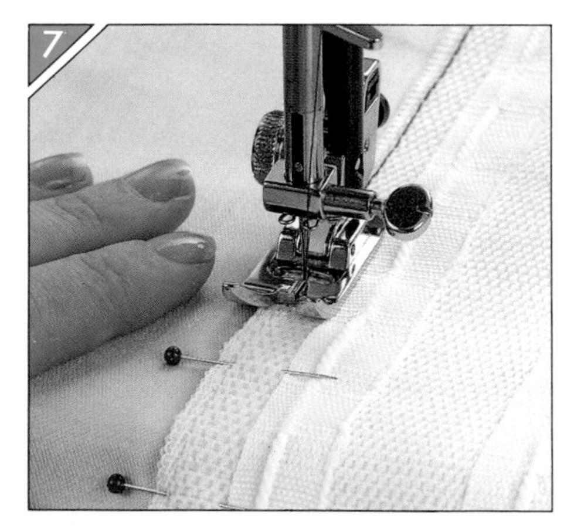

■ Knot the cords at one end and stitch this short side and then both long sides of the heading tape (**7**). Leave cords free at the other end to gather the valance.

When the valance is the correct width, tie the loose cords together and insert curtain hooks at regular intervals.

· PELMETS ·

A pelmet is a stiff panelled heading to curtains, unlike the valance which is draped. It must be based on a rigid support for the fabric covering, which may be a sturdy wooden "box" mounted above the windows or a specially-made stiffening designed as an interlining to fabric for this type of effect. Self-adhesive backing is available, which makes the work of stiffening the fabric quite simple, or you can use traditional buckram, a woven cloth treated to maintain rigidity, in combination with a heavy interlining.

Because the pelmet is rigid you can cut the lower edge to any shape – regular scallops or zigzags, or a broad arc at the centre of the window sweeping down to flat panels at either side over the drawn-back curtains. The simplest way to apply trimmings is to stick on braid or fancy edging with a fabric adhesive after the pelmet has been made up.

Construction of pelmets
Cut buckram or pelmet stiffening to the pelmet shape. Cut the fabric, lining and soft interlining to the shape adding on 1.5cm for turnings all round. Place the interlining on wrong side of fabric and stitch together around edges. Tack the stiffening centrally to wrong side of fabric and interlining. Turn the edge of fabric over the stiffening, clipping where necessary, and glue in place. Press slightly wider turnings to wrong side on lining and **slip-stitch** to back of pelmet.

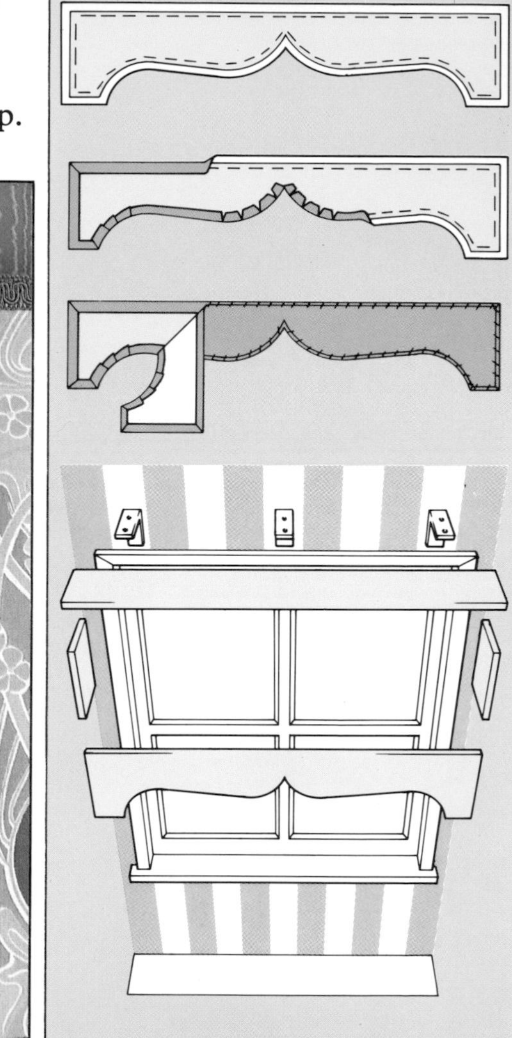

Fixing to the window
The fabric pelmet is mounted on to a wooden pelmet board which has small side boards (returns) attached at each end. The pelmet board is fixed above the window with angle irons and is positioned so the top of the board will be level with the top of the pelmet. Attach the pelmet with touch-and-close fastening along top of pelmet and front and side edge of the board, or with tacks.

· TIE-BACKS ·

Tie-backs can be purely practical – to keep the curtains out of the way when they are drawn back during the day – or they can make a distinctive decorative feature. You can use any of a number of corded and tasselled tie-backs available from department stores, or make your own from the same fabric as the curtains or a matching or co-ordinating choice. Alternatively, you can create an individual design of plaited ribbons, patchwork strips, braid, appliqué or any ornamental device that occurs to you. In this case, you may also wish to make the function of the tie-backs more decorative, by looping lightweight curtains gracefully to hang in graduated folds, for example.

Tie-backs
The stiffened fabric type are usually shaped with a gentle downwards curve at the centre which fits around the inner edge of the curtains. The tie-backs are constructed in the same way as a fabric pelmet. They are held in place by curtain rings, stitched to the wrong side at each end, which fasten onto a hook on the wall.

CHAPTER THREE

BLINDS

An alternative or addition to curtains, blinds offer stylish options for window dressing.

· BLINDS ·

Blinds offer a range of stylish and versatile window treatments, used as the only window covering or teamed with curtains. The look can vary from plain and simple to frankly exotic, according to the type of blind you prefer and your choice of fabric and trimmings. Choose the most appropriate style for the effect you wish to create – a Roman blind for smart graphic effect, a frilled Austrian blind for a pretty look; a festoon blind for sumptuous elegance. For simpler styling, a permanent half-length cottage blind blocks a drab view or protects your privacy if the window is overlooked. A basic roller blind is just a flat length of fabric, but clever choice of colour and pattern or an inventive way with trimmings and edgings can enliven the plain construction of the blind.

Practical and economical, blinds are often chosen for their functional advantages. Because they don't obstruct the window area in the same way as draped or billowing curtains, they are the ideal choice for windows situated above a desk, worktop or sink, or in a "working" area such as a bathroom or playroom. They are also particularly suitable for rooms which tend to be dark, as they don't cut out so much of the light when they are pulled up to the top of the window.

Choose fabric to reflect the mood of the blind. A small geometric print goes well with the clear uncluttered lines of the otherwise plain Roman blind. Bright yellow will add a sunny aspect, with the plain fabric showing the scallops and gathers of an Austrian blind well. Semi-sheer farics are ideal for blinds which will remain pulled down permanently, and the light shining through will accentuate the graceful scallops of a festoon blind.

CHOOSING FABRIC

When considering fabric for blinds, hold a piece up to the light to see the effect: patterned fabric can lose its impact and small patterns seem less well-defined; the colour of a plain fabric can appear washed out with the light shining through rather than on to the surface. Make a careful choice of the weight of the fabric, not only to suit your room styling but to take into account the different effects of the blind when it is drawn up or down.

ROMAN BLINDS hang flat when pulled down, but draw up into horizontal pleats. They should be made from a reasonably substantial fabric, but not one with a stiffened finish. Any good quality curtain weight cotton is suitable, and this gives a very wide choice, from plain colours and weaves to geometric patterns, chintzes and lightly textured finishes. Roman blinds are usually lined – use cotton sateen or an insulating curtain lining – to add body, keep in the warmth of the room and prevent the construction of the blind being shown up by light shining through the fabric when the blind is down

AUSTRIAN AND FESTOON BLINDS have a gracefully swagged appearance. Fullness comes from a curtain heading tape used at the top of the blind and a cord system which draws the blinds up into elegant loops of fabric. A festoon blind is constructed to have a permanently ruched effect even when drawn down fully. Both types look very pretty if made from lightweight voile, net, lace or fine cotton. This just filters the sunlight and offers some privacy, particularly effective if hung in combination with heavier curtains. But if the blind is the only window covering, you can equally well use a medium or heavyweight fabric. Cotton curtain weights are fine, but anything up to a heavy brocade for an Austrian blind can be used on a large window.

Either style can be left unlined, but if they are to be lined the main fabric is backed with curtain lining and the two fabric layers are treated as one in making up the blind. Any trimmings such as piping or frills can be added in self-fabric or a co-ordinated or contrasting choice, but they should be of a compatible weight and suitable for the same method of washing or dry-cleaning which will be applied to the main fabric.

A COTTAGE BLIND is ruched vertically across the window covering half the window area. It is mounted at the top on a fine rod or curtain wire and threading the fabric over the rod creates the ruching. Light or medium-weight fabrics are suited to this simple effect – attractive printed cottons and lightly embossed or textured fabrics for solid colour and pattern; sheers, nets and laces for translucency; broderie anglaise and other machine embroidered fabrics for a pretty, fancy finish.

A ROLLER BLIND should be made from a firm fabric which hangs smoothly and rolls up evenly. Specially stiffened blind fabrics are available in a good range of colours and patterns, many with border print features. Holland and PVC resist dirt and can be sponged clean. Otherwise, you can use any suitable cotton curtaining and treat it with a liquid or aerosol stiffener. Do this before cutting and test the stiffener on a sample piece of fabric first.

Choosing blind fabric

Light shining in through a window or darkness outside will alter the look of fabric used for blinds. See the effect of light and darkness on an all-over miniprint with a dark coloured background (left), a plain cotton seersucker (centre), and a lightweight flocked voile (right).

· POSITIONING AND MEASURING UP ·

Roman, Austrian and festoon blinds are usually attached to a wood batten so that the screw eyes holding the cords which draw up the blind can be fixed to the underside of the batten. Roman blinds are attached directly to the front face of the batten, but Austrian and festoon blinds have a curtain heading tape which can be hung from curtain track mounted on the batten, giving extra support to the weight of the fabric and making it easy to remove the blinds for washing or cleaning. It is also possible to buy a special blind track which incorporates the "eyes" for the cord system, making the batten unnecessary.

Blinds can be positioned inside or outside the window recess. If the blind is teamed with curtains, hang it inside the recess and make sure it won't catch on window fittings. A blind mounted outside the window recess can be positioned to make the window appear taller, the bottom of the blind just lapping the window frame when pulled up. This treatment also enables you to compensate for a window that is not quite square at the corners. The width of the blind should extend 10-15cm beyond the window recess on either side to avoid chinks of light showing when it is drawn down.

A cottage blind is positioned on the window and need not extend beyond the frame. A roller blind hangs from brackets which you can fix to the frame or just outside it. The way you hang any blind may affect the finished size. Before you measure up and buy fabric, make sure it is feasible to mount brackets or battens at the position where you want the blind to hang. It may be obstructed by a heavy window frame moulding and you should also check that window locks or handles won't affect the hang of the blind fabric when it is pulled all the way down.

Mounting blinds

Top: a roller blind mounted on the wall outside the window recess.
Centre: a Roman blind mounted within the window recess, with decorative tied-back curtains mounted outside the recess.
Bottom: net curtains mounted within the window recess, with an Austrian blind outside the recess.

CALCULATING FABRIC

Using a wooden rule or metal tape, measure the width and length of the area to be covered by the finished blind.

FOR A ROMAN BLIND add 4cm to the width for side hems and 11cm to the length for bottom and top turnings.

FOR AN AUSTRIAN BLIND the width is dictated by the heading tape you use and the length of the track on which the blind hangs, as for curtains. Measure the track length and multiply by 1½-2½, depending on the heading tape you choose (see page 32). Make a small allowance for side hems and joins in the fabric if necessary. If the fabric has a pronounced pattern, remember to allow extra for pattern matching. To the measured length, add 6cm to allow for top turning and hem.

FOR A FESTOON BLIND, calculate the fabric width as for the Austrian blind. If you want a lightly ruched effect down the length, allow twice the measured length; for a fuller effect allow three times the length. In either case, this includes enough fabric for a lath casing and a frill at the bottom edge.

FOR A COTTAGE BLIND, measure the area of window to be covered and add 4cm to the width for side hems. To the length, add enough to make a casing for the curtain wire or rod on which the blind is threaded at top and a hem at the bottom.

FOR A ROLLER BLIND, add 2cm to the width for side hems (ready-stiffened fabrics that will not fray need no hems) and add 30-35cm to the measured length to allow for a lath channel at the bottom and attachment to the roller at the top.

CALCULATING TAPE REQUIREMENTS

Roman, Austrian and festoon blinds are drawn up by a system of cords passing through loops or rings on rows of tape stitched vertically on the back of the blind. You can use plain tape and stitch on small plastic curtain rings, or buy special blind tapes with loops or rings woven into the construction of the tape itself at regularly spaced intervals. To calculate how much tape is needed, make a scale drawing of the blind and work out how many vertical tapes should be evenly spaced across the width to draw it up neatly. You must position tapes down either side of the blind close to the edge; those in between should be spaced equally across the width of the gathered blind no more than 30cm apart.

The heading tape for an Austrian or festoon blind must run the width of the fabric; allow 1cm at each end to turn under for a neat finish.

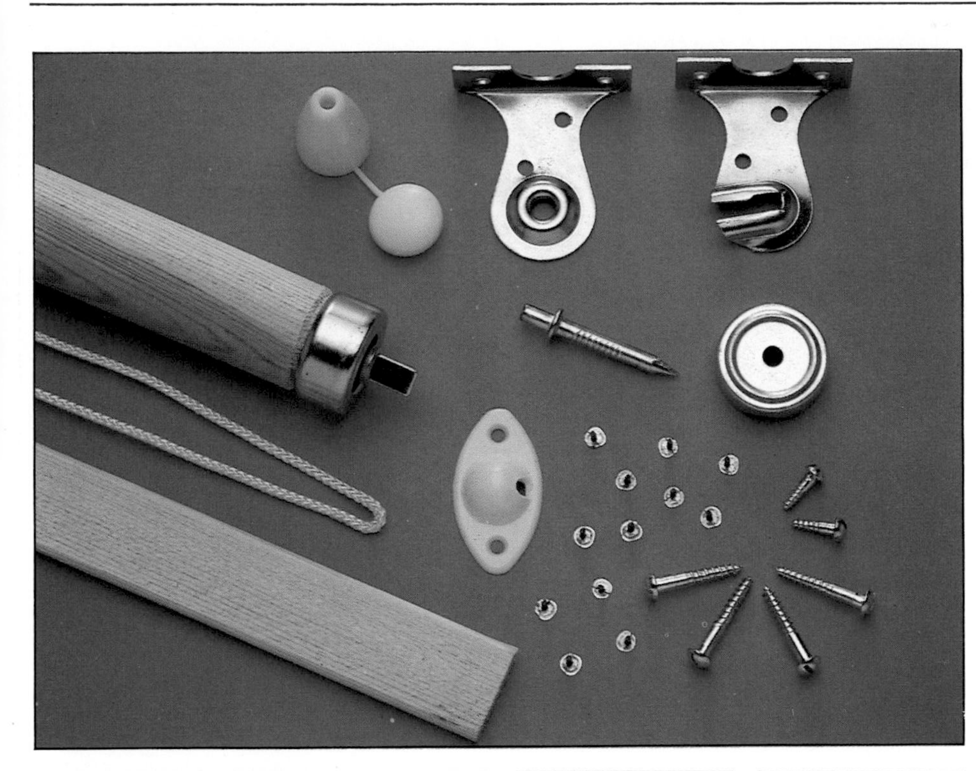

Roller blinds

A roller blind kit includes the roller with a square pin at one end, which encloses the winding mechanism. A separate round cap and round pin is provided for the other end, which is hammered in place after the roller has been cut to size. The slotted bracket for the square pin should be fitted at the left of the blind and the round pin bracket at the right. A wooden batten is attached to the lower edge of the blind. A cord holder fixes the pulling cord to the batten, and a puller is supplied for the other end of the cord. The fabric is fixed to the roller with tacks. All the fixing screws needed are provided with the kit.

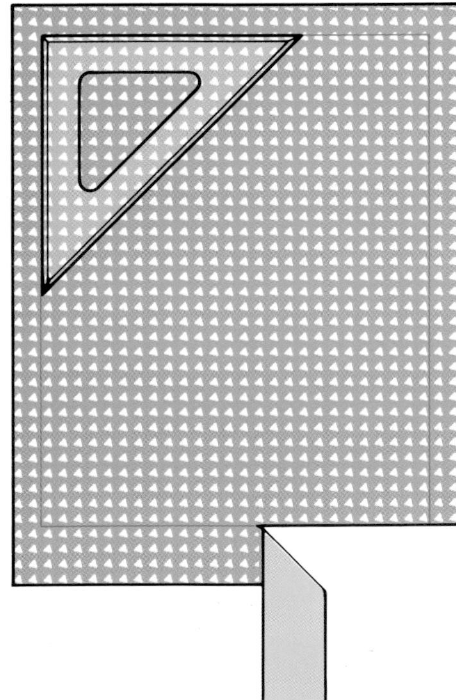

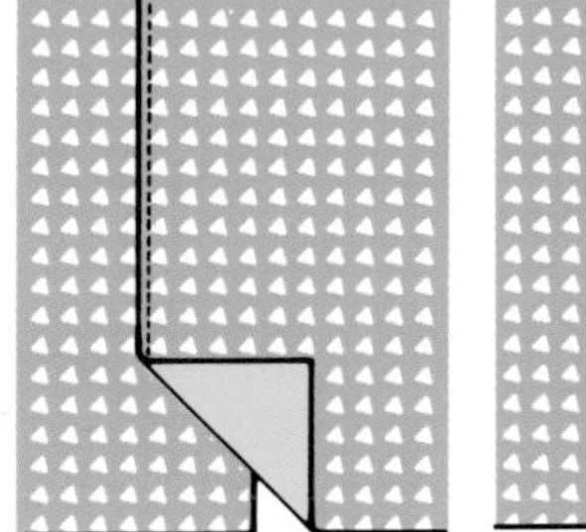

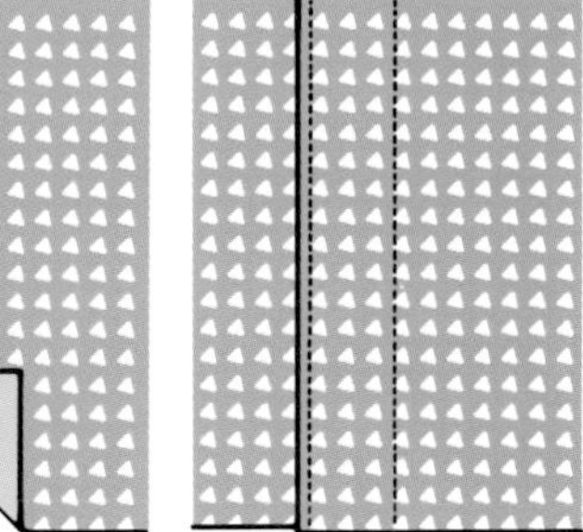

Joining sections

When it is necessary to join fabric widths, match any pattern carefully allowing for a 1cm overlap. Overlap edges and machine stitch unstiffened fabric near both edges. Alternatively join stiffened fabric by overlapping edges in the same way and fastening with an adhesive strip.

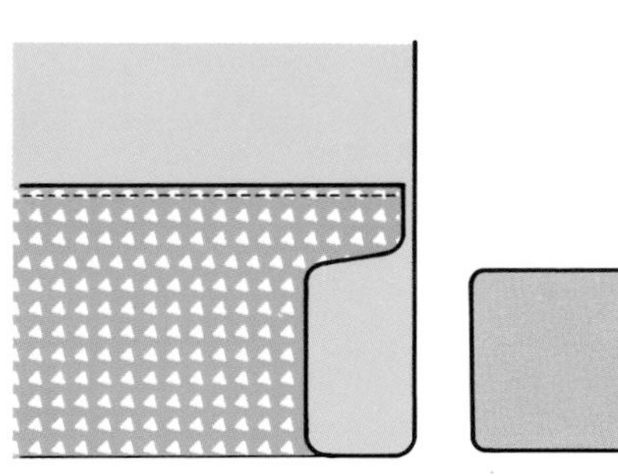

Fitting the batten

Cut the batten to 1cm less than the width of blind. Fold a single hem, 5mm wider than batten, to wrong side and stitch. Thread batten in and **slipstitch** ends.

Cutting out the blind

Measure the length and the width of the area to be covered. Add at least 30cm to the length so the roller will be covered when the blind is pulled down. Arrange the position of any pattern on the fabric carefully. Mark out the blind using a long ruler and a set square at the corners to ensure they form perfect right angles.

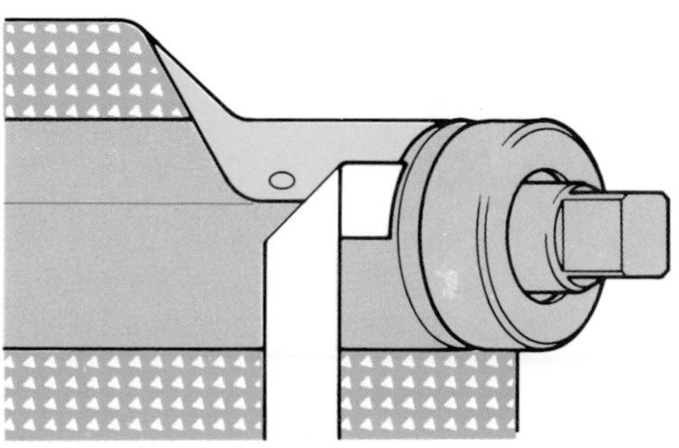

Completing the blind

Place the roller on right side of fabric with edge of fabric along the line marked on roller. Fasten with adhesive tape then hammer in tacks and remove tape. Thread the puller and cord holder onto cord and fasten cord holder to batten. Fix wall brackets allowing 5cm above in a recess so the blind can run freely. Roll the blind tightly around the roller and place the roller into appropriate brackets.

Roman blinds

Before cutting out the blind fabric, work out the position for the top batten from which the blind will be hung. Measure the length from the top edge of the batten position to the required finished blind length. Then add the hem allowances (see page 64) to the length before cutting out. First fold and stitch the side hems, then the top hem of the blind.

Measure width of blind and divide the amount by 30cm, rounding up or down to the nearest whole number. This will give the number of sections between the vertical tapes. Fold the blind into the appropriate number of sections and press in creases at folds as guidelines for the tapes. Cut tapes to fit over side hems and creases, making sure each lower ring or loop is 12cm up from edge. Make lower hem.

Tie cord firmly to the lowest ring or loop on the first tape. Thread the cord up through the ring or loops, then across the top to the side edge and down the length of the blind. Make sure the edge with the loose cord is the edge from which you wish to pull the blind. Thread cords through all tapes in this way, each time taking the cord across the top edge and down the side edge of the blind.

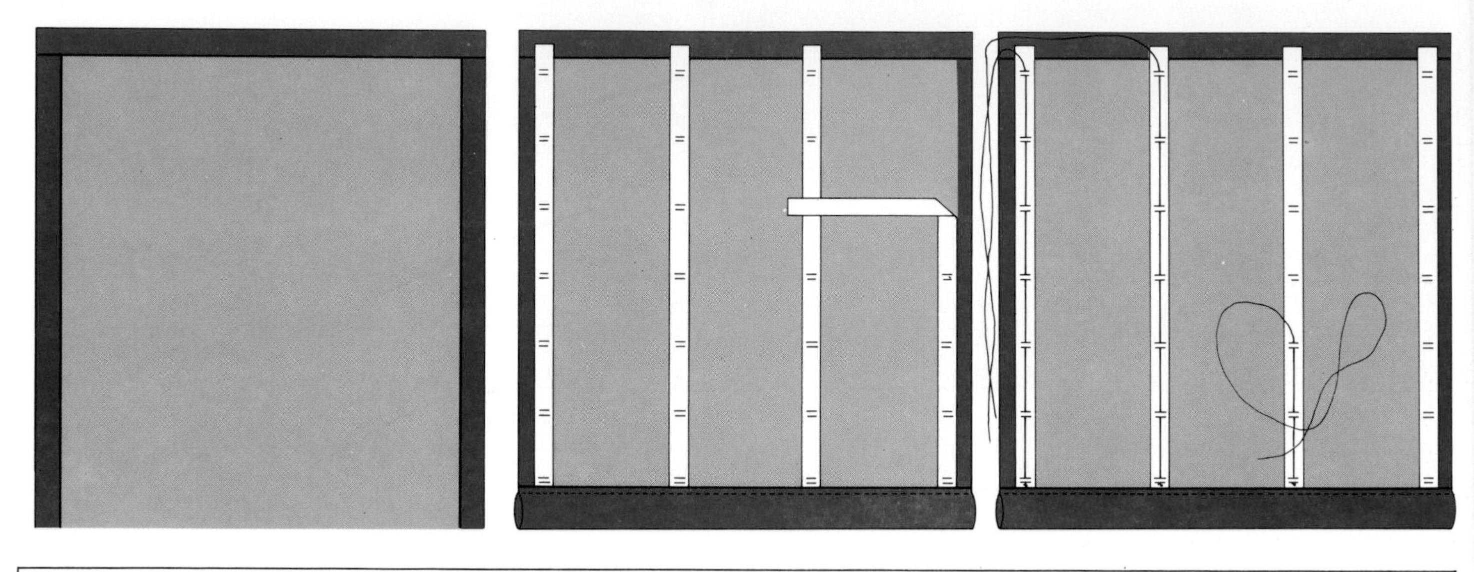

Fixing and rigging a Roman blind

Fix wall brackets to the batten, and lay batten across top edge of blind. Choose screw eyes which are large enough to thread all the cords through. Screw the eyes into the underside of the batten to line up with each cord. Wrap top hem of blind over top edge of batten and attach with tacks or staples. Thread each cord through its appropiate eye, then across through the other eyes to the side edge. Knot cords together near top of side edge. Fix the batten in place. Knot cords again at the ends, or leave a single cord as the puller and trim others at top knot.

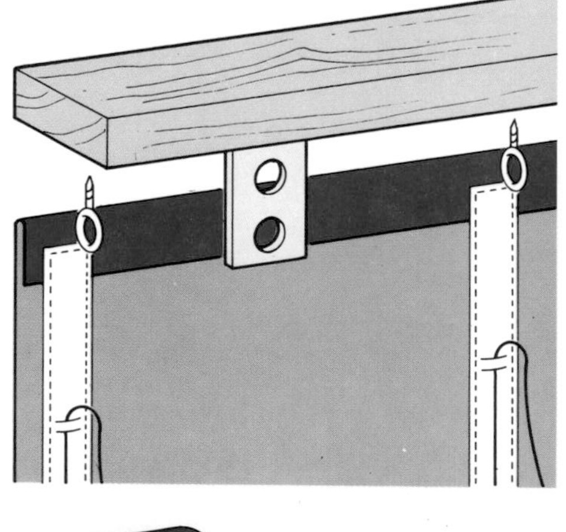

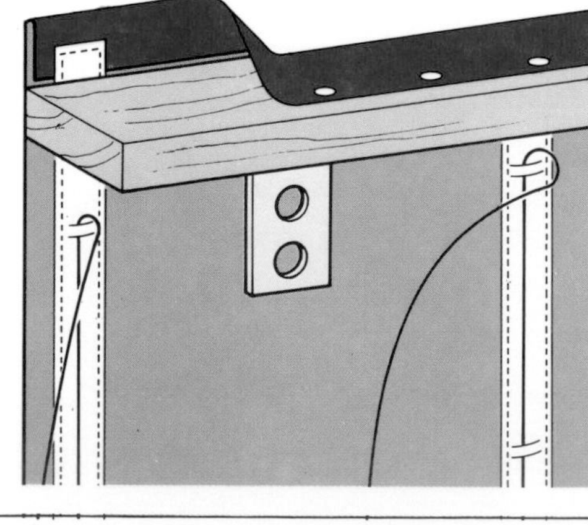

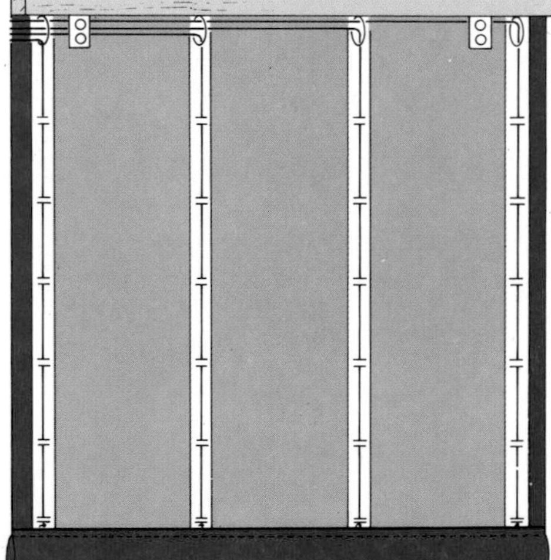

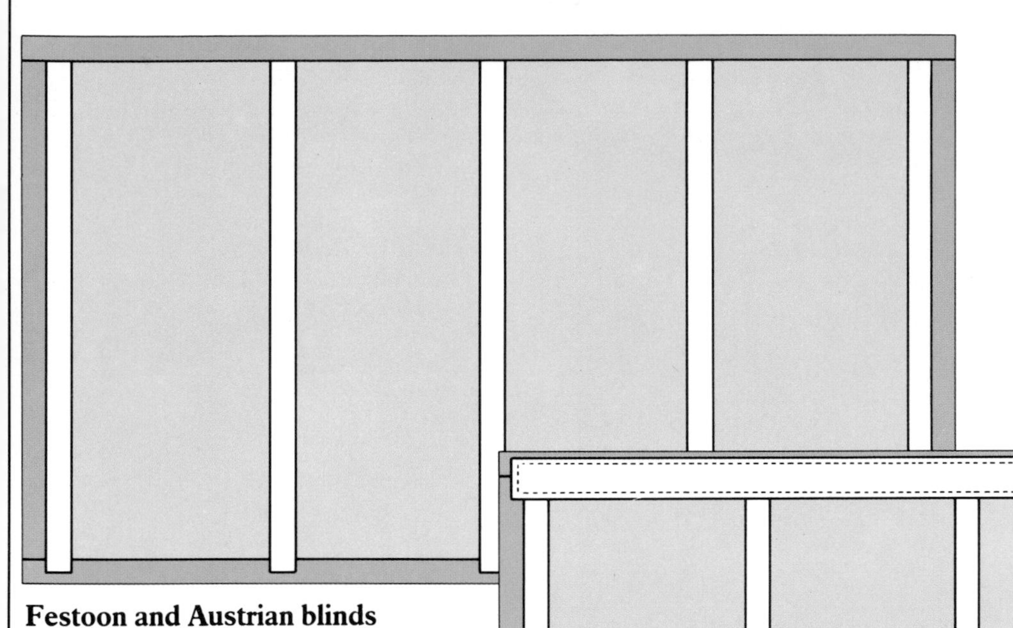

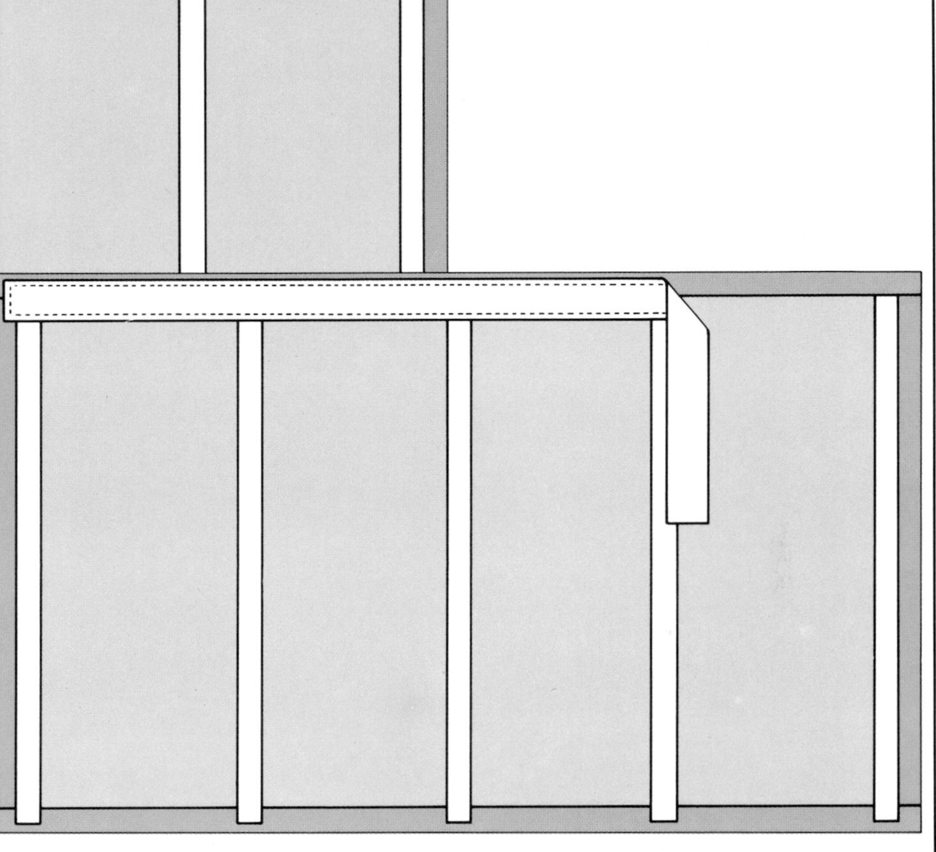

Festoon and Austrian blinds

These blinds are gathered at the top with a heading tape like curtains, and the gathering will pull the tapes effectively closer together on the finished blind. The festoon blind, which also has extra lengthwise fullness, requires less widthwise fullness so the tapes are placed closer together. The Austrian blind has more fullness with the tapes placed further apart. In both cases the tapes should be about 30cm apart when the blind is gathered, though the distance can be varied to suit the window size and shape.

First make the side and lower hems. Then position the vertical tapes. On tapes with loops or rings ready attached make sure a loop or ring is positioned near the lower edge and that the loops or rings line up horizontally on each tape. Then fold the top hem over and stitch on the heading tape. Gather the heading tape to window size. Attach and thread the cords in the same way as the Roman blind.

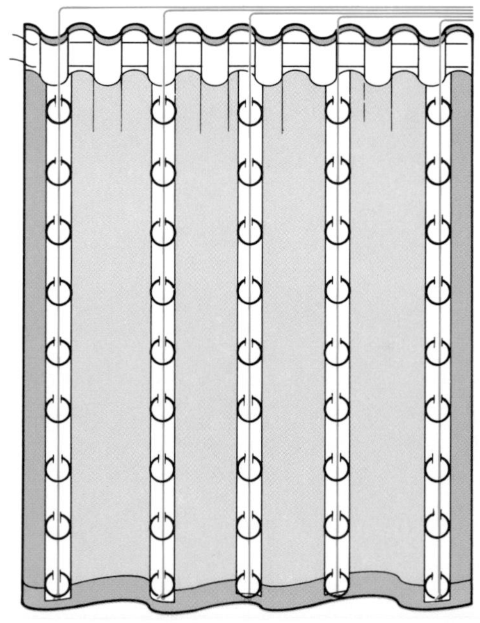

Hanging the blind

A special Austrian blind track is available which includes eyes which can be attached to the track for the cords. Alternatively the blind could be mounted onto a wooden batten with a curtain track fixed to the front of the batten and eyes screwed to the underside in line with the cords. Thread the cords in the same way as a Roman blind.

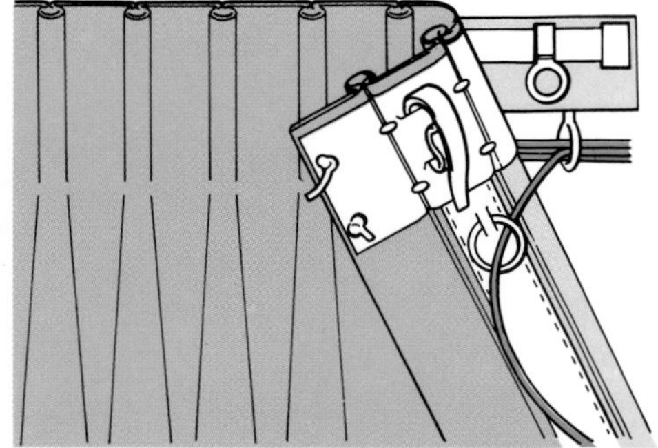

· ROMAN BLIND ·

A Roman blind hangs flat against the window when drawn down and folds into deep horizontal pleats as it is raised. Roman blinds give an elegant, tailored look to the room, but are not difficult to make, particularly if you use a blind tape with woven-in loops or rings already attached. This fixes the size of the pleats, so if you wish to create deeper or narrower folds, you can machine stitch plain tapes down the back of the blind and sew on small curtain rings by hand.

The geometric styling of the blind is particularly suited to strong colours and definite patterns, but when choosing patterned fabrics, bear in mind that the pleating will interrupt any large motifs or one-directional designs. All-over miniprints are ideal and you can find these in good medium-weight cottons which are firmly woven and will fold crisply when drawn up. Plain, bold colours also create a good effect – clean lines are the essential feature here.

Calculating fabric amounts

Length: Measure the window drop. Add 14cm for hem allowances and a little extra for making horizontal tucks in the fabric.
Width: Measure the width of the window area. Add 6cm for side hems. Allow extra for seams allowances if you are joining widths of fabric.
To calculate tape requirements, see diagram on page 62.

You will need

- Fabric
- Matching sewing thread
- Looped blind tape
- Wooden lath 4cm deep, 1cm shorter than width of blind
- 5cm×2cm wooden batten the width of the blind
- Staples or tacks

Types of blind tape

There are various types of blind tape but they all work on the same principle. The tape has rings or loops placed at regular intervals along the tape. A cord ties into the lowest ring or loop and threads up through the other rings or loops which pull up to form the back folds of the blind when the cord is pulled. The tapes shown below left and centre, have rings or loops ready fixed and these are suitable for Roman and Austrian blinds. The tape shown right, is a narrow curtain heading tape with hand fixed rings. This tape can be gathered making it suitable for a festoon blind.

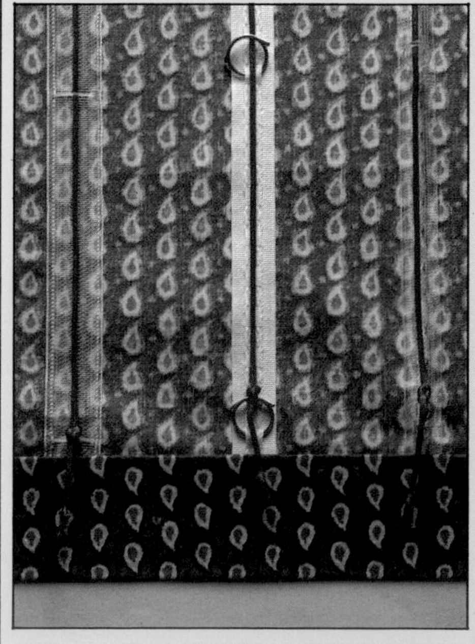

Making up

■ Cut fabric to required size. Turn a double 1.5cm hem to the wrong side along each side edge. Pin, tack and stitch. Turn a double 2.5cm hem along the top edge of the blind. Pin, tack and stitch (**1**).

■ Fold and press the fabric at 25-30cm intervals across the width to provide guidelines for positioning vertical tapes. Cut strips of looped blind tape to the length of the blind plus 1cm. Pin, tack and stitch the first strip close to the side hem (**2**), turning under 1cm at the top to neaten the raw edge.

■ Stitch tapes down the back of the blind following the foldlines, making sure the loops in the tapes line up horizontally across the width of the blind.

Across the bottom of the blind turn and press 1cm, then fold up a 5cm hem. Pin, tack and stitch to form a casing hem (**3**). Slot the wooden lath through casing, **Slipstitch** hem ends together.

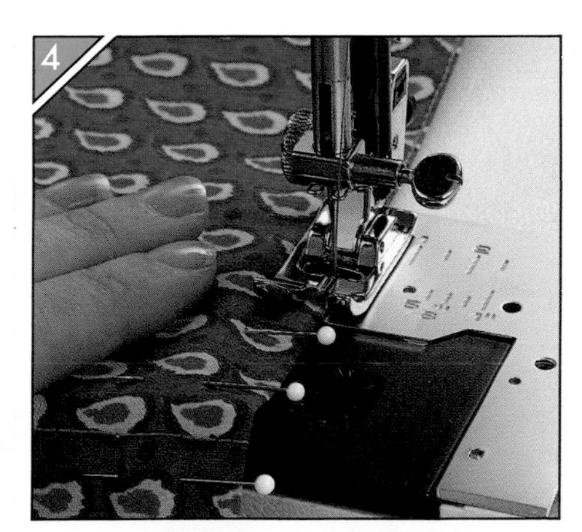

■ To help form neat, tailored folds when the finished blind is drawn up into pleats, tack and stitch 3mm deep horizontal tucks across the width of the blind to correspond to alternate rows of loops on the vertical tapes. Make the first tuck at the level of the second loop from the bottom of the blind (excluding the casing hem). To make the tuck, fold and press the fabric wrong sides together and stitch 3mm from the fold (**4**). Press the folds accurately, following the straight grain of the fabric, to ensure that they will make clean, evenly spaced horizontal lines across the blind when it is hung.

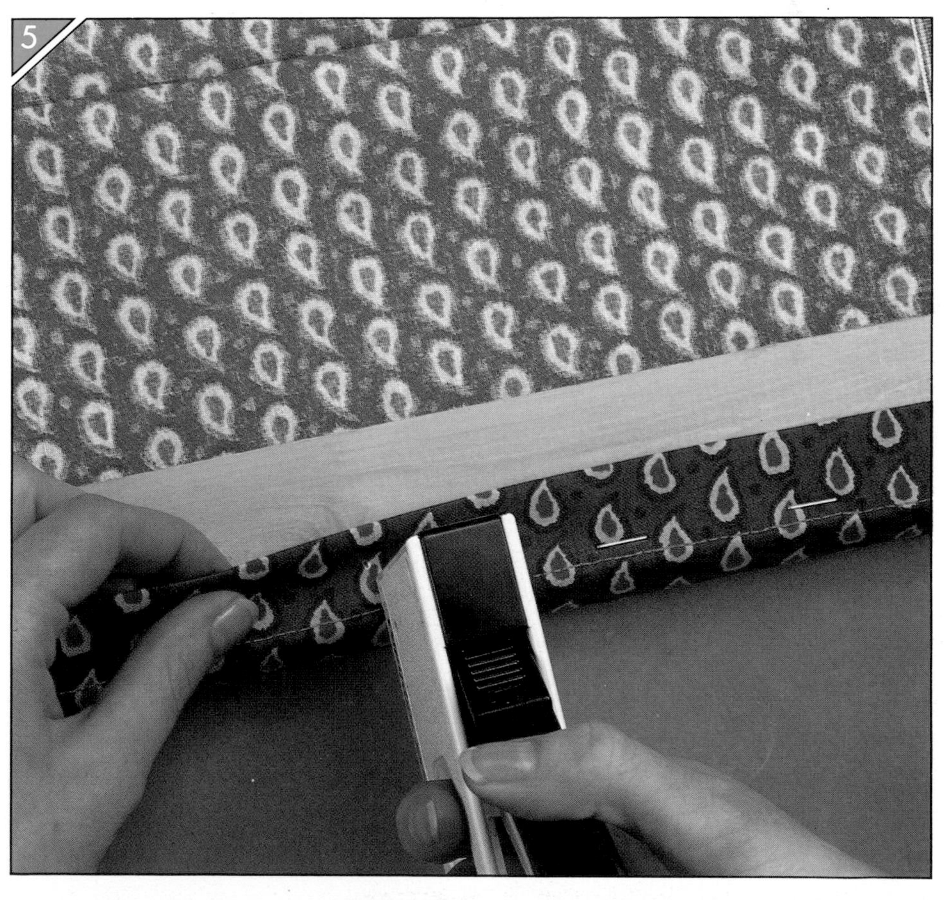

■ Cut the wooden batten to the width of the blind. Spread out the blind right side down and place the batten across the top edge. Turn the top hem over on to the broad side of the batten and staple or tack across the width (**5**). To insert the cord system and mount the blind, see the diagram on page 62.

· AUSTRIAN BLIND ·

An Austrian blind creates remarkable impact with its loosely folded swags. The fullness comes from a gathered or pleated heading combined with the generous looping as the blind is drawn up. You can choose a light, medium or heavy fabric – the blinds adapts to the distinctive character of its material. Light and medium weight cottons in bright colours or patterns have a sunny or vivid effect. A lightly textured or satinized surface provides an extra dimension, and sheers are also excellent, giving a beautifully softened look. Alternatively, the blind can be made of a heavy-weight fabric which creates a more sculptured effect as the looping occurs, subtly emphasized if the fabric has a distinct surface sheen.

The decorative styling can be further elaborated by the addition of a frill across the bottom of the blind, even running the length of both sides as well for a really sumptuous finish.

Calculating fabric amounts

Length: Measure the window drop. Add 6cm for hem allowances.

Width: Measure the width of the window and multiply by 2-2½ to allow enough fabric width to form heading pleats. Add 4cm for side hems.

To calculate tape requirements, see diagram on page 63.

You will need

- Fabric
- Matching sewing thread
- Looped blind tape
- Curtain heading tape
- Cord

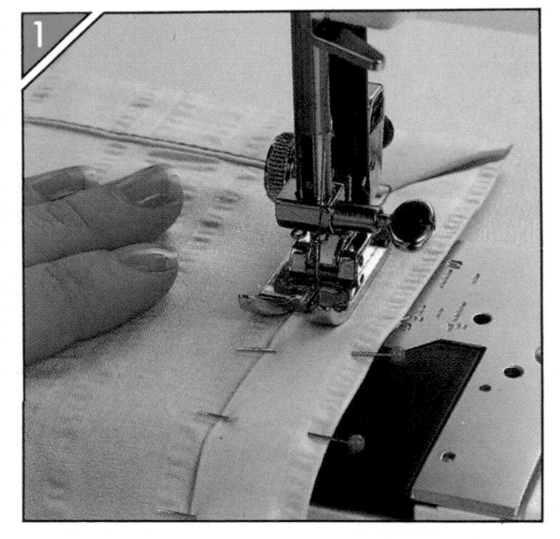

Making up

■ Cut fabric to required size. Along the bottom and both sides of the fabric turn a double 2cm hem to the wrong side. **Mitre** the corners. Pin, tack and stitch the hems in place (**1**).

Cut strips of looped blind tape to the length of the blind plus 1cm. These strips of tape are to be positioned down the length of the blind at regularly spaced intervals of about 60cm across the width. Make sure there is a loop 1cm up from the bottom of each length of tape and that the strips are matched exactly so that when in position the loops will line up horizontally across the blind.

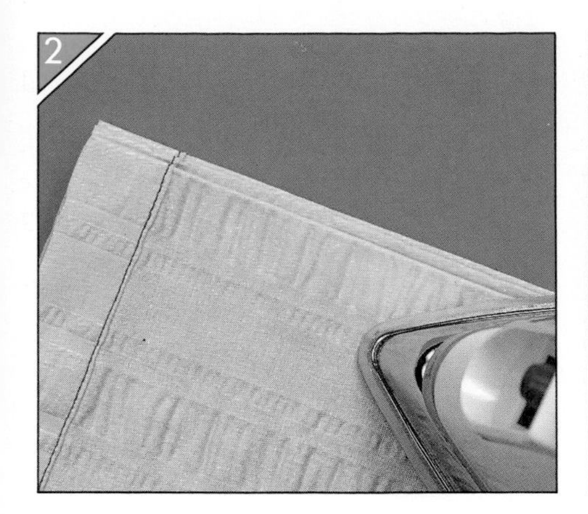

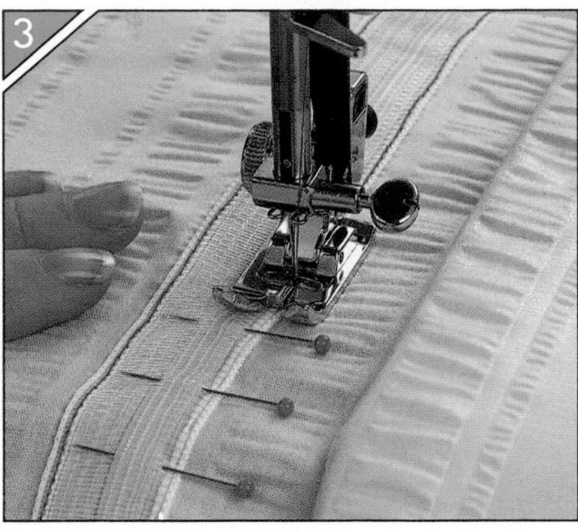

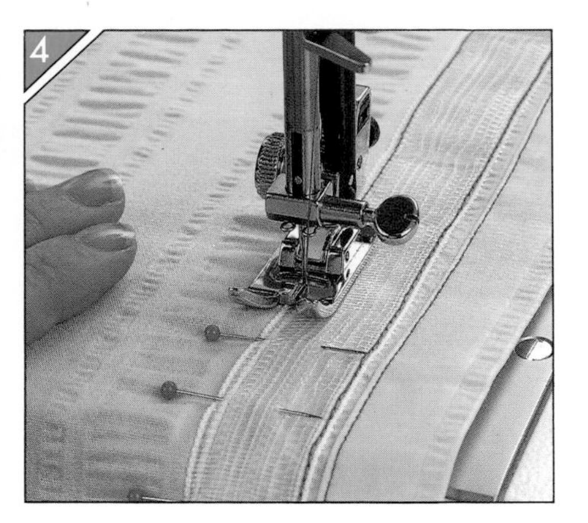

■ Fold the fabric vertically concertina fashion at approximately 60cm intervals across the width and press (**2**). The fold lines provide the guide to positioning the vertical tapes. If there are any joins in the fabric, arrange for the seams to be covered by the tape, but do not allow the spacing between vertical strips to become irregular.

■ Place the first length of tape down the length of the blind 2.5cm from the side edge, close to the side hem. Turn the end of tape under for 1cm at hem edge, pin, tack and stitch down both edges of the tape (**3**), working both lines of stitching in the same direction so the tape does not pucker.

■ Continue stitching the tapes at regular intervals across the width of the blind. Neaten the lower end of each tape by turning under 1cm at the hem of the blind. As the tapes are positioned, check that the loops are matched down each length to line up horizontally and conceal any seams under the tapes (**4**).

■ Turn 2cm of fabric to the wrong side across the top of the blind and press. Pin and tack heading tape across the top of the blind to cover the raw edge of the turning. Stitch heading tape in place (**5**).

Gather or pleat the heading tape until the blind is window width. Thread cords through the loops in the vertical tapes, as shown on page 63, before mounting the blind in place.

Adding a frill

To make the blind more opulent a frill of purchased broderie Anglaise edging or a fabric frill can be added to the side and lower edges. First decide the required finished frill depth and trim this amount plus 2.5cm from the appropriate edges of the blind. For the ***frill*** *length allow $1^1/_2$ times the length of the blind edges. For a double fabric frill, allow twice the required finished depth plus 3cm for the depth of frill. Cut and join enough strips to make the frill the required length. Gather up the edge of the frill to fit the blind arranging extra gathers at the corners. With right sides facing, stitch the frill to the edge taking 1.5cm seams. Trim the seam to 1cm and zigzag stitch the raw edges together.*

· FESTOON BLIND ·

A festoon blind is similar to an Austrian blind, but though the swags are made by drawing up the fabric on a similar cording system, the festoon blind has additional ruching which keeps its effect even when the blind is fully let down. Narrow curtain heading tape is used for the vertical tapes on the blind and it is drawn up to make even gathers down the length which remain permanently in place. Small split curtain rings are inserted at regular intervals to accommodate the cording system.

The ruched finish works extremely well in light and medium weight fabrics – sheer, slightly textured or with a shiny surface. A translucent fabric creates romantic styling, and a lightweight blind can be teamed with heavily draped, floor length curtains to create a luxurious effect. If the blind is used alone, a heavier fabric and rich, strong colour emphasizes warmth and privacy in the room when the blind is down.

Calculating fabric amounts

Length: Measure the window drop and multiply by 1½ for medium weight or 3 for lightweight fabrics. Allow 5cm for the top turning and frill seam.

Width: Measure the width of the window area and multiply by 1¼ for medium weight or 1½ for lightweight and sheer fabrics. Add 4cm for side hems and 1cm seam allowances if you are seaming widths of fabric together.

For the frill: You need enough 20cm deep strips of fabric to make up one long strip 1½ times the width of the blind fabric. To calculate tape requirements, see diagram on page 63.

You will need

- Fabric
- Matching sewing thread
- Narrow, lightweight curtain heading tape
- Small curtain rings
- Curtain heading tape
- Cord

■ **Making up**

(The steps are shown in solid fabric rather than the sheer fabric shown in the main picture, to illustrate the detail clearly.)

■ Cut fabric to required size. Turn a double 2cm hem to the wrong side down each side edge. Pin, tack and stitch in place.

To make the frill, fold the seamed strip of fabric in half along its length, right sides together with raw edges matched. Stitch a 1cm seam across both short ends. Turn out to the right side and press. Work two rows of gathering stitchings through both layers of fabric along the top edge of the frill (**1**).

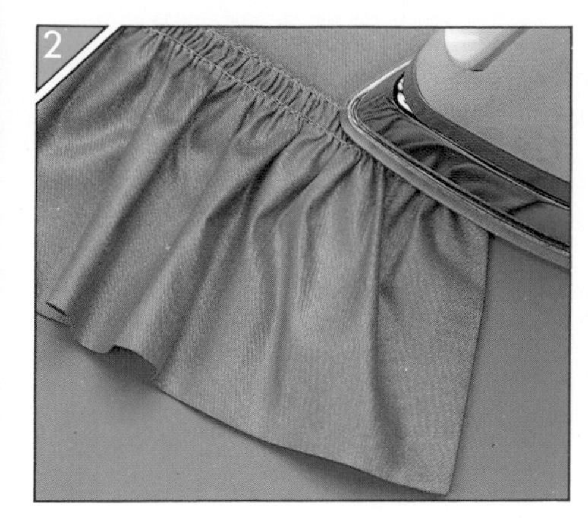

■ Pull the gathering threads until the width of the frill equals the width of the blind. Even out gathers and knot thread ends. Right sides together, align the raw edge of the frill with the bottom edge of the blind fabric. Pin, tack and stitch the frill in place (**2**). Press frill seam upwards on to the wrong side of the blind.

Fold the blind fabric at regular intervals of 25-40cm across the width and press the folds. These provide guidelines for positioning the vertical strips of heading tape. Lengths of tape should be spaced evenly and positioned over the side hems and over any seams joining fabric widths.

■ Cut the appropriate number of strips of tape to the length of the blind (excluding frill) plus 1cm. Pin lengths of tape in position following the foldlines, turning under 1cm to neaten the ends at the seamline of the frill. Beginning with the tape at the side hem, tack and stitch each length of tape in place (**3**). Press the fabric from the wrong side using a steam iron or dry iron and damp cloth.

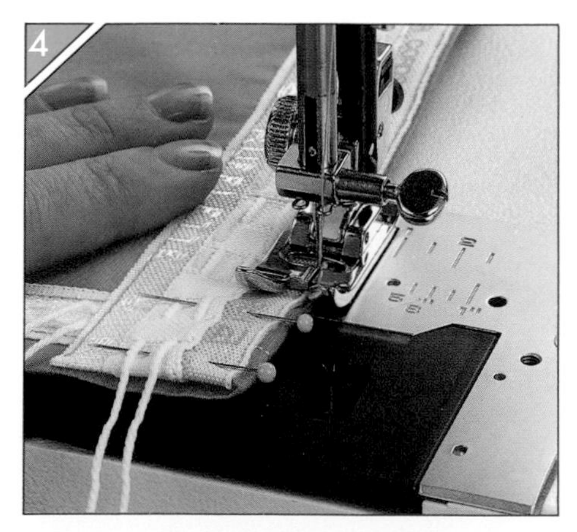

■ Turn 4cm of fabric on to the wrong side across the top of the blind. Position curtain heading tape along the turning to cover the raw edge. Pin, tack and stitch in place, but keep the gathering cords on the vertical tapes clear of the horizontal stitching line on the heading tape, tuck raw ends of tape under to neaten (**4**).

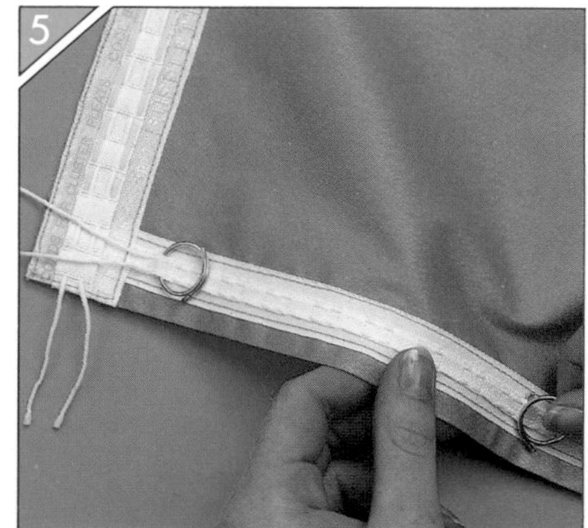

■ Slot small curtain rings into the vertical lengths of tape at evenly spaced intervals of about 20cm (**5**). The top rings should be just below the heading and the bottom rings should sit about 10cm from the bottom of the blind. Space them accurately so that the rings line up horizontally across the blind width.

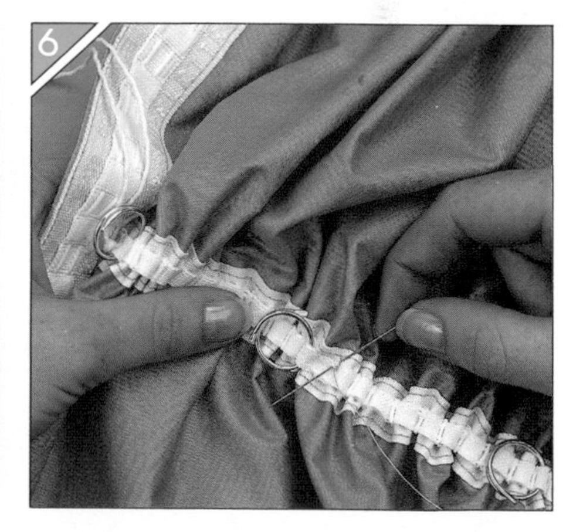

■ Pull the cords in the vertical tapes to gather up the blind evenly to the required drop. Tie off the cords. Hand stitch neatly just below each ring to secure cords to fabric (**6**), to prevent slippage when the blind is in place. Gather the heading tape at the top of the blind to the required width. Thread cords through the rings as showns on page 62.

· COTTAGE BLIND ·

This pretty half-length blind effectively disguises an ugly window or blocks an undesirable view but it is a permanent feature, suitable for a bathroom or small landing window, for example, where you do not need to vary the amount of light entering. It can be mounted on curtain wires or on narrow rounded or flattened curtain rod, threaded through a casing on the fabric at top and bottom and attached to the window frame on either side. A cottagey print in glazed cotton is a highly suitable fabric choice; the treatment also lends itself to sheers or fancy fabrics such as Swiss muslin or broderie Anglaise.

Traditionally, a cottage blind over the lower half of the window is given a finished look by the addition of a short valance at the top. If you choose a print fabric with a clearly defined border section, this border used as the valance makes a pretty link between the top of the window and the bottom of the cottage blind.

Calculating fabric amounts
This blind is made from one piece of fabric and does not require a tuck to be made for the wire. It is therefore ideal if you wish to use a patterned fabric.
Length: Measure the window drop. Add 3cm for hem allowance and 6.5cm for making the top casing.
Width: Measure the width of the window area. Add on 1¼-1½ times width for fullness and 2cm for each side hem.

You will need
- Fabric
- Matching sewing thread
- Curtain wire and eyes

Making up

■ Cut the blind fabric to the required size. Place fabric face down and turn a double 1cm hem along both of the side edges of the blind. Pin, tack and stitch in place. With the fabric still face down, turn a double 1.5cm hem along the lower edge of the blind. Pin, tack and stitch in place (**1**).

■ Wrong sides together, turn under the top of the blind by 1cm then another 5.5cm to make a double hem. Press in the fold. Pin, tack and sew in place 5mm from the inner edge (**2**). This will form the casing for the wire, which is inserted to make sure that the blind hangs evenly.

■ Measure 3cm down from the fold at the top of the blind. Pin, tack and stitch across the width of the blind at this point (**3**). Make sure that this line of stitching is parallel to the first line of casing stitching. This completes the casing.

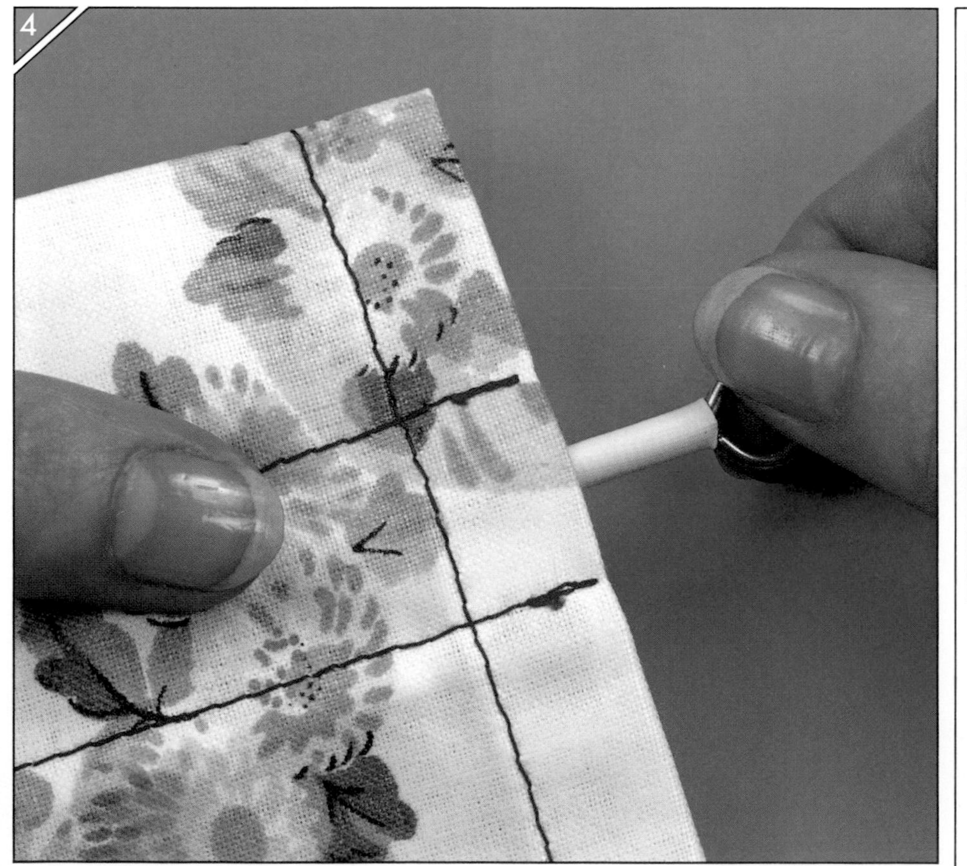

■ Trim curtain wire to correct length. It will need to be slightly shorter than the distance between hooks so it is held taughtly. Screw eyes into ends of wire and thread the wire through the casing (**4**).

Making an unlined valance

The gathered valance, which is traditionally made to hang above a cottage blind, is unlined. The valance is cut to the same width as the blind, and its length may vary between a quarter to half the blind length depending upon the size of the window. Add on the same top and bottom hem allowances as on the blind. The valance is made in the same way as the blind. Position the hooks, which will hold the curtain wire, about 3cm down from the top of a recessed window. This will allow the self fabric frill at the top of the curtain to stand up above the wire.

· DESIGN IDEAS ·

Blinds are a versatile form of window dressing in which the choice of fabric and trimmings can make all the difference to the effect, from the smartly simple roller blind to the extravagant opulence of the ruched and draped festoon blind. A well-chosen border, frill or decorative edging can transform a plain blind into an interesting focal point, adding textural detail or contrast colour which can dress up an inexpensive fabric and provide the perfect finishing touch.

The clean lines of a Roman blind require an unfussy trimming, such as a deep fabric border or flat braid stitched to sides and hem, or across the pleats where it must be perfectly aligned. The softer styling of Austrian and festoon blinds suggests ribbon trims, decorative tassels, bobbles or fringe to edge the bottom hem, or a softly ruched frill echoing the swagged effect of the blind. Cottage blinds can be smart and simple or heavily frilled and ornamented, depending on the effect you wish to create; matching edgings on a cottage blind and valance link top and bottom of the window. In a small window area you can afford a lightly fanciful effect, such as ribbon knots with attractively trailing long ends of ribbon, specially pretty on sheer fabrics.

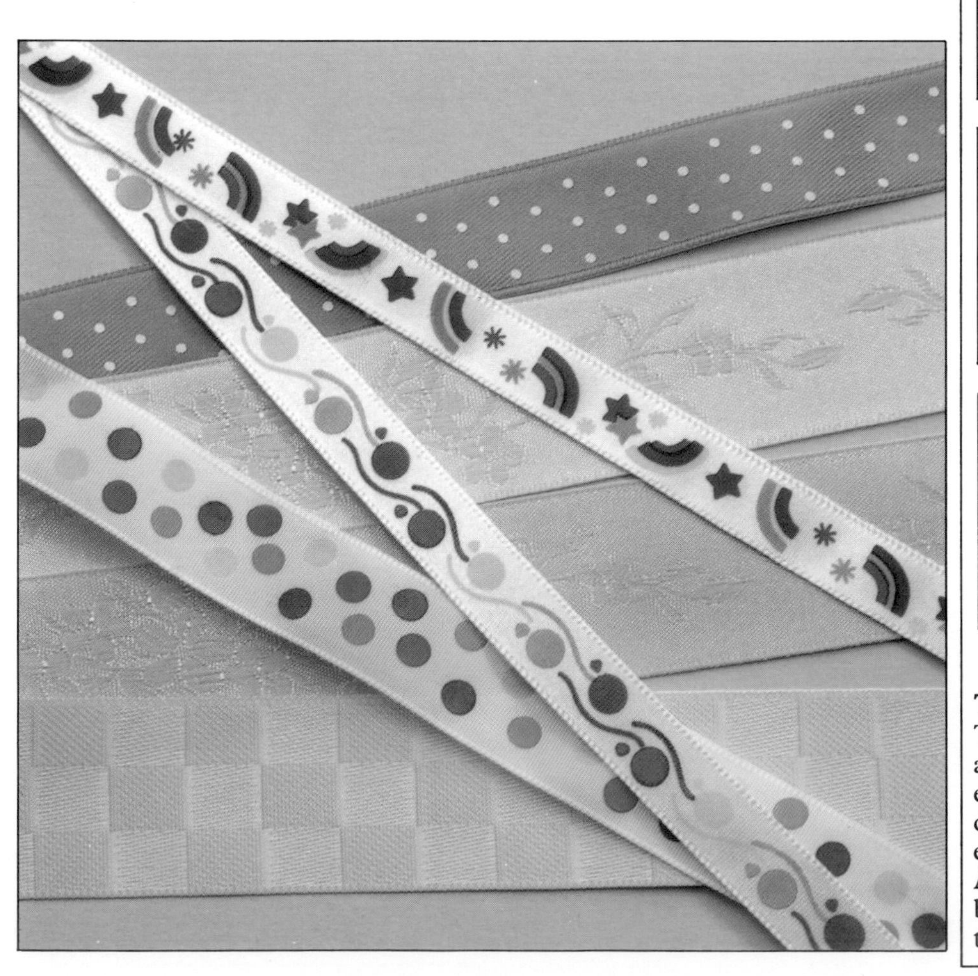

Fabric ideas

The choice of fabrics for blinds is endless, from traditional patterns to modern geometrics, from heavyweight cottons to filmy, translucent drapes. Traditional floral patterns go well with cottage styling – soft easy chairs, pretty rugs and wooden furniture – whereas bold abstracts need a more severe approach to line and contour in the room design. Small prints create a bright, fresh appearance appropriate to kitchens, bathrooms and children's rooms.

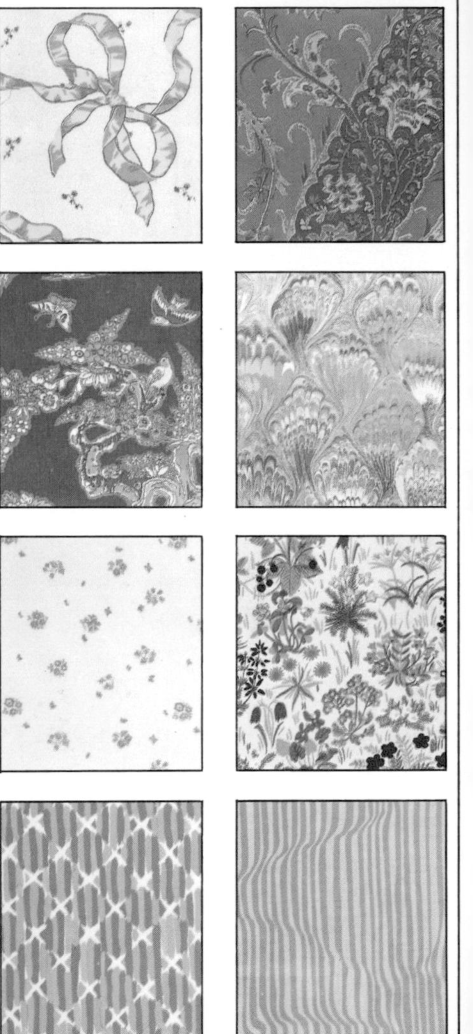

Trimmings for blinds

The crisp lines of a roller or Roman blind are suited by decorative braid trims, embossed and subtly coloured or sharply defined with bright motifs. Tasselled edgings neatly finish the looped hem of an Austrian or festoon blind, complemented by silky pull cords hung with ornamental tassels, bobbles, or wooden acorns.

CHAPTER FOUR

· BED LINEN ·

Smart and contemporary or frilled and pretty, home-made bed linen will add a personal touch to the bedroom setting.

· BED LINEN ·

The bedroom is a personal retreat, the place where individual preference can be indulged without restraint. Fabric furnishings provide style and comfort, from the simplest pillowcase to a formal, fully fitted bedcover. But bedlinen should also be highly practical, to allow for frequent changing and washing. Fortunately the great range of easy-care and washable fabrics offers plenty of scope for bright and sleek or soft and luxurious effects; but if you want to make a once-for-all, sumptuous choice of fabric for the outer bedcover, you can move into the dry-clean fabric range to find special effects of pattern and texture on more exotic fabrics.

Clever choice of fabric and design for bedlinen will add to the mood of the room setting. Bright primary colours and smart geometric prints will give a modern look, which could be softened to a more cottagey feel by the addition of frills. Large bold prints will add a focal point to a fairly plain room, while a traditional print will team well with more formal plain pillowcases and matching valance. Or for a softer more romantic setting choose frills and flounces.

BASIC BEDLINEN

The labour-saving approach to bedmaking favours a fitted bottom sheet teamed with a duvet, but the heavy softness of the traditional sheets and blankets combination is still an inviting prospect – flat sheets are quick to make, or you may prefer a fully fitted lower sheet and partly fitted upper sheet with fitted bottom corners.

The availability of extra-wide sheeting fabric has made it a very practical proposition to sew sheets, pillowcases and duvet covers in your own choice of colour and pattern. Sheeting looks cheery in bright colours and stunning in rich deep-dye hues, fresh and restful in pastels or subtly subdued designs. Polyester/cotton blends are the most practical form of sheeting, but if you can find and would prefer to use pure cotton for its fresh, crisp feel, note that you will probably need to add a considerable shrinkage allowance when calculating the amount you need.

Pillowcases use little fabric and this is one occasion when you can get away with using printed dress fabrics to create an attractive toning or contrasting pillowcase – or just add a pretty print frill or deep lace border to a plain-coloured sheeting pillowcase for a personal finish.

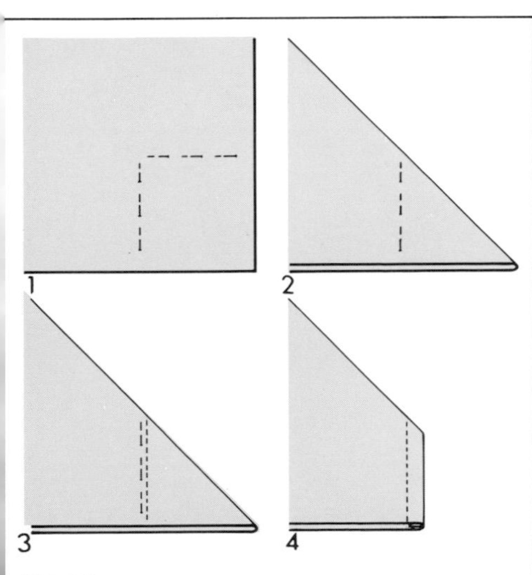

Making a corner

Wrong side up, measure 36cm in from each edge at the corners of the fabric. Mark the lines with pins (**1**). Fold the corner wrong sides together, aligning the pins and pin together (**2**). Stitch 1cm inside the line of pins (**3**). Trim the corner within 5mm of the stitching line (**4**). Fold seam again with right sides together and stitch 1cm from the fold to enclose the raw edges.

VALANCES

A valance neatly and attractively covers the sides and foot end of the bed base. It can be designed to team with the sheets and bedcover or to match other soft furnishings in the room, giving a very finished look to the overall room scheme.

The valance can be made in one of three ways. A tailored valance with inverted pleats at the corner uses the least fabric and gives the made-up bed a crisp, smart appearance, a useful alternative to the overall fitted bedcover. Gathered or pleated valances are well suited to the decorative, less formal styling of a patterned quilt or comforter, or to the practical, unfussy look of a duvet. Sheeting and medium-weight cottons or synthetic fabrics are good for gathers and fine pleats. Heavier chintzes and slubbed or textured-weave fabrics can be used, but are best applied to the corner-pleated version as they will look too bunchy if gathered into a flounce. Alternatively, if you have a rather luxurious bedcover you may prefer a silky or filmy valance, or a deep frill of all-over lace.

BEDCOVERS

Bedcovers range from the easy, informal throw-over cover or lightweight quilt-style comforter to a neat fitted cover with a deep flounce or formally tailored pleats.

Cotton and cotton/synthetic mixes are also a good choice for washable outer covers. Designs range from simple stripes or scattered motifs to rich paisleys, abstracts and mock-patchwork patterns. For a more traditional effect there is a wide range of chintzes, brocades or glistening velvets; hardwearing, informal styles come from brightly coloured canvases or various weights of corduroy. Linen and light wool fabrics are also a possibility, but check the cleaning instructions carefully. Silk is a luxurious choice, but you could consider substituting from the selection of less expensive, practical silk-look synthetics. Laces and sheers need simple styling – as a plain throw-over spread or fitted cover with a neat gathered frill.

Trimmings and fastenings for washable fabrics should also be washable, and colour-fast. Check for possible shrinkage and deal with this before making up. If you plan to add self-fabric trimmings, wash all the fabric first. Braids, ribbons, lace or fringing should be washed before they are attached, unless you are sure they are colourfast and will not shrink.

Measuring up

If you are making a pillowcase out of one piece of fabric simply measure the length and width of the pillow; add 3cm seam allowance to the width and 21cm to the length for seam allowance and flap. For a sheet, add the mattress length, plus twice the depth, plus 50cm for tucking in; by the mattress width, plus twice the depth, plus 50cm for tucking. For a bedcover you will need to take measurements over the made-up bed including pillows.

Take the measurements accurately and make a note as you go. It is handy to have a rough outline plan ready, upon which you can add the measurements. When measuring areas longer than the tape measure, mark the point reached with a pin, then continue measuring from the marker pin. Remember to remove pins.

· FLAT SHEET ·

A flat sheet can be used as bottom or top sheet, so it is useful whether your top cover is a duvet, fitted cover or comforter. It is simple to sew, bringing the satisfaction of a good-looking and highly practical result for little effort. This makes it perfect for the beginner, teamed with easy-to-sew pillowcases, an encouragement to go on to more ambitious projects.

Polyester/cotton is strong, smooth, shrink-resistant and fully washable, available in a good range of colours and a number of attractive patterns, often with different colourways. It is made to standard widths corresponding to bed-size and is certainly the most practical fabric for sheets.

Alternative fabrics for sheets

If you have a taste for something a little different, look among the full range of suitable fabric weights for printed cottons, synthetics or even a washable cotton satin for a luxury effect. Handle the fabric to get a sense of its crease-resistance and durability.

Such fabrics will probably not be available in the width you need for full bed-size, so it will mean seaming sections together. Rather than joining two fabric widths, which will make a centre seam that falls down the middle of the bed, cut one section in half lengthwise and seam on either side of a central panel, so the seam lines can be placed towards the edges of the bed.

Calculating fabric amounts

Length: Add mattress length to twice mattress depth; add 50cm for a 25cm tuck-in allowance at each end.
Width: Add mattress width to twice mattress depth; add 50 cm.

You will need

- Sheeting fabric
- Matching sewing thread
- Fine pre-shrunk piping cord, measuring the width of the fabric plus 5cm, for a top sheet only.

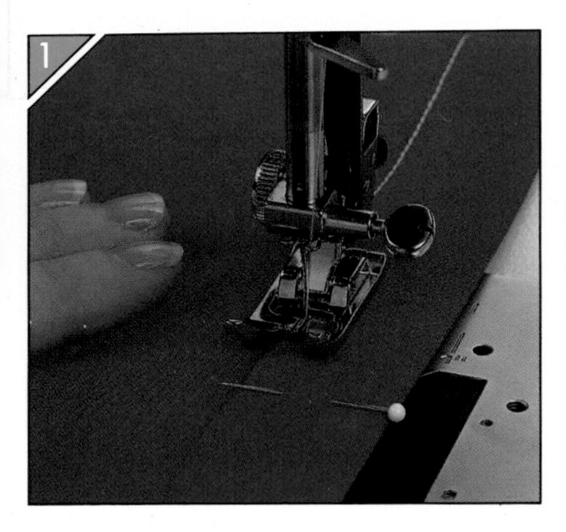

Making up

■ Cut fabric to required size. Turn a double 1.5cm hem along both long sides and stitch. Along one short edge turn under a double 2.5cm hem, stitch (**1**).

■ At the other short edge, turn under and press a double 8cm hem. Pin, tack and stitch 1cm from the fold. Stitch again 1.3cm from the fold to form a narrow channel (**2**). This deeply hemmed edge forms the turn-down on a top sheet. If you are making a bottom sheet to be tucked in at both ends of the mattress, stitch a double 2.5cm hem at both short edges of the fabric.

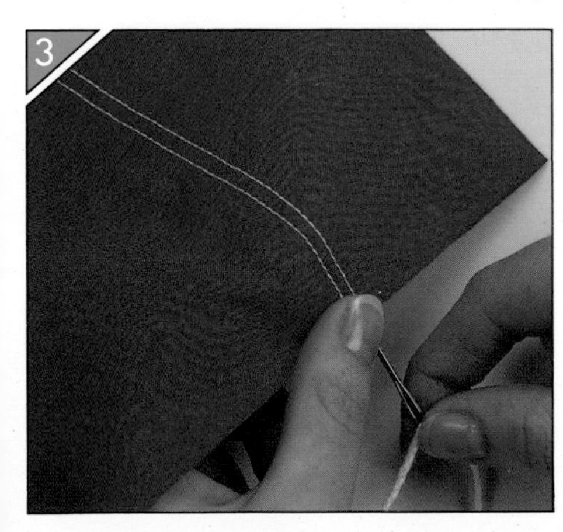

■ Using a long bodkin, thread fine piping cord through the channel (**3**) across the full width of the sheet. Secure the ends of the cord by stitching them to the side hems and neatly oversewing the openings at either end of the channel.

Stitching with a twin-needle

A twin-needle attachment is a quick way to form the double row of stitching which makes the channel for the piping cord. It is simply inserted in place of the ordinary machine needle and threaded from two separate reels; as the needles are in fixed positions, the lines of stitching are evenly spaced and of the same tension along their full length.

Using patterned fabric

To avoid showing the wrong side of a printed fabric at the turn-down of the top sheet, stitch a self-fabric or contrasting facing to create a neat, attractive finish. Cut a deep rectangle of fabric the same width as the sheet. Turn a narrow hem along the width at one edge, then seam the other three sides of the facing to the sheet. Turn out and press.

· FITTED SHEET ·

A fitted sheet covers the mattress neatly and makes bedmaking quick and simple – the perfect base for a duvet but just as good for the lower sheet in a sheets-and-blankets combination. You can also adapt the technique to make a top sheet with fitted corners at the foot end of the bed only – plan the most convenient style for the size of your bed and its accessibility when you have to change the bedlinen. Easy-care, purpose-made sheeting fabric is the most practical choice.

Calculating fabric amounts

Length: Add mattress length to twice mattress depth; add 36cm for an 18cm tuck-in allowance at either end.

Width: Add mattress width to twice mattress depth; add 36cm.

You will need

- Sheeting fabric
- Matching sewing thread
- 1m of 6mm wide elastic

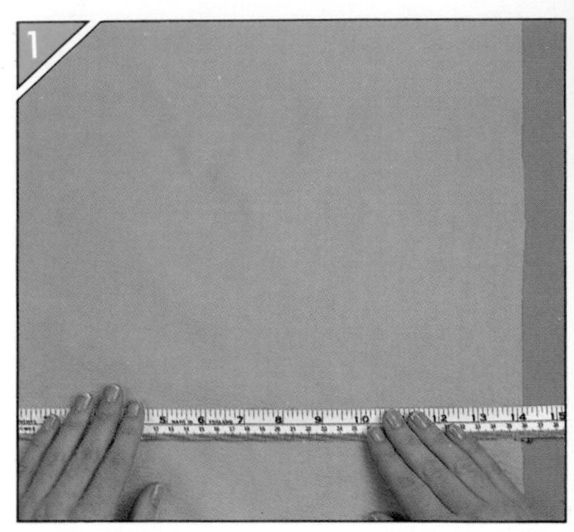

Making up

■ Cut fabric to the required size. Measure 36cm along the edge from each corner on all sides; mark with pins (**1**). From the position of each pin, chalk a line on the fabric at right angles to the edge and mark where the lines meet.

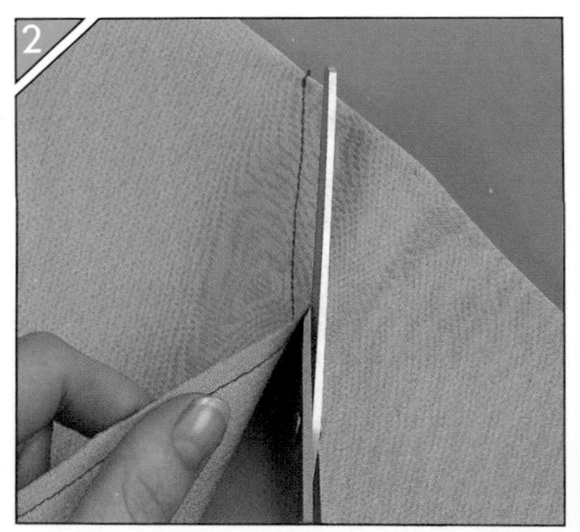

■ With the wrong sides facing, fold one corner between the point where lines intersect and the corner, so the 36cm marker pins and chalked lines match. Pin together along the chalked lines. Stitch 1cm inside inside the pinned line. Trim the corner of the fabric to within 5mm of the stitching line (**2**).

■ To complete the corner seam, press the seam open, then repress with right sides facing and the seam at the edge. Pin, tack and stitch 1cm from the fold (**3**) to enclose the raw seam edges and form a **French seam.**

Repeat steps 1, 2 and 3 to complete a seam at each corner.

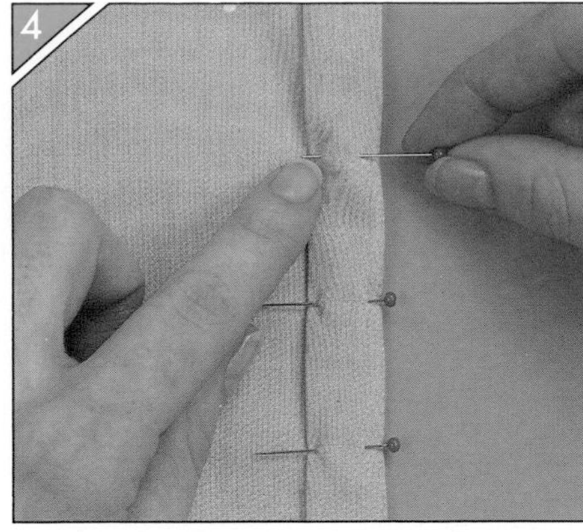

■ Turn under 1.5cm all around the outer edge of the sheet. Turn again to form a double 1.5cm casing hem. Pin securely (**4**). Mitre the corners and slip stitch the mitres carefully so there is a clear channel inside the hem to thread the elastic through.

■ Measure 34cm along the pinned hem on either side of each corner seam; mark with pins. Stitch the casing hem along the straight edges and also around the corner section, leaving a gap of 1.5cm at each mark (**5**) to thread the elastic through when gathering up the corners.

■ Cut four 23cm lengths of elastic. Thread elastic into the casing hem at each corner, using a narrow bodkin. As the elastic is shorter than the casing, the fabric is gathered up at each corner of the sheet. Pin each end of elastic through the casing hem at each opening (**6**). Then tuck the ends of the elastic inside the casing hem. Repin the elastic ends parallel to the edge so you can machine across the ends.

■ Stitch ends of elastic securely, using two rows of machine stitching across the depth of the hem (**7**). Close up the openings in the casing with machine stitching, or **sliphem** by hand.

· PLAIN PILLOWCASE ·

The simplest type of pillowcase is made from a folded length of fabric with a foldover flap on the inside which tucks over the inserted pillow. The flap keeps the pillow neatly but firmly in place.

The pillowcase can be made in the same sheeting fabric as the sheets, or you may prefer a complete colour contrast. Plain colours can be enlivened with ribbon trims, applique shapes or embroidery to form designs at each corner or a pretty border along the short edge of the pillowcase. These trimmings can be stitched to the flat fabric before the pillowcase is made up, so the ends of a ribbon, for example, are securely enclosed within the seams to make a neat finish.

The simple styling is well suited to use of patterned fabric to enliven the look of single-colour sheets; alternatively if the sheets have a pattern, you may find the fabric is available with the same motif in opposite colourways, which creates a well co-ordinated look that can be carried through in similar colouring for the duvet or bedcover.

Calculating fabric amounts

Use a single piece of wide sheeting for each plain pillowcase.

Length: Measure the length of the pillow; double the measurement and add 21cm for flap and hem allowance.

Width: Measure the width of the pillow and add 3cm for seam allowances.

You will need

- Sheeting fabric
- Matching sewing thread

Making up

■ Cut the fabric to the required measurements. Along one short edge of the fabric piece, turn a double 5mm hem on to the wrong side. Pin, tack and stitch (**1**).

■ On the other short edge, turn 5cm on to the wrong side and press. Turn in 1cm at the raw edge; pin, tack and stitch in place (**2**). This edge with the deep hem will be on the front of finished pillowcase.

■ Lay the fabric flat, right side down. Fold over the narrow-hemmed edge to make a flap 15cm deep. Press and pin in place (**3**).

■ Fold the fabric in half widthways with wrong sides together, aligning the wide-hemmed edge with the fold of the flap. Pin, tack and stitch the side edges, taking a 5mm seam allowance (**4**).

■ Turn the pillowcase with right sides facing. Pin, tack and stitch the side edges 1cm from the first seam to enclose the raw edges (**5**). Turn the pillowcase right side out and press.

Different finishes

Lace trims, tucks and delicate floral embroidery add a delightful personal touch to pillowcases. Add the decoration after stitching the front hem but before completing the pillowcase.
Lace and ribbon trim: stitch a strip of wide lace across the front hem edge, then stitch ribbon along the centre.
Lace and tucks: Add 1cm for each tuck to the length of the pillowcase. Form the tucks by folding the fabric with wrong sides together and stitching 5mm from the fold. Space the tucks and stitch lace trimming between.
Embroidered motif: For a scalloped edge, trim 6cm from the front edge. Cut the scalloped shape and oversew the edge with a small close zigzag stitch. Embroider the motif by hand or machine.

· FRILLED PILLOWCASE ·

Unlike a plain pillowcase, this is made with separate pieces for front and back, and the frill is another separate unit. Made up in plain sheeting, it is more decorative because of the frill, but by clever choice of fabrics you can create designer styling with no extra effort. An attractive co-ordinated effect is achieved by making the pillow from the same fabric as the sheets and adding a contrast colour or pattern for the frill. Alternatively, the pillowcase itself can form the contrast, with the frill providing the co-ordinated link with the other bedlinen. If you have a piece of sheeting left over and it is not large enough to make a full pillowcase, you can use it for the back of the case and make the front section and a matching frill from a separate length of fabric.

The frill is made from a doubled-over fabric strip, so the wrong side does not show and you can use any printed cotton. If the main fabric is a pastel colour, floral designs make pretty frilling; for a bold effect make sheets and pillowcases in a plain dark or primary colour and choose a bright abstract print of small-scale design to make the frill, or go for a clearly contrasting colour. The same pattern with reversed colourways is another simple and stylish design solution.

Calculating fabric amounts

Front: Measure the length and width of the pillow. Add 3cm to each measurement for 1.5cm seam allowances all round.
Back: Add 6.5cm to the length of the pillow and 3cm to the width.
Flap: Allow the width of the front section, including seam allowances, and a depth of 17.5cm.
Frill: Decide on the depth for the finished frill (usually between 2cm and 8cm); double the depth and add 3cm for seam allowances. Allow a total length twice the total measurement around the pillow (altogether four times length and four times width). This can be achieved by seaming strips of fabric of the required depth; when cutting, allow for seaming on each strip.

You will need

- Sheeting fabric
- Matching sewing thread

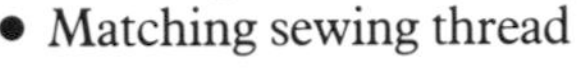

Adding purchased lace frills

Many types of lace edging can be used instead of a fabric frill. Heavy cotton lace in snowy white or soft cream will add an expensive antique look to a matching plain case. Crisp cotton broderie Anglaise trimming will give a fresh pretty finish to plain or patterned fabric. The wider the lace the more sumptuous the effect will be.

For a gathered frill you will need four times the length and four times the width of the pillowcase of lace. When choosing the lace allow for 1.5cm of the width to be lost in the seam. Some heavily decorated laces look better not gathered to show the design of the lace at its best. These will still need some extra length to form gathers or deep inverted pleats at each corner to give the lace enough fullness to fit around the corner when turned right side out.

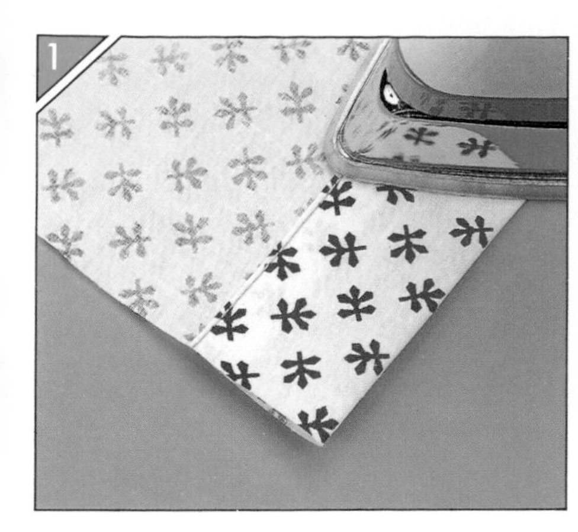

Making up

■ Along one short edge of the back piece, turn 5cm on to the wrong side and press. Turn under 1cm at the raw edge; pin, tack and stitch in place. Press (**1**).

Along one long edge of the flap, turn a double 5mm hem on to the wrong side. Pin, tack and stitch in place.

To make the **frill**, seam the strips of fabric together to the required length. With right sides together, join the short raw edges with a flat seam to form a circular band of fabric.

■ Fold the frill band in half lengthways with wrong sides of the fabric facing and pin. Divide the frill into four equal sections and mark with pins.

Gather each frill section in turn by running two even rows of stitching between pin markers (**2**). Pull up the threads to make even gathers.

■ Divide the outer edge of the front piece of the pillowcase into four equal sections and mark with pins. Match the pin markers on front piece and frill, adjusting the gathers in each section as necessary. Pin, tack and stitch the frill in place 1.5cm from the raw edges (**3**).

■ Place the back piece over the frilled front piece, right sides facing; align the hemmed edge of the back with the seamline on the front. Over this, place the flap right side down, matching the long raw edge of the flap with the raw edge on the front. Pin and tack all around the pillowcase, turn it over and stitch from the front, on the frill seamline (**4**).

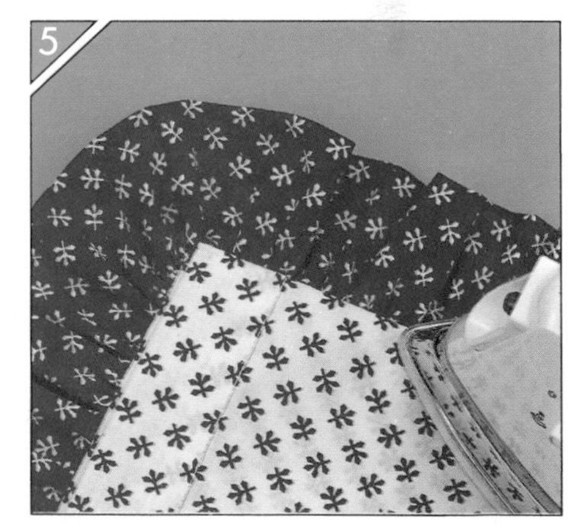

■ Trim and neaten the raw edges. Turn the pillowcase right side out, tuck in and smooth the flap on the inside of the case. Press seams and hems (**5**) so the frill stands out evenly around the pillowcase.

• DUVET COVER •

A duvet is designed to make life simpler – it is warm in winter, lightweight in summer and eliminates the more tedious aspects of bedmaking. In line with this quality, the duvet cover should also be easy to care for – lightweight and washable but standing up to daily use. Polyester/cotton sheeting is just as good for a duvet cover as for sheets, with the advantage of widths suitable for single to king-size bedcovers.

The basic cover is very simply made and fastened with press stud tape or touch-and-close fastening for quick removal. It consists of two rectangular fabric pieces, so you can make it all in one colour or pattern, or choose different fabrics for the two sides to create a toned or contrasting effect. If you want an unusual material for the upper side, you can seam panels of standard-width fabric and cut a single width of sheeting for the lower side. Make sure the fabrics are compatible for washing; wash the top fabric before cutting out to eliminate any shrinkage. This method also lends itself to a patchwork or strip-pattern effect for the upper side of the cover.

Calculating fabric amounts

Length: Measure duvet length (usually 200cm) and add 7cm for hem and seam allowances.

Width: Measure duvet width and add 4cm for seam allowances.

You will need

- Sheeting fabric
- Matching sewing thread
- Press-stud tape or touch-and-close fastening

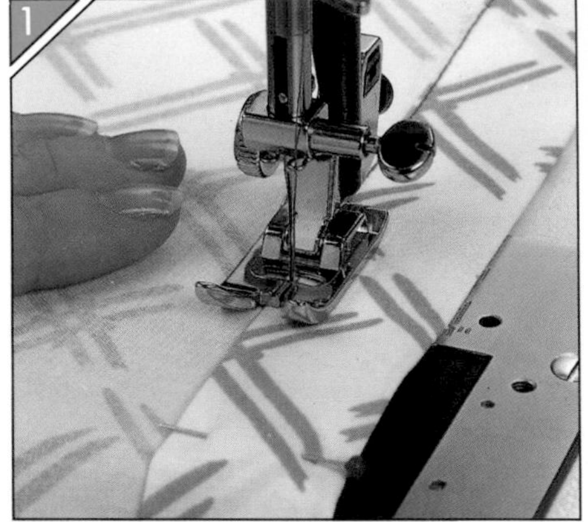

Making up

■ Cut two pieces of fabric to the required size. Turn a double 2.5cm hem along the bottom edge of both pieces. Pin, tack and stitch the hems (**1**). Press hems.

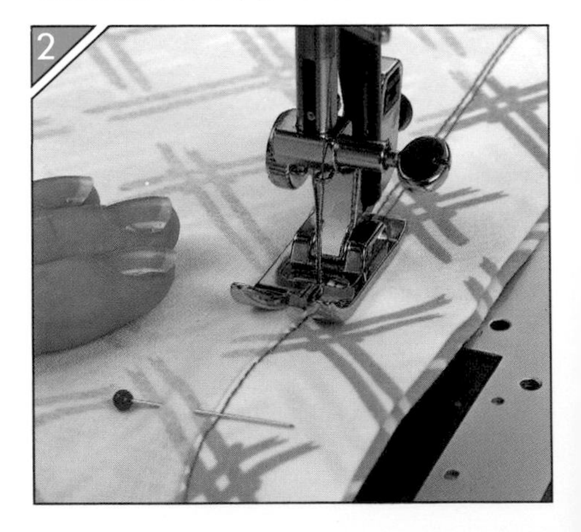

■ Spread one piece of fabric on top of the other with right sides facing (or fold in half the single length of fabric) and align the hemmed edges. Pin and tack the hemmed edges together for a length of 30cm at either end, leaving a central opening. Stitch the tacked sections 2.5cm from the outer edge of the hem (**2**).

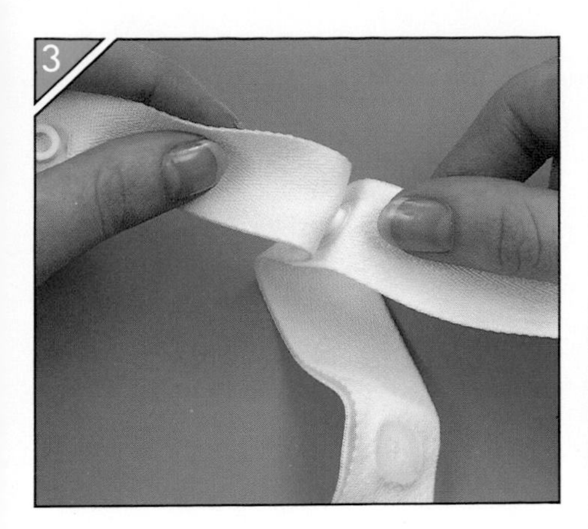

■ Cut a length of **press stud tape** 3cm longer than the opening. Run the tape along the hemmed edges of the cover before cutting the required length, taking care that the press studs will be evenly spaced along the opening with a stud placed close to the seamed sections at either end so the closure will not gape. Undo the press studs to separate the tape into two lengths (**3**). Alternatively, use touch-and-close fastening cut to opening length plus 3cm. Apply the fastening in same way as press stud tape.

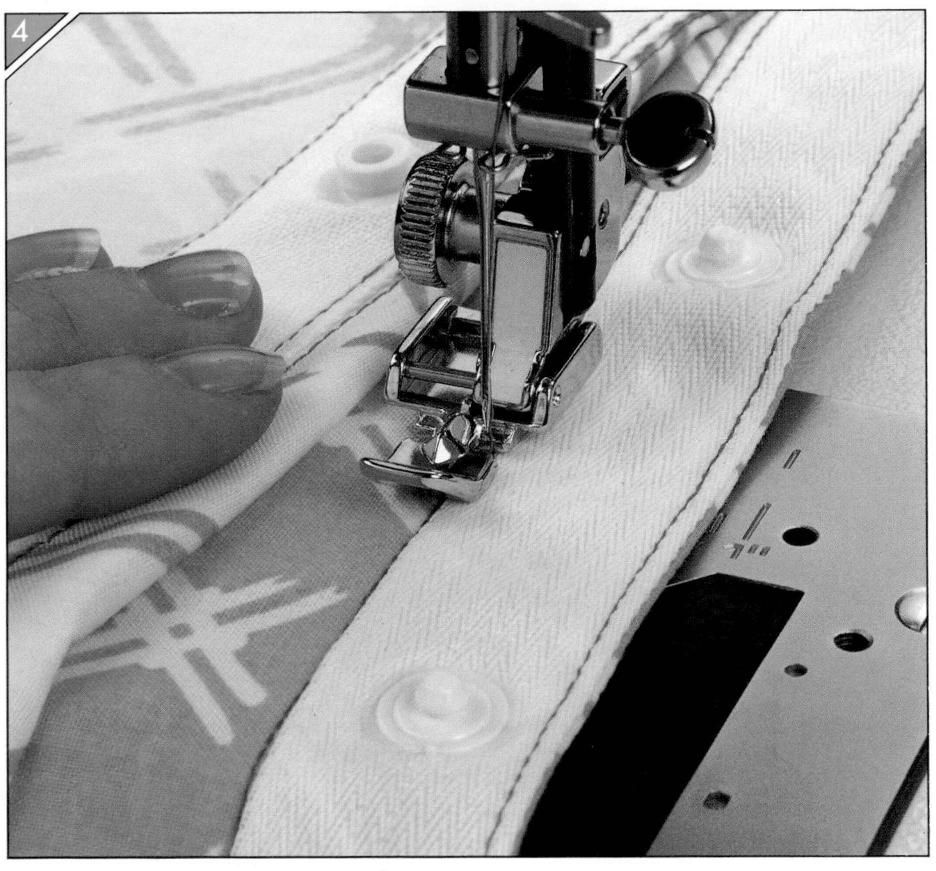

■ Pin one length of tape along one side of the opening, with 1.5cm surplus tape at either end. Tack and stitch in place. Use a zip foot on the machine when stitching the tape. Repeat on the other side of the opening, checking that the studs are matched along the length (**4**). This is simply done by fastening the tape, then pinning through the second strip between the studs before unfastening.

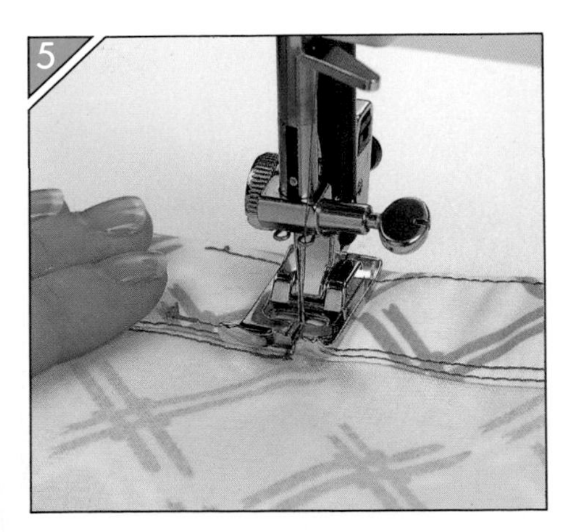

■ Fold the cover with right sides facing. Pin, tack, and make a double row of stitching vertically across the hem at each side of the opening to enclose the raw edges of tape (**5**). Finish the stitching securely as it will be under strain when the duvet cover is changed.

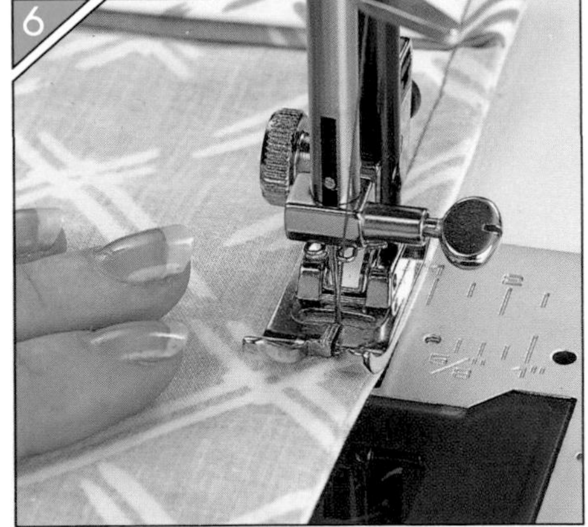

■ Turn the cover to wrong sides facing and make a **French seam** around the three open sides- pin, tack and stitch 5mm from the raw edge; trim seam to within 3mm of the stitching; turn the cover with right sides facing and stitch again to enclose the raw edges (**6**).

· GATHERED VALANCE ·

A gathered valance creates an informal style while providing a neat cover-up for the bed-base. Alternatively, you can pleat the "skirt" evenly or make a tailored valance with inverted pleats at the corners (see pleating for the Fitted Bedcover on page 94) for a smart, crisp appearance. For all styles, the skirt of the valance is sewn to a flat section of fabric that spreads across the bed base underneath the mattress. This can be made from the same fabric as the skirt or a co-ordinated material. For economy, if the base section of the valance will not show, an old (but not threadbare) sheet can be used or a plain calico. To neaten the edges and prevent any of the sheeting being seen around the edges of the mattress, you can stitch 8cm wide strips of the skirt fabric around the base section before making up.

Plain and patterned cottons, including sheeting fabric, are a practical choice for a gathered valance. A plain basic style can be enlivened with a braid, ribbon or fabric border stitched to the skirt.

Calculating fabric amounts

Main panel: Measure the mattress top and add 3.5cm to the length and 3cm to the width.

Skirt: Measure the height from the floor to the top of the bed base and add 6.5cm. This gives the depth of the skirt. The total length of fabric needed for the skirt is four times the mattress length plus twice the width.

You will need

- Sheeting fabric
- Matching sewing thread

Making up

- Cut the main panel on the lengthwise grain of the fabric. Curve the two base corners by drawing around the edge of a plate (**1**). Cut the curves.

- Cut strips of fabric to the measured depth of the skirt; as many as you need to achieve the total length, with 1.5cm seam allowances. Join them into one long strip using **French seams.**

Turn a double 2.5cm hem on to the wrong side of the fabric at the lower edge of the skirt. Pin, tack and stitch the hem in place (**2**).

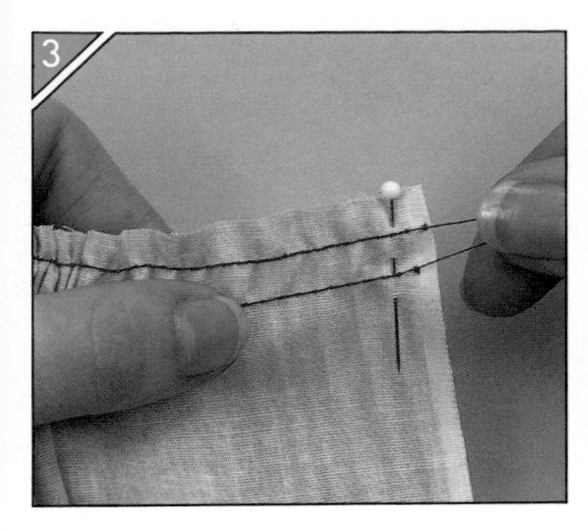

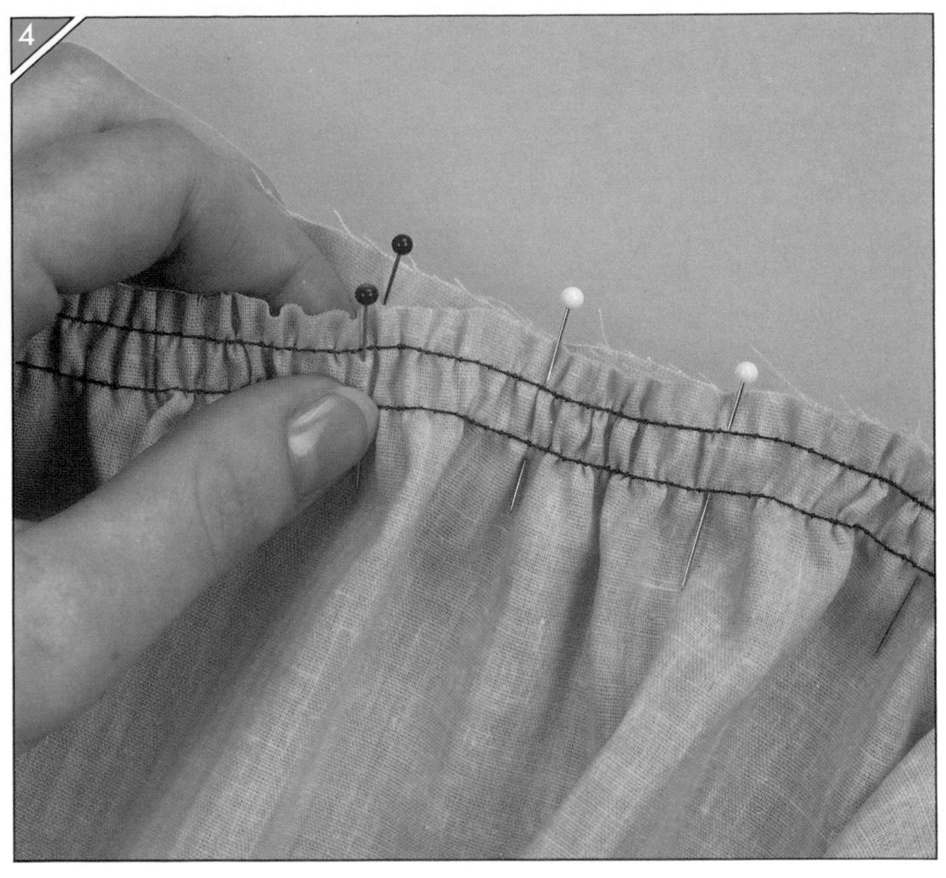

■ Divide the total length of the skirt into six equal divisions and mark them with pins at the top edge. Work two rows of **gathering** stitches between the pinned marks in each section. Pull up the threads to gather each section evenly (**3**). You can secure the threads by winding them around the pins in a figure of eight to keep the gathers in place.

■ Measure the sides and bottom edge of the main panel and divide the total measurement by six. Mark the six equal divisions around the three sides with pins. Match the pinned marks on the skirt to the pins on the main panel. Pull up the gathers in each section of the skirt as necessary until the lengths are exactly matched. With right sides of the fabric facing, pin together (**4**).

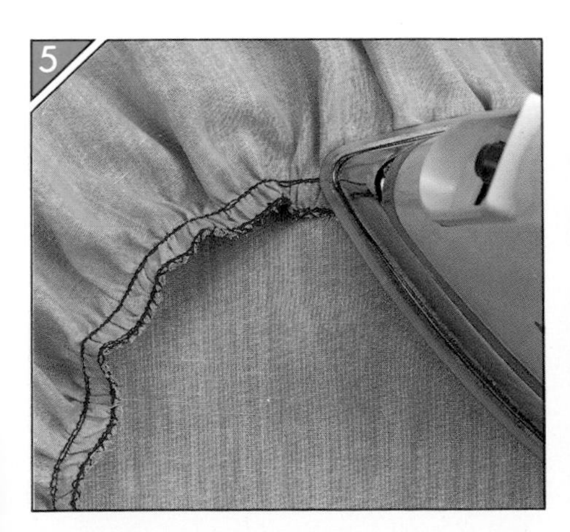

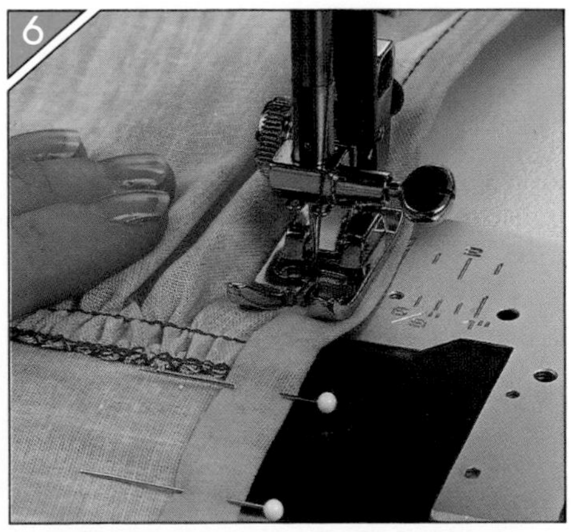

■ Tack and stitch the skirt to the main panel 1.5cm from the raw edge. Trim down the seam allowance to 1cm and stitch again close to the first line of stitching. Neaten the raw edges by working over them with machine zig-zag stitch. Press the neatened seam towards the main panel (**5**).

■ At the remaining raw edges of the main panel and valance (to be placed at the top end of the bed) turn and press a double 1cm hem on to the wrong side of the fabric. Pin, tack and stitch in place (**6**).

· THROW-OVER COVER ·

A throw-over cover is almost as simple to make as a flat sheet, but clever choice of fabric can give a very rich effect. Medium weight cottons are suitable, in mock-patchwork designs, traditional chintz or paisley patterns, pretty florals or bold geometrics. For a warm winter look, choose light wool, textured weave or figured fabric in glowing colours; alternatively lighten the styling with pale colours or a washable all-over lace.

The length of the cover can be cut to the measurement of the bed length and drop to the floor – designed to be literally thrown on simply to cover the bedding – or you can add extra length at the top end so the cover can be neatly tucked under and drawn up over the pillow in a slightly more formal finish.

Calculating fabric amount
Measure the bed with all the bedclothes in place, including pillows.
Length: Measure from the top of the mattress to the end of the bed, then the depth to the floor. Add 10cm for hem allowances. If you want the cover to tuck under and over the pillows, add an extra 50cm to the length.
Width: Measure the width of the mattress and depth to the floor; double the depth. Add 10cm for hem allowances.

You will need
- Fabric
- Matching sewing thread

If you are joining sections of fabric, provide for two seams on either side of a central panel rather than an unsightly central seam. The cover shown is made from two widths of fabric, one cut in half for the side panels. Choose a standard fabric width which when doubled makes at least the measured width of the top of the bed and drop on either side, and buy twice the measured length.

Using thick fabrics

The throw-over bedcover is designed for medium to lightweight fabrics, but, if you would prefer a warmer cover for winter nights, it can be adapted simply for thicker fabrics. Heavy-weight wool, ready quilted fabric and even fur fabric could be used. The double hem around the edge would be too bulky for such fabrics, so omit the hem allowances and finish the edges with fold-over braid. This braid is purchased ready folded in half. The raw edge of the fabric is simply sandwiched into the braid, with the slightly narrower half of the braid on the right side and machine stitched in place through all thicknesses. Trim the corners of the cover into a curve first by drawing round a plate, so the braid will fit around the corners easily.

Making up

■ Cut two widths of fabric to the required length, allowing for pattern-matching if necessary. Trim off the selvedges from both sides of each length. Cut one piece in half lengthways to make side panels.

Fold under 1.5cm seam allowance along the edge of one side panel and place it over the seam allowance on one side of the central panel, matching any pattern. **Ladder stitch** together from the right side (**1**).

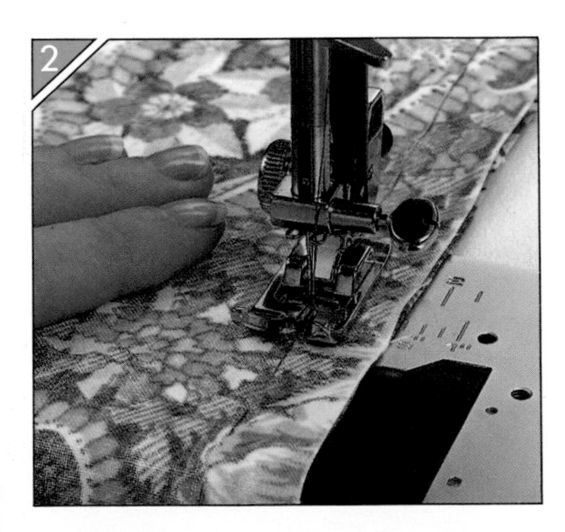

■ Repeat the previous step to attach the second side panel to the central panel. Machine stitch the pieces together making **flat seams** following the lines of ladder stitching (**2**). Neaten the raw edges of the seams and press open. Trim the side panels if necessary, allowing 5cm for the hem on each side.

■ Turn and press a 5cm single hem all around the edge of the cover, then fold in the raw edges 1.5cm and press. **Mitre** the corners by opening out the folded hem and cutting across the corner diagonally just outside the fold line. Fold the hem back in place and press (**3**).

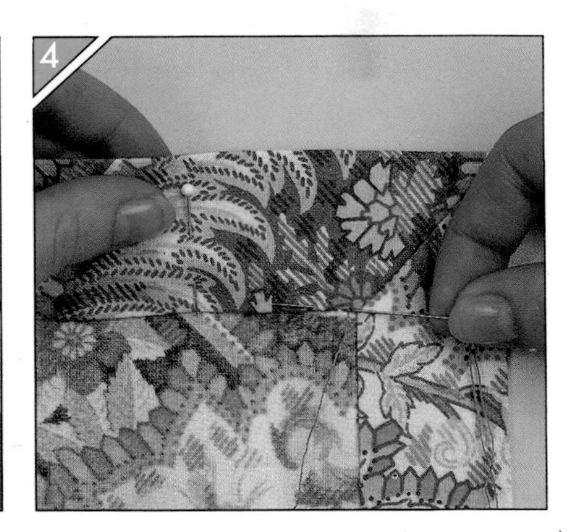

■ Pin the hem in place and finish with hand stitching. Slipstitch the edges of the mitred corner together and use **hemming** or **blind hem stitch** to secure all four side hem (**4**). Press the completed cover from the wrong side using a steam iron or dry iron and damp cloth.

· COMFORTER ·

A comforter is a lightweight quilt that can be used as a top cover over the other bedding, or as a single covering for warm nights combined with a top sheet. It looks particularly attractive when teamed with a valance, as it hangs just below the line where the mattress sits on the bed base. A comforter is reversible so you can make the front and back panels from different fabrics, to change the style just by turning it over. The inner layer of wadding provides softness and enough weight to make this more substantial than a throw-over cover. Simple hand stitching at regularly spaced intervals ties the layers together across the length and width, and the edges are neatly bound. The binding can be made with joined self-fabric bias strips or you can use a plain-coloured bias binding.

Use washable fabric and wadding. You will need to join pieces of wadding to make up the full width and the best choice of fabric is one which wears well but is not too dense or heavy. The tied effect of the quilting can be made a feature if the fabric is plain.

Calculating fabric amounts
Length: With bedding in place, measure from the head of the bed to just below the mattress at the foot of the bed.
Width: Measure across the bed and down to just below the mattress on either side. You need two panels of fabric and one panel of wadding to these dimensions. Allow an extra 2cm on widths for joining sections of fabric or wadding. Allow extra fabric to make bias strips.

You will need
- Fabric
- Wadding
- Thread
- Stranded embroidery cotton

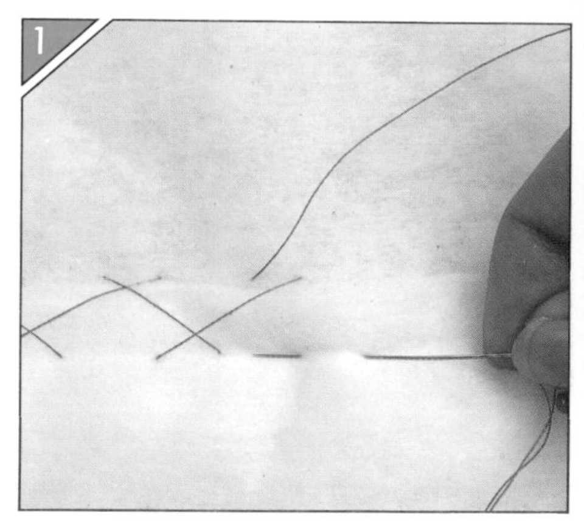

Making up
■ Cut wadding to length and stitch sections together to make up the full width of the comforter. Overlap the edges of the wadding pieces and join them with a broad **herringbone stitch** (**1**).

Making bias binding
First mark out the bias strips, 5cm wide, diagonally on the wrong side of fabric as shown on page 166. Join the bias strips to make the required length plus a little extra for the final join. Press the raw edge of the strip over to the wrong side as shown below.

■ Continue pinning and tacking the layers, using rows of large stitching 25-30cm apart, working from the centre outwards on both sides of the first row of stitching. Take the tacking lines right to the edges of the fabric. When this is completed, tack all around the edges of the comforter 1cm from the raw edges of fabric (**3**).

■ Cut fabric to the correct dimensions for the front and back panels, joining widths with **flat seams** if necessary. Spread out the back panel right side down and lay the wadding on top, matching the edges. Spread the front panel over the wadding right side up. Starting at the centre, pin and tack all three layers together across the width (**2**). Use large stitches and a contrasting coloured thread.

■ Make enough self-fabric bias strip (see left) to run around all four sides of the comforter. (Alternatively, use 2.5cm wide bias binding.) Fold the bias strip over the raw edges of the joined fabric and wadding layers. Pin and tack, overlap the ends of the binding and turn in the raw edge. Machine stitch the **binding** in place neatly (**4**).

■ Remove the tacking threads and mark the positions for ties across the comforter with pins. Space them regularly about 25-30cm apart across the length and width. To make a tie, thread a needle with embroidery cotton and make a short stitch through the layers of fabric, leaving a 5cm end of thread. Make a second stitch in the same place (**5**).

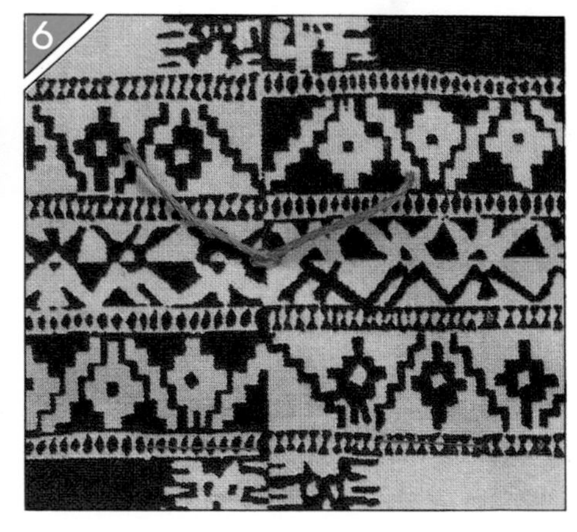

■ To complete the tie, knot the ends of thread and trim them to equal lengths (**6**). Work right across the length and width of the comforter tying the layers of fabric together at the pinned marks.

· BEDCOVER WITH CORNER PLEATS ·

A smartly tailored bedcover is cleanly styled and practical, concealing the bedding completely. Inverted pleats at the corners make it easy to lift and relay the cover, but on the bed it settles neatly into a crisp, boxy finish. This is a useful style for one-room living; the bed is neat and unobtrusive when fully covered during the day and if you remove the pillows the bed can effectively be turned into a sofa. But even if your bedroom does not have to double as a living room, you may simply prefer the more severe look of a pleated rather than frilled cover, and the tidy effect of a fitted cover rather than the more basic throw-over cover.

The handsome styling depends upon choice of a fairly firm, crease-resistant fabric that folds elegantly into the pleats and disguises minor lumps and bumps in the bedding underneath the top spread. Piped seams are an optional extra, but they do create a professional finish.

Calculating fabric amounts

Main panel: Measure the top of the bed with bedding in place. Add 20cm to the length, for a tuck-in under the pillow, and 3cm to the width for seam allowances.
Skirt: The skirt is cut in three panels, one for each side and one for the foot of the bed. Measure from the top of the bed to within 1cm of the floor and add 6.5cm for seam and hem allowances. This gives the depth of the skirt panels. For the side panels, measure the length of the bed and add 40cm for the corner pleats and pillow tuck-in. For the foot panel, measure the width of the bed and add 40cm for corner pleats. Extra fabric will be needed for matching patterns at the joins of the skirt.

You will need

- Fabric
- Matching sewing thread

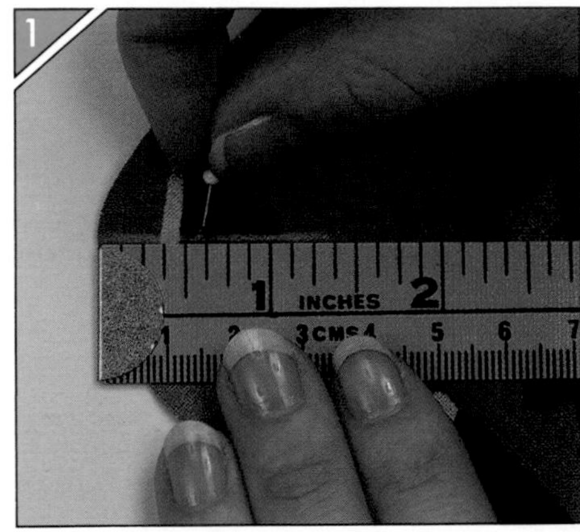

Making up

■ Cut out the main panel on the length-wise grain of the fabric. If the fabric pieces have to be joined to give sufficient width, use **French seams** to eliminate raw edges on the wrong side.

With a tailor's chalk pencil, draw a short line at an angle of 45 degrees from each of the base corners. Curve the corners slightly. To mark the position of the corner pleats, measure 1.5cm in from the raw edge along the chalk line at each corner. Mark with a pin (**1**).

■ Cut out the panels for the skirt and join them into one long strip. Be sure to join the side and foot panels in the correct sequence. Make French seams taking a 1.5cm seam allowance: with right sides together, stitch a 5mm seam, then turn the fabric wrong sides together and stitch 1cm from the fold to enclose the raw edges (**2**).

■ Turn a double 2.5cm hem on to the wrong side of the fabric at the lower edge of the skirt. Pin and tack, then **hem** by hand (**3**). Press the hem.

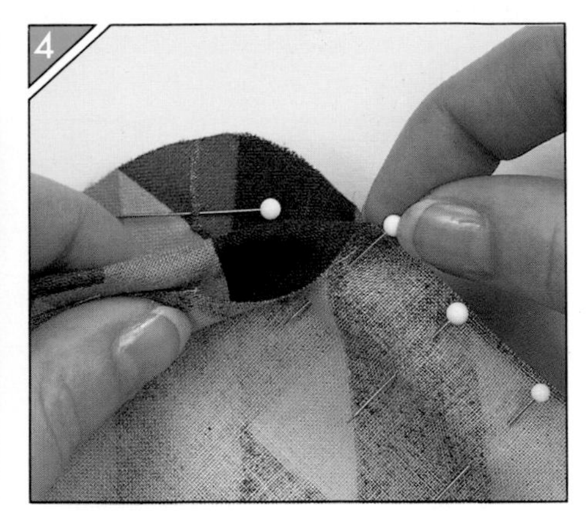

■ Mark the centre of the top edge of the foot panel with a pin. Mark the centre of the foot edge of the main panel in the same way. With right sides facing, and matching the two pinned marks, pin the foot panel of the skirt to the edge of the main panel, up to the pinned marks at the corners (**4**).

■ Starting at the top end of the main panel, pin the side panels of the skirt to the main panel, down to the pinned marks at the base corners (**5**). There is now a surplus amount of fabric in the skirt at each corner which will be used form the inverted pleats.

At each corner, fold the surplus fabric into a pleat, matching the centre of the pleat to the pinned mark at the corner of the main panel (**6**). Clip once into the seam allowance of the pleat so it will turn smoothly around the curve on the corner of the main panel.

■ Tack and stitch the skirt in place (**7**), taking care to stitch through all the layers of fabric at the corner pleats. Neaten the raw edges along all the seams with machine zig-zag stitch.

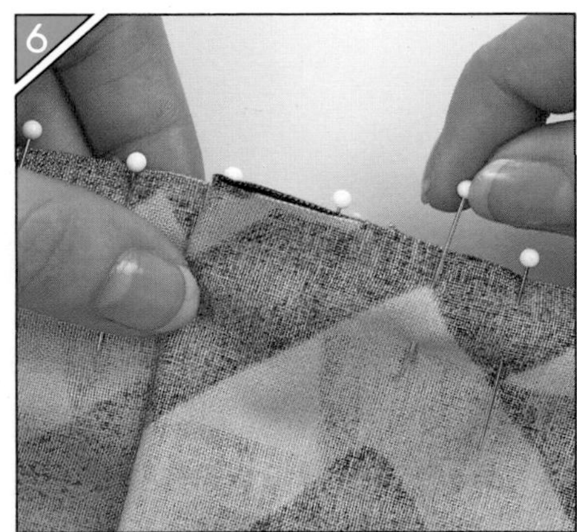

■ Along the raw edge across the top of the bedcover, turn a double 1cm hem to the wrong side. Pin, tack and stitch the hem in place (**8**). Press the finished cover, folding the pleats and pressing in the creases to make them hang smoothly.

Pressing the pleats

On the wrong side, measure the width of the pleat from the centre seam to outer folds. Mark the same distances at the lower edge with pins. With right sides uppermost, arrange the pleat on the pressing board so the marking pins are at the outer folds and the centre fold edges meet exactly at the seam. Press centre and outer folds removing the marker pins as they are reached. Do not press over pins.

· FLOUNCED BEDCOVER ·

A fitted bedcover with a deep flounce has a soft style enhanced by subtle colouring. You need a firmly woven fabric which handles easily and has good draping qualities. Cotton with a satinized finish gives a slightly luxurious feeling; a figured fabric would also be a good choice, or you might prefer a light wool for comfort with a plain or slightly textured weave. Quiet, fresh pastels, cool, muted tones or warm autumn colours all lend themselves to the semi-formal styling of the cover. It is simply designed and not difficult to make; the rounded corners fitting neatly at the bed base are the kind of detail that helps you to achieve a clean, professional finish.

Calculating fabric amounts

Main panel: Measure length of the made-up bed top and add 20cm to allow for the height of the pillows; measure the width and add 3cm for seam allowances.

Flounce: Measure from the top of the bed to within 1cm of the floor and add 6.5cm for seam and hem allowances. This makes the depth of the flounce. The full length of fabric needed is four times the length of the bed, plus twice the width, plus 4cm for side hems at the bedhead end. Cut strips of fabric to the measured depth of the flounce and seam them together to make up this length. Extra fabric will be needed if you are matching patterns at the seam joins.

You will need

- Fabric
- Lining fabric for the main panel
- Matching sewing thread

Making up

■ Cut out the main panel on the length wise grain of the fabric. (If fabric widths are being joined to make the full size, seam two half-widths on either side of a central panel, rather than making a central seam.) Cut lining fabric to the same size. Curve the two base corners on both fabric and lining by drawing round the edge of a plate with tailor's chalk (**1**). Trim the corners along the marked lines making sure the curves join into the straight edges in a smooth line.

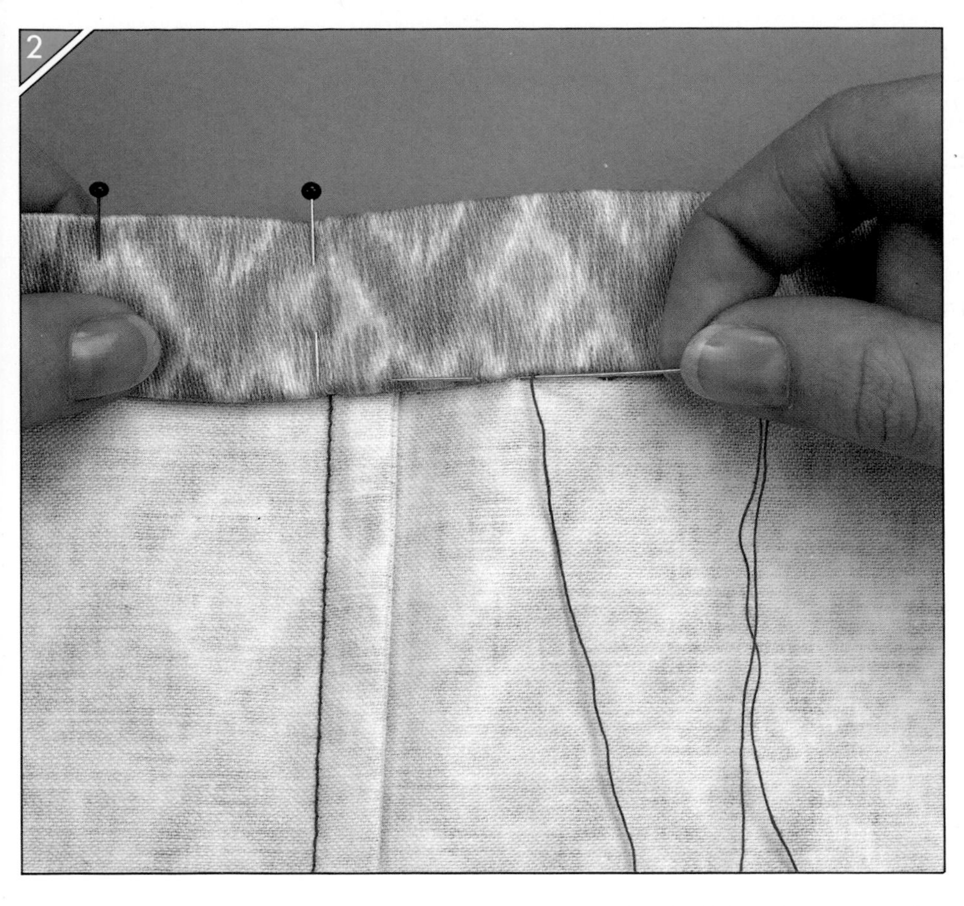

■ Cut the strips for the flounce and join them into one strip using **French seams**. Take 1.5cm seam allowances and match pattern details on the seams.

Turn a double 2.5cm hem on to the wrong side of the fabric at the lower edge of the flounce. Pin, tack and **sliphem** in place (**2**).

■ Divide by six the total length of the two long sides and lower edge of the main fabric panel. Mark the divisions with pins. Divide the length of the flounce by six and mark with pins. Work two rows of **gathering** stitches along each section of the flounce.

Pull up the gathering stitches to match the sections of the flounce to the divisions on the main panel. With right sides of the fabric together, pin the flounce around the three sides of the main panel, matching the pinned marks (**3**).

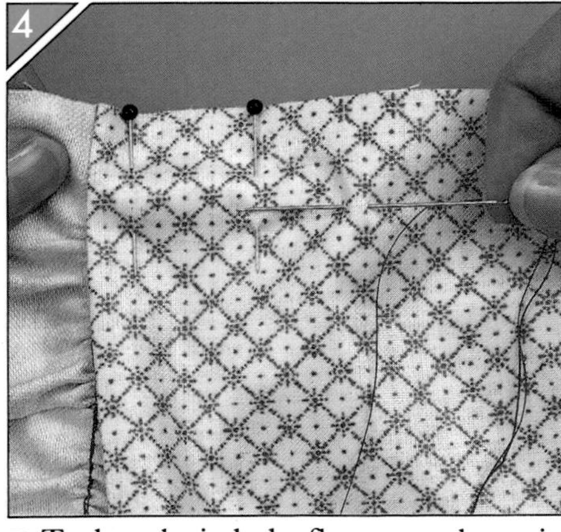

■ Tack and stitch the flounce to the main panel 1.5cm from the raw edges. Trim seam allowance to 1cm and stitch again close to the first stitching line. Press the seams.

Position the lining fabric over the main panel with wrong sides facing. Turn under the raw side edge of the lining where it meets the flounce seam. Pin and tack them together along the top edge (**4**).

■ Turn and press a double 1cm hem on to the wrong side of the cover across the side edges of the flounce and the tacked top of the main panel. Pin the hem and machine stitch it in place (**5**).

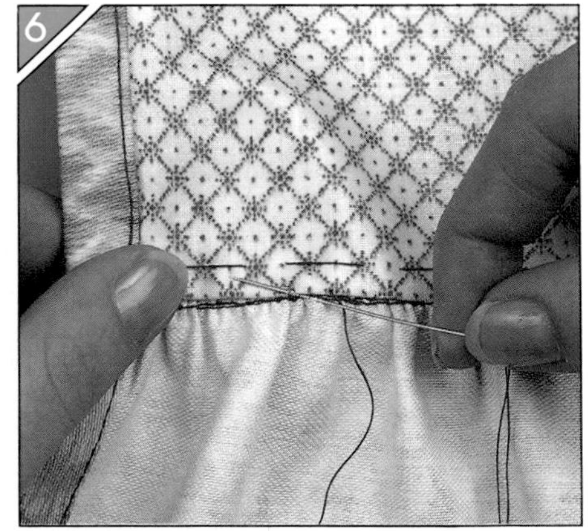

■ Turn under the sides and lower edge of the lining and pin it to the wrong side of the flounce, to cover the flounce seam. Tack the lining in place and secure the turned edges with **hemming** stitch (**6**). Work along the line of the flounce seam so the hemming is not visible on the right side of the cover.

· DESIGN IDEAS ·

Most items of bedlinen are relatively simple to sew, and their clean, straight edges and flat planes offer many tempting opportunities for decorative additions. A pretty and effortless way to add colour detail to plain sheets and pillowcases is to apply a ribbon or braid trim or ready-made frill to the pillowcase edge and sheet turn-down – a few straight lines of stitching and you have a smartly individualized design. More ambitious sewers can consider placing appliqué motifs on borders and corners, working scalloped edges and an attractive cutwork design, or applying different types of embroidery stitches in rich colours echoing the scheme of other bedding and furnishings. It is best to work this sort of decoration on the fabric pieces before making up a pillowcase. A frilled pillowcase gains a crisp, professional finish if piping is inserted between the front section and the frill.

These ideas are also appropriate for the outer bedcover, depending on its fabric and design. The throw-over cover, which is quick and easy to make, can be finished with scalloped edges, a narrow frill, or braid trims to enliven the basically plain styling.

Fabrics and trimmings
Lace, eyelet embroidery and shiny ribbons make beautiful decoration for traditional-style bedlinen in white or pastel colours, edging the pillowcase or sheet turn down. For modern styling, fabrics in bold abstract patterns and distinctive strong colours are an increasingly popular choice, complimented by the rich deep-dyedhues available in plain sheeting fabric.

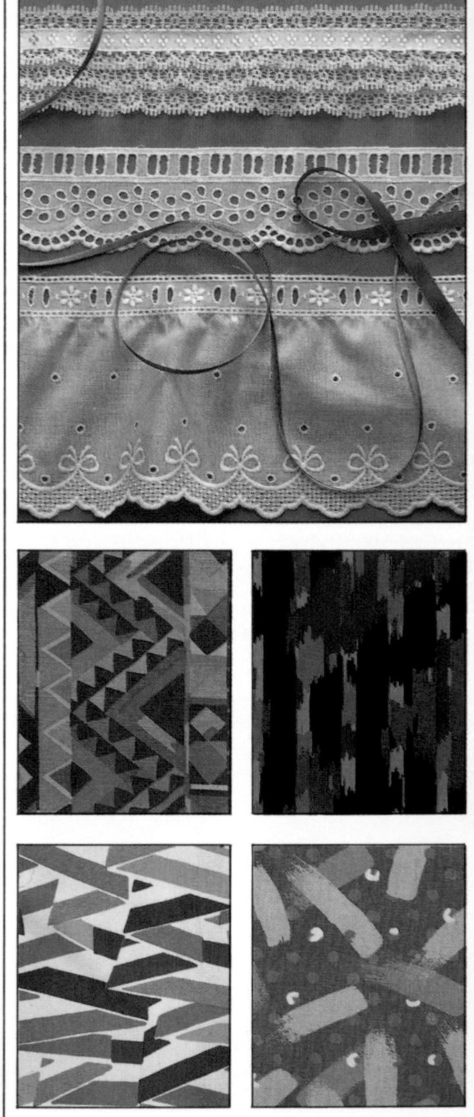

White bedlinen still has an inviting look despite the recent proliferation of fabric colours and patterns. Soft quilting and deep frilling with a discreet colour contrast (left) creates luxurious styling by day or night. The very different effect of fresh pastels and co-ordinating patterns (right) is equally eye-catching.

CHAPTER FIVE

TABLE LINEN

Formal starched white or modern bright prints, whatever the style a fabric cloth and co-ordinated table linen will complement the setting.

· TABLE LINEN ·

Tablecloths and fabric napkins are not necessities of modern living, but they set a mood and style – bright and fresh, cool but decorative, elegantly luxurious – which can be enjoyed whether you are entertaining twenty people or dining alone. Alternatively you may prefer to use tablemats made from your own choice of fabric, or to combine mats with a cloth to create a fully co-ordinated effect. Tablemats are simply constructed and can be made as plain or elaborately decorative as you wish.

Co-ordinating table-linen will enhance any table. Matching quilted mats and napkins in bold, bright colours will complement modern table-ware; a co-ordinating print will enliven plain crockery; or for a more traditional setting choose plain white with a little surface texture to form the perfect backdrop for elaborate table-ware.

FABRICS

For practical cloths choose washable fabrics – cotton/synthetic blends are also minimum-iron which is pleasantly labour-saving. Plain colours lend themselves to smooth, easy styling and can be enlivened with decorative trimmings, appliqué and embroidery. A lawn, calico or other plain-weave cotton is a suitable choice, or a textured fabric such as seersucker which adds interest to plain colouring.

MEASURING UP

Unless you are copying the size of an existing cloth, the basic measurements you need are the size of the tabletop and the required drop from the edge of the table downwards. To judge a good length for everyday use, sit at the table on a chair in regular use and measure from the edge of the table to your lap. A little below lap-length – usually a drop of about 25-30cm – is about right to avoid a skimpy appearance. The drop should hang gracefully even if it is short; too little fabric will stand out awkwardly from the tabletop. For a full length cloth, measure from the top of the table to within 1cm of the floor.

When calculating the full amount of fabric needed, add twice the drop to table length and width, or to the diameter of a round table, and add hem allowances. The hem is most easily kept to a narrow depth for convenience in sewing, but you can make it deeper to add more weight, which helps the fabric to hang elegantly, especially on a floor-length cloth. Alternatively, you can bind the edges of the cloth, so no hem allowance is needed. This is effective on a round cloth, where a bias binding accommodates the curves neatly.

Ideally, a tablecloth should be made from a single width of fabric, but if you need to seam widths together, make a central panel with equal side panels. This applies to rectangular and round cloths, never allow a seam to fall across the centre of the table.

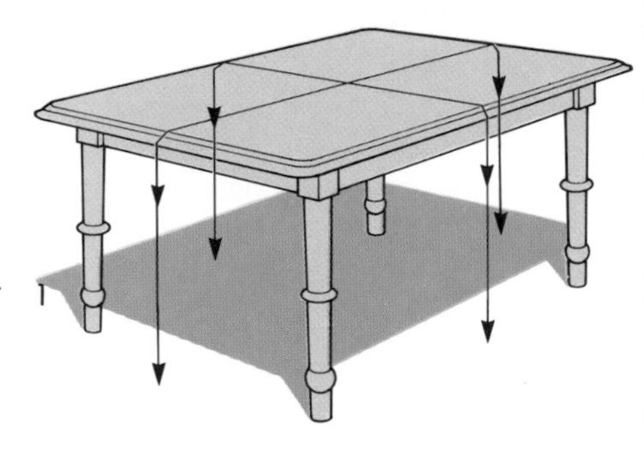

Add twice the calculated drop to the width and length of the table (**1**). Join strips of fabric either side of the main panel (**2**).

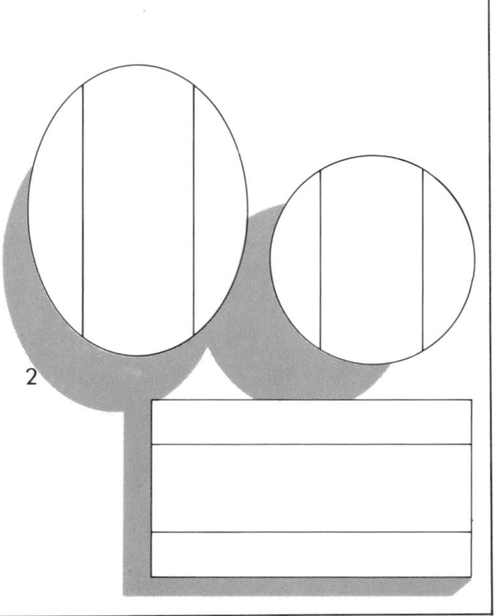

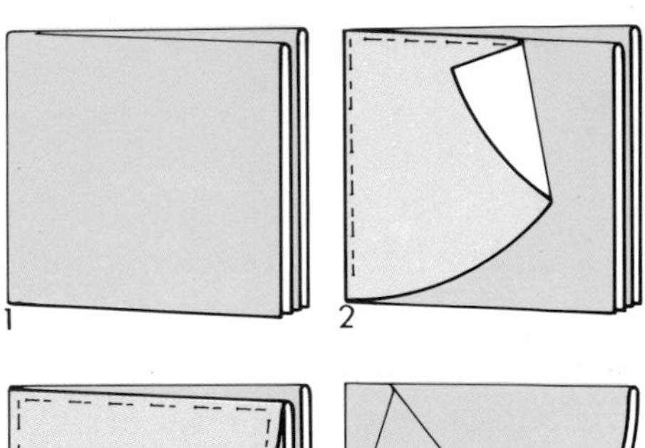

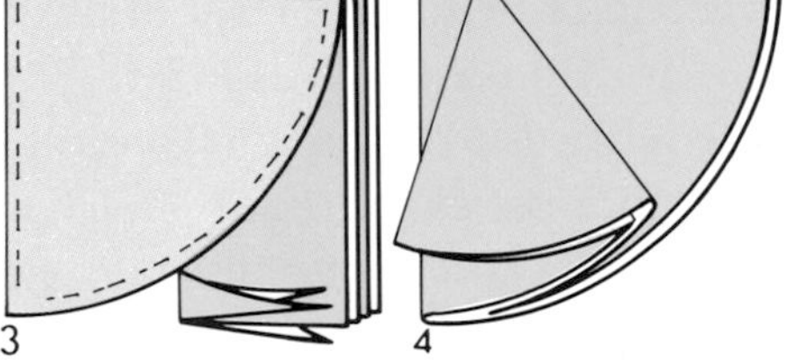

Cutting a circular tablecloth

Cut a square piece of fabric with sides equal to the diameter of the circles; you may need to make joins. Fold the fabric in four (**1**). Cut a paper pattern the same size as the folded fabric. With a pencil and string, draw a quarter circle from one corner of the square to the opposite corner. Cut along the line and pin the pattern to the fabric (**2**). Cut around the pattern, making sure that you cut through all four layers (**3**). Remove pattern and unfold fabric (**4**).

Printed cottons offer a wide range of different effects, from small, busy all-over patterns in cool morning colours to rich, dark, swirling designs subtly glowing in a room lit for a leisurely evening at home. Gingham is a lively choice for the kitchen, the woven white-and-coloured checks pretty but informal; you can choose a tiny dogtooth or broad chequerboard effect in fresh green or yellow, strong blue or red, brown or black. PVC coated fabrics are a useful option for wipe-clean kitchen cloths, available in plain colours and a variety of patterns.

The crisp and heavy textures of linen are pleasantly traditional, especially the natural creamy colours, lending themselves to discreet embroidered or cutwork borders and corner motifs. Pure linen needs extra care, but linen/synthetic mixes or linen-look fabrics are easier to handle.

Plain fabrics and woven-in patterns are suitable for matching napkins, and also for making tablemats, which may be designed for use with other tablelinen or to be placed directly on the tabletop. As tablemats are made from a double layer of fabric, you can choose one-sided prints if preferred. Medium to heavy, hardwearing materials are a good choice for mats in everyday use – fabrics such as denim, canvas or hessian which are available in a range of colours and light or dark neutral tones. Brightly coloured binding or a patterned braid edging lightens the purely practical emphasis. To make a thick mat you can insert a layer of wadding, or use ready-quilted fabric instead.

SPECIAL EFFECTS

Tablelinen needs to wear well and come up fresh when washed, but you may also wish to make beautifully decorative cloths for side tables or for the main table when it is not in use for dining. Lace makes an ideal throwover cloth, perhaps draped on a floor-length cover of velvet or a rich silk or taffeta underlayer. Layered cottons look attractive as a daytime cover-up for a round table, in co-ordinated prints or contrasting colours, depending upon the effect you want to create. The top cloth should be considerably shorter than the lower layer and can also be a different shape. This treatment lends itself to decorative edgings such as scallops, braids, ribbons, cutwork embroidery or appliqué, to emphasize the layered effect.

· RECTANGULAR TABLECLOTH ·

Whether your table is square or oblong, a tablecloth gives a clean, finished effect, for daytime freshness or evening elegance. Basically, it is simply a hemmed rectangle of fabric, but the hem is neatened with mitred corners, a technique which, once learned, is useful for a number of soft furnishings projects to give a professional touch.

Plain or printed cottons are a practical choice of fabric. If you are making up the cloth from seamed panels, you have the option to use one fabric for the central panel and a co-ordinated colour or pattern for the outer panels, rather than the same fabric throughout. The traditional choice of white makes a crisp base for your table settings, and gives a sparkling effect for an evening dinner party, but you may prefer a darker colour or busy pattern for daytime use which need not be kept quite so pristine.

Calculating fabric amounts

Measure the length and width of the tabletop. To each measurement add twice the drop from the edge of the table. Add 6cm to length and width for hem allowances.

For a large table, you may need to join widths of fabric. If so allow twice the length. Also allow extra for positioning and matching any pattern.

You will need

- Fabric
- Matching sewing thread

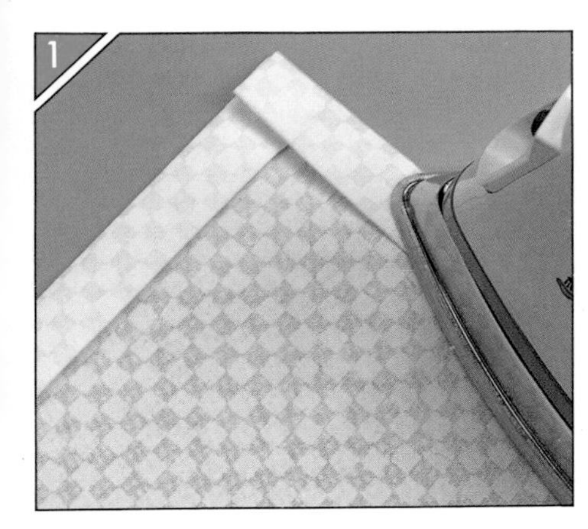

Making up

When joining fabric widths, avoid an unsightly central seam. Cut two pieces of fabric to the correct length and width, allowing for pattern matching if necessary. Use one as the centre panel and cut the second piece in half lengthways. Pin and tack the half-widths to the sides of the central panel, then stitch together using **flat fell seams**.

■ Cut fabric to size, or join widths as above. Along each edge of the fabric, turn 1.5cm on to the wrong side and press. Fold over 1.5cm again to make a double hem and press (**1**).

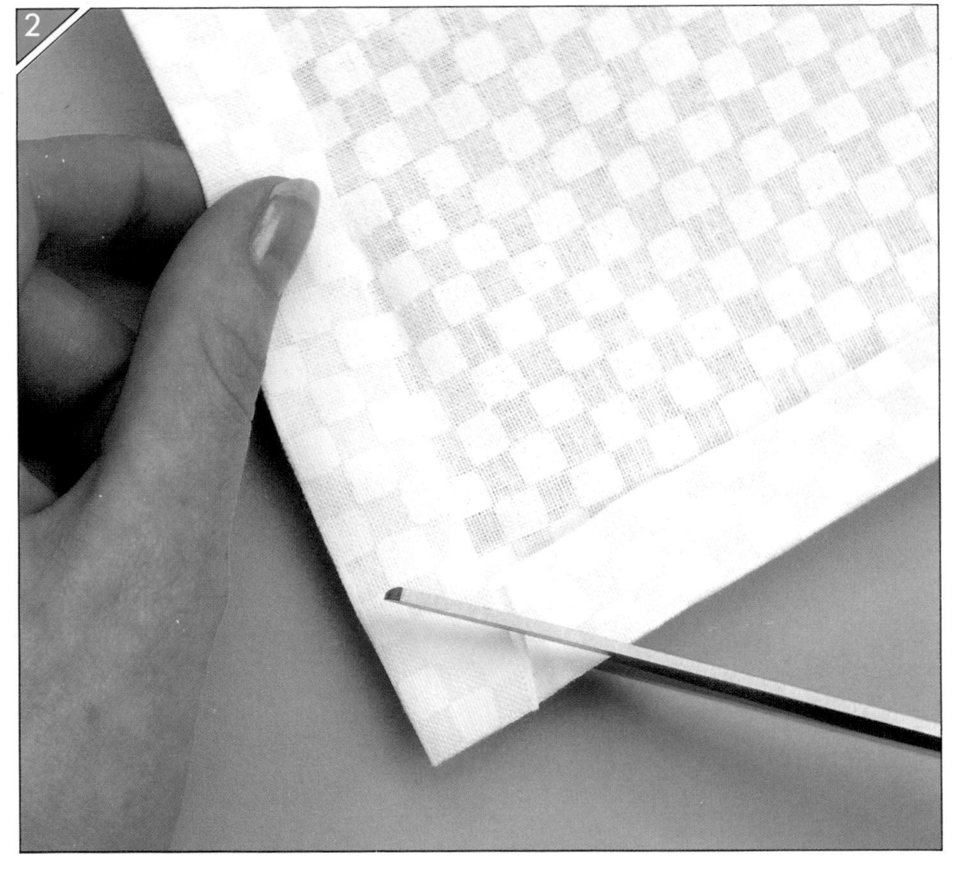

■ Open out one fold of the hem. Cut diagonally across each corner fold to within 6mm of the corner point at the inner fold (**2**). Fold the fabric back on itself with right sides together and match the cut edges at the corners. Match the folded edges of the hem, and pin the edges together near the fold to keep the edges exactly level.

■ Pin and stitch a narrow seam along each diagonal cut. Stitch the seam 6mm from the raw edge, with the stitching line passing through the inner corner point (**3**). Press seams flat and turn the corners out to the right side.

■ Re-fold the double hem along the pressed lines. At each corner, the diagonal seam forms a neat mitre when pressed in place. Pin, tack and stitch all round the edge of the tablecloth (**4**). At the beginning and end of the stitching line, pull threads through to the wrong side and fasten off. Press the hem.

Pattern matching

When seaming panels to make a tablecloth, allow extra fabric for pattern matching. Cut the central panel and place it against the remaining fabric, aligning the pattern motifs before you cut the side panels (take seam allowances into account). Pin and tack the seamlines before stitching, matching the motifs precisely.

· ROUND TABLECLOTH ·

A round cloth is cut from a square of fabric: the fabric is folded in four and cut using a paper pattern of a quarter-circle. For everyday use a short cloth is neat and stylish, but a round cloth looks particularly elegant in a floor-length version, especially when made of a medium weight fabric which falls into graceful folds all around the table.

Fresh cottons are a good choice for informal styling, all-over flower prints and random abstracts with small motifs minimize problems of pattern matching if you need to join widths of fabric. For a more formal effect, choose a plain-weave linen or linen-look fabric or a lightly textured weave.

Round cloths lend themselves particularly to a decorative layered style. Choose co-ordinated or contrasting colours and patterns and simply cut two paper patterns to make a floor length underlayer and a top cloth with half-length drop.

Calculating fabric amounts
Measure the diameter of the tabletop. Add twice the depth of the drop plus 3cm for hem allowances.
A round tablecloth creates the best effect if cut from a single width of fabric, but if you need to join widths, use the method described for the rectangular tablecloth (see page 104).

You will need

- Fabric
- Matching sewing thread
- Large piece of strong brown paper
- String
- Pencil

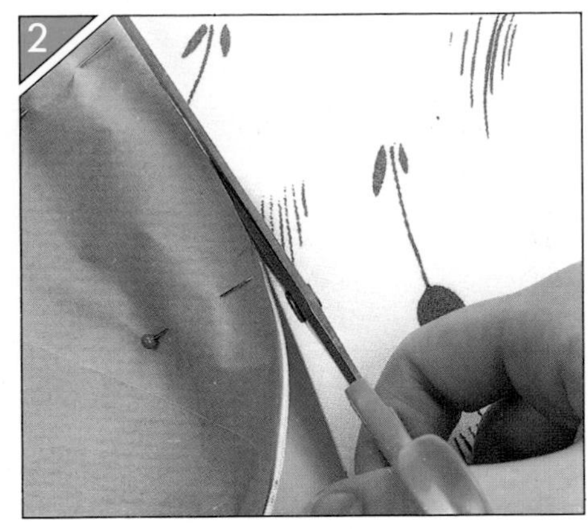

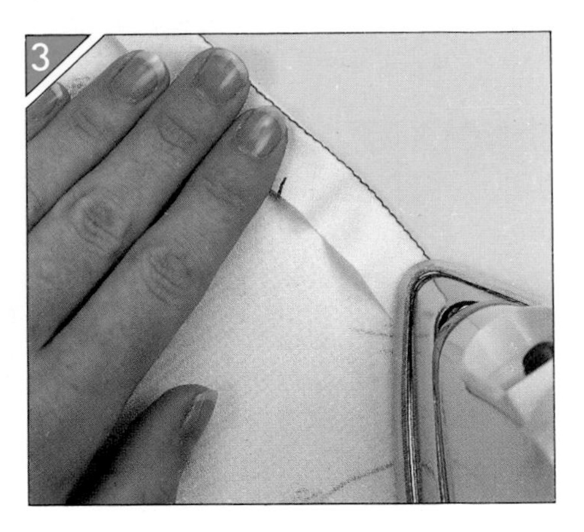

Making up

■ Tie the string to the pencil and measure the radius (half the diameter) of the tabletop along the length of string. Hold the measured point on the string at one corner of the brown paper. Stretch out the length of string and move the pencil to draw a quarter-circle on the paper (**1**). Cut along the pencil line.

■ Fold the fabric in four and pin on the paper pattern, aligning the straight edges of the paper with the folded edges of the fabric. Cut the fabric, following the paper pattern (**2**).

■ Stitch around the outside edge of the cloth 1.5cm in from the raw edge. This marks the line for the hemmed edge. Press the edge on to the wrong side all around the cloth along the stitched line (**3**). The stitching will tend to roll over naturally just inside the fold giving a good smooth curve.

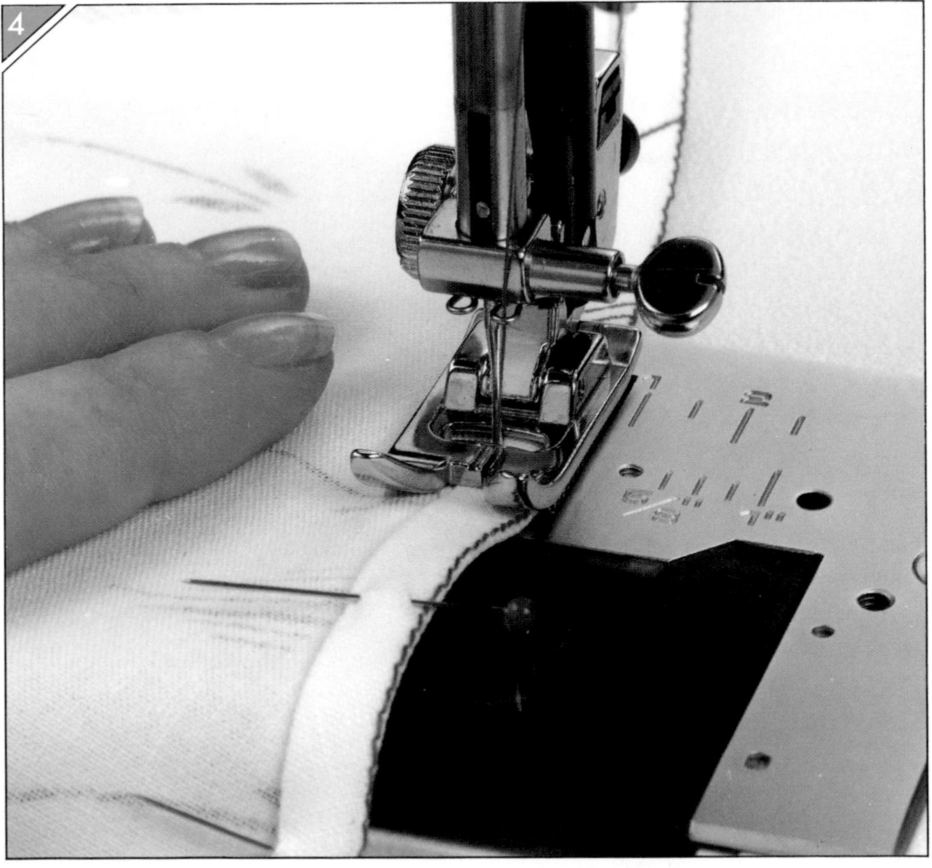

■ Carefully turn under the raw edge of the fold to make a double hem. Pin and tack the folded edge. Stitch all around the hem of the tablecloth, keeping the stitching line close to the inner fold (**4**). Remove the tacking and press.

For an alternative edging

Follow the first two steps to cut out the circle of fabric. Trim down the hem allowance to 5mm evenly all around the cloth. ***Bind*** *the raw edge with a contrast colour bias binding. Fold the binding over the raw edge, easing it around the curve. You can pin and tack the binding in place and machine stitch once all the way round; or machine stitch one edge of the binding on to the right side of the fabric, then fold it over and* ***sliphem*** *the other edge on the wrong side, following the line of machine stitching. Press the finished edging carefully.*

· TABLEMATS ·

Placemats and mats for serving dishes can be as plain and practical or as decorative as you wish, made as a basic rectangle or with neatly rounded corners. A quilted effect can be stitched by hand or machine, with a layer of polyester wadding sandwiched between two pieces of fabric, or you have the option of a very handy shortcut, using ready-quilted fabric and simply binding two layers together. Fabric mats are not entirely heatproof, so don't put down dishes straight from the oven without slipping a cork or plastic mat underneath the fabric one, but they provide sufficient insulation to protect the tabletop from most warm plates.

If you are making a tablecloth, buy an additional length of fabric for a set of matching napkins; otherwise, this is an ideal opportunity to use up offcuts of fabric and remnants of attractive cottons which are too small to be of use for any major projects. Make them co-ordinate or contrast with tablecloth or placemats; keep them plain or add embroidery, appliqué or braid trims to create a stylish finish.

Calculating fabric amounts

If the tablemat is for the plate only, measure the diameter of your dinner plate and calculate the dimensions accordingly. If the tablemat is for the complete place setting, a rectangle of about 45cm × 30cm will be required.

You will need

- Covering fabric
- Sewing thread
- Wadding

Napkins

Cut two identical squares between 45cm and 50cm square. Fold and press a double 7mm hem on all four edges of the napkin, taking care to fold in the corners neatly. Pin, tack and stitch the hemmed edges close to the inner fold.

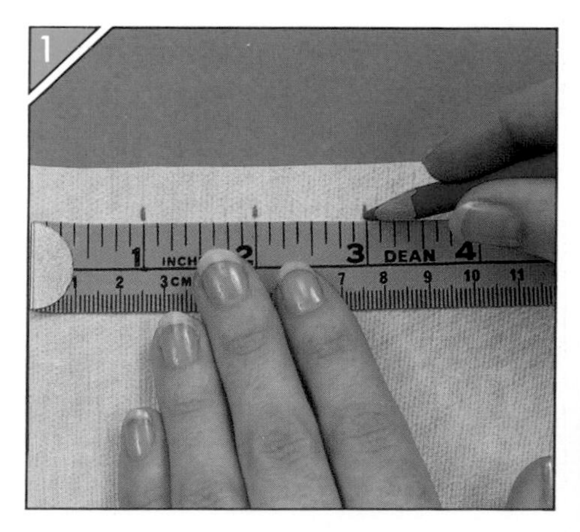

Making up

■ Cut two pieces of fabric to the required size. With a hard pencil or tailor's chalk, mark evenly spaced lines about 2.5cm apart along a shorter side (**1**). Draw lines from short side to short side.

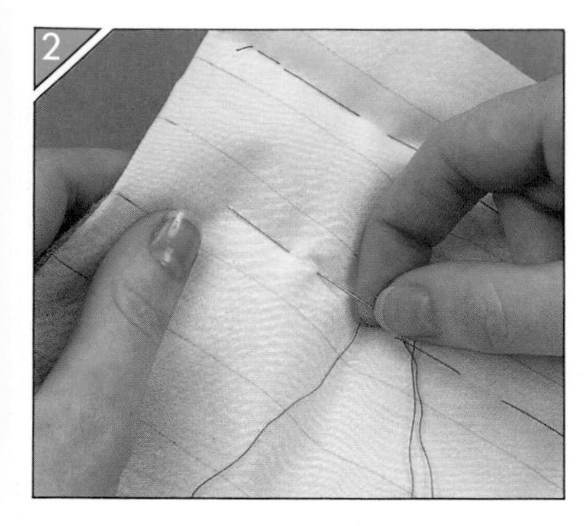

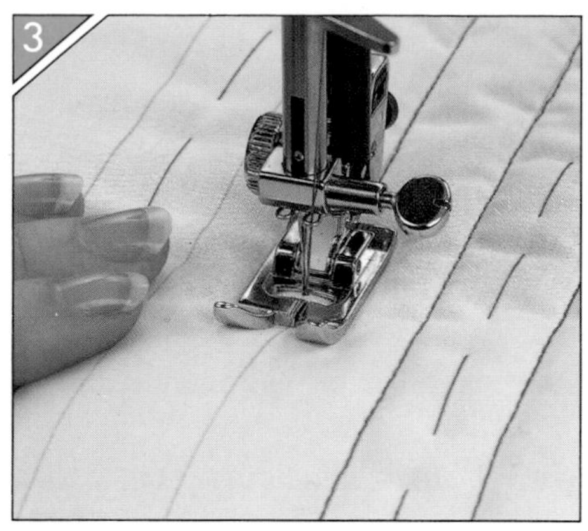

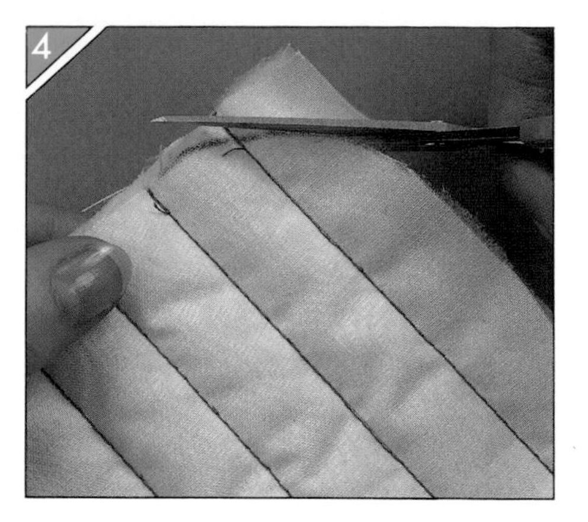

■ Cut the wadding to the same size as the fabric and sandwich between the wrong sides of the two pieces of fabric. Holding the three rectangles firmly between finger and thumb, pin together carefully. Stitch rows of tacking stitches between alternate drawn lines (**2**).

■ Using the pencilled or chalked lines as guidelines, sew parallel rows of long machine stitches from one short side of the rectangle to the other (**3**). You might like to use a contrasting thread for working the quilting stitches.

■ Cups, saucers and plates can all be used as a guide to round the corners of the tablemat. Decide how tight a curve you require and place the appropriate circular object on the first corner. Draw around it with tailor's chalk and repeat for each corner. Cut along the curved lines (**4**). Finally, trim the corners neatly.

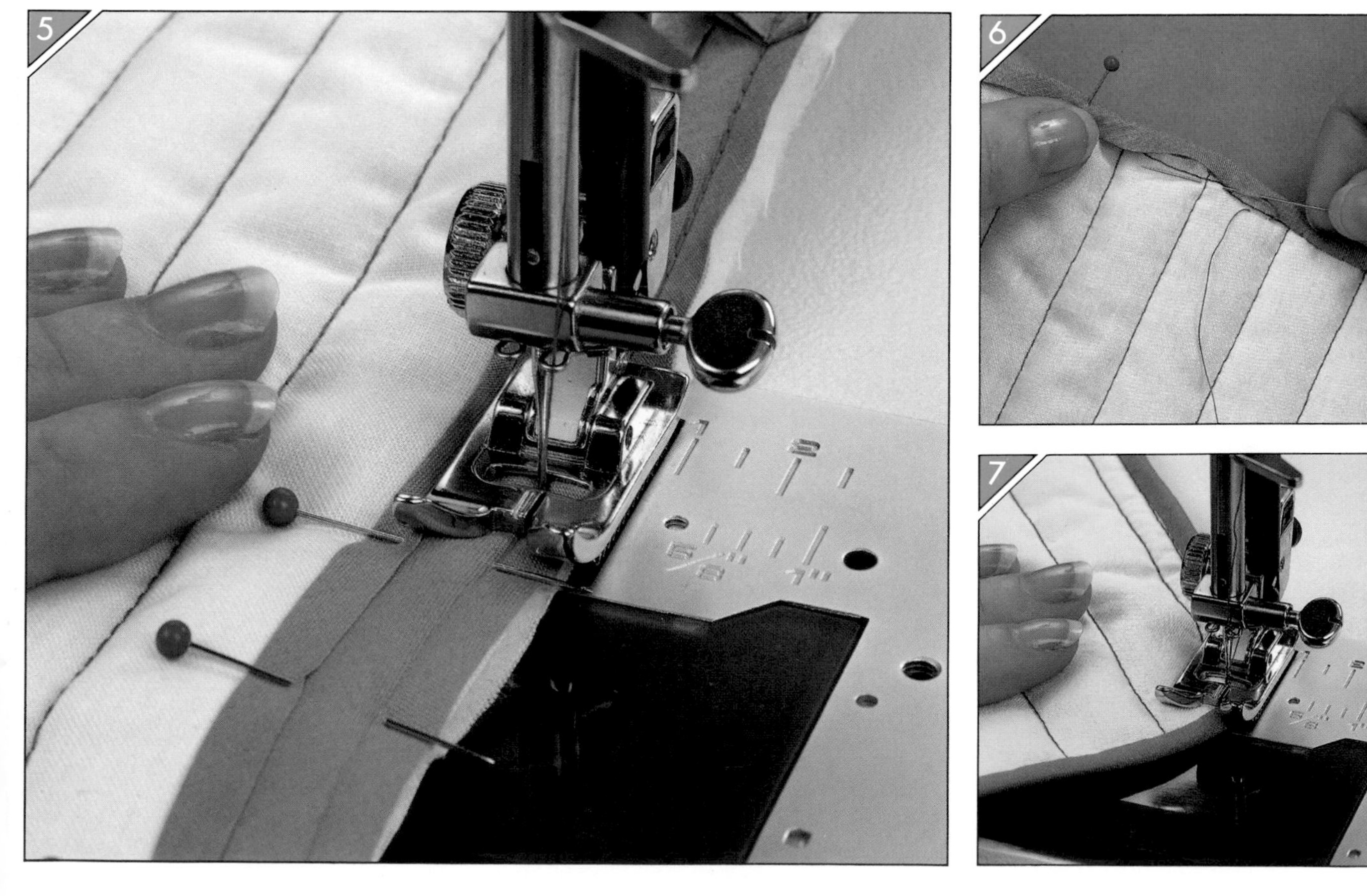

■ To give a neat and stylish finish to the tablemat, edge it with binding. If you used a contrasting colour for the quilting stitches, it is a good idea to use binding of the same contrasting colour. Open out one folded edge of binding. Pin binding around mat with right sides facing and raw edges level. Stitch in place along the crease on binding (**5**).

■ Fold over the edge to the wrong side. Press and stitch binding in place (**6**). On the right side, machine stitch on the inside edge of the binding to strengthen around the edge (**7**).

· DESIGN IDEAS ·

Making your own table linen is an opportunity to set the mood and atmosphere of your dining, whether for a leisurely summer breakfast or an elegant dinner party. The choice of fabric should flatter your tableware and blend in stylishly with other furnishings, and small design details such as the trimmings and edging for tablecloths, placemats or napkins can make all the difference, lending a personalized touch that makes even the most basic table linen extra special.

Pick up cues on colour and detail from the existing elements of your table. An attractively patterned dinner service may suggest an unusual colour combination; gleaming silverware and delicate china look good against spotless white or subtly creamy table linen enhanced by the most discreet trimming such as a narrow satin binding, lace edging, or toning embroidery at borders and corners. Modern cutlery and sturdy china benefit from bold colours and equally modern fabric designs. Dark hues and large-motif patterns can create a dramatic setting.

Borders and edgings

A neat, attractive way to create unusual styling for a tablecloth is to add a deep border in a co-ordinated or contrasting fabric. Wide strips of fabric stitched around the edges of the cloth can be doubled over with the corners cleanly mitred to create a professional finish. Plain colour with a strong abstract or geometric border creates a good effect, while pretty flowered fabrics gain an eye-catching finish when edged with an all-over mini-print in co-ordinated colours. The extra fabric helps the tablecloth drop to hang elegantly and is an excellent idea for a rectangular cloth. This type of border is not suitable for a round cloth as the depth of the fabric strip does not sit neatly around the curved edge: a good alternative is a narrow binding or deep frill, using the same principle of varying colour or pattern.

Co-ordinated fabrics

Table linen has a fresh, stylish look if co-ordinated fabrics are used for the different items. Crisp cotton fabrics are available in a wide range of attractively integrated designs, in colours ranging from clear pastels to rich dark hues and patterns from traditional chintzes to all-over geometrics or lightly scattered motifs. Generally, co-ordinates also include plain-coloured fabric suitable for napkins and binding or border trims.

CHAPTER SIX

· CUSHIONS ·

Traditionally piped or softly frilled, a matching set or mixture of fabrics, whatever their shape, cushions will add an inviting relaxed atmosphere.

· CUSHIONS ·

Cushions are for comfort and are the best means of highlighting and adding contrast to a room scheme. You can let your imagination run riot on cushions because they can be of any shape, with an outer cover of almost any type of fabric, and as plain or elaborately decorative as you wish. Unlike the sofas and chairs on which they sit, cushions can simply be moved to another room if you get tired of them, or you can make up a different type of cover for little extra investment, so it's worth trying out ambitious design ideas on this small scale. At the least you will end up with some unusual and individual focal points in your room, and at best it may get your confidence up to put a larger project into action. The great thing about cushions is that you can plan them to co-ordinate with a new scheme of room decoration, or just make them up as you have time and simply add to your collection whenever an appealing small piece of fabric comes your way. A jumble of pretty cushions gives your familiar furnishings a whole new and different look.

Cushions of all shapes and sizes will add comfort and a warm welcoming atmosphere. Fabric remnants can be used for individual cushions, and careful choice of different, but complementary, fabric will give a lively effect. The cushions can be made plain or trimmed with piping, a frill, tassels and even appliquéd lace fabric.

Cushion fillings

There are various types of cushion fillings. Some, such as down, are more luxurious and suited to expensive fabrics and tailored cushions. Others, such as foam filling, are a cheap, sturdy alternative for less formal cushions. Shown clockwise from top right: down , foam filling, synthetic wadding and polystyrene beads .

CUSHION PADS

Ready-made pads for round and square cushions and bolsters are readily available in a range of standard sizes and you will also find pads for neat little neck cushions and some decorative shapes such as hearts and fans. But you can make up a cushion pad to any shape you please, just by seaming up a calico or other plain-weave cotton inner cover and stuffing it with a suitable synthetic wadding or natural down.

Make up a paper pattern before cutting the fabric, to guarantee the shape works out as you expect. Straight-sided shapes are easily constructed – an L-shape, triangle or cube for example. Use dinner plates as guidelines for curves and draw any irregular shaping freehand, going over the line until it looks right. Remember that the shape will be narrowed and distorted slightly when it comes to inserting the wadding, unless you add a gusset, so allow fairly generous contours. If you are making a symmetrical cushion, you need only draw up one half of the pattern piece and cut out on a folded piece of fabric, as is commonly done in dressmaking.

SYNTHETIC WADDING is available in various types and qualities, usually of polyester or acrylic, both of which are fully washable. The best grades are siliconed for extra softness and there are special "firm-fill" grades which may be a good choice for an unusual shape of cushion. Check the washing instructions on the particular type you choose and make sure it is compatible with the pad cover fabric.

DOWN is light, soft and resilient, an expensive choice but you will find that a little goes a long way. It is an appropriate filling for a cushion to be covered with a light and luxurious fabric such as silk. Feathers are less expensive than down but also less resilient. Goose and duck are best for this purpose, also available mixed with down for a lighter feel. The inner cover must be made with downproof cambric which does not allow the down to work through when the cushion is in use.

FOAM FILLINGS are not as soft or flexible, whether you use a block of foam or foam chips, but they are good for informal styles which will have to withstand some rough and tumble, in a child's bedroom or playroom, for example, or for use with garden furniture.

POLYSTYRENE BEADS are tiny balls of polystyrene. They are lightweight but not soft, and are best used for informal shapes and floor cushions.

FABRICS AND TRIMMINGS

For an outer cushion cover, almost anything goes, although lightweight and loose-weave fabrics should be lined for firmness and dry-clean only fabrics are obviously less practical than washable ones. Crisp cottons are a good choice if you are adding self-fabric frills to round or square cushions. For bolsters and boxed cushions (see page 120), you should use firm and hardwearing fabrics, though bolsters are traditionally given a rich effect with satin or satinized-fabric covers drawn up with silky tassels and cords. As you don't need a great length of fabric for cushions, it's a good opportunity to use luxury fibres, fancy weaves and unusual hand-printed patterns, which can give a real lift to the room if you have decided on a plain and economical choice for sofa and chair covering fabric.

Trimmings range from neat piping inserted into outer seams to fringes, lace frills, braids or quilted appliqué motifs. Patchwork cushions are particularly appealing – you can make up one or both halves of the cover in patchwork, or appliqué a patchwork section on to a plain piece of fabric.

· SQUARE CUSHION ·

The simple symmetricality of a square lends itself to a wide range of fabrics and decorative treatments. If you have a plain sofa, select a lively range of well co-ordinated patterned fabrics; on patterned upholstery you can choose rich, plain colours and add luxurious fringing, silk cord edging or fancy braids. Piped edges give a smart effect, or to soften the shape, insert a pleated or gathered frill in the seams (see Frilled pillowcase, page 84).

The neatest and most secure way of fastening a square cushion cover is by a zip placed across the back of the cushion. Alternatively, you can insert a zip in the side seam, or use press stud tape or touch-and-close fastening in one side of the cover, but there is inevitably a slight distortion of the edge with these methods. Square cushion pads are available in a range of sizes, but it's a simple matter to seam and fill your own if you want a particular size, perhaps to fit comfortably into an upholstered armchair.

Calculating fabric amounts
Front cover: Measure the length and width of the cusion pad. Add 1.5cm seam allowance all round.
Back cover: You will need to cut two pieces of fabric for the back of the cushion so that you can add the zip. Divide the area of the cushion pad in half widthways and add 1.5cm seam allowance to the centre edges of both halves.

You will need
- Fabric
- Matching sewing thread
- Cushion pad
- Zip fastener
- Piping cord (optional)

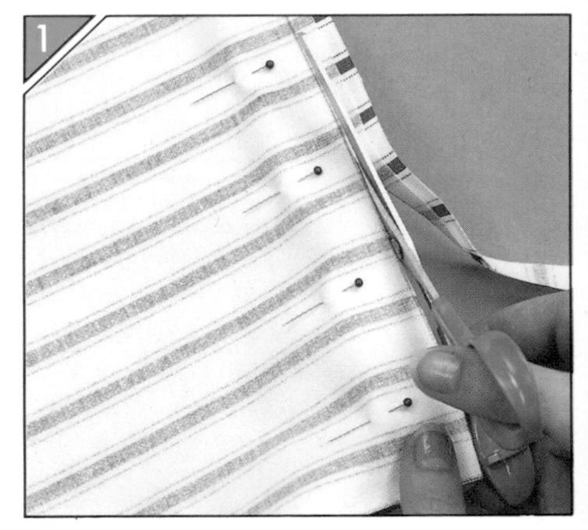

Making up
■ Using a ruler and tailor's chalk, mark the square for the top of the cover and the two rectangles for the back on the wrong side of the fabric on the straight grain. If the pattern needs matching, mark out one back piece and use this as a guide to match the pattern when cutting the second back piece (**1**). Cut out the three sections, matching the pattern if applicable.

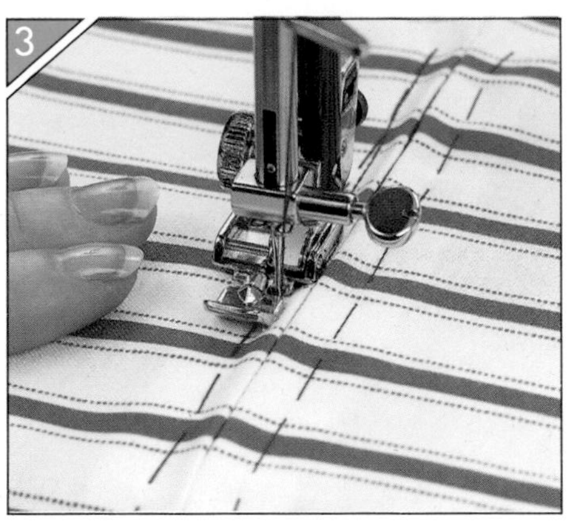

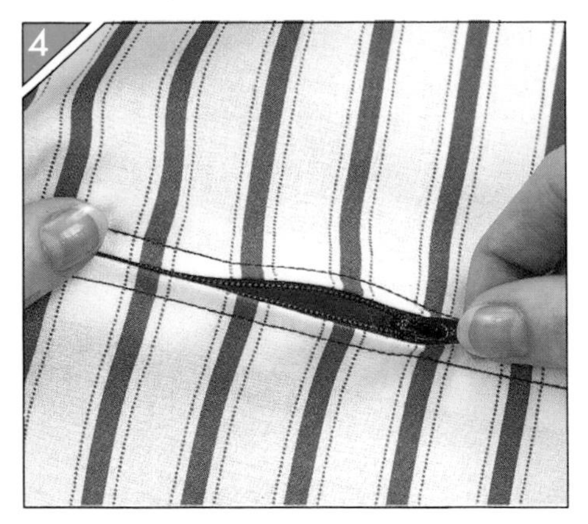

■ Place the two back rectangles together with right sides facing. Pin and tack a flat 1.5cm seam along centre edges. Stitch for at least 5cm in from each end leaving the centre of the seam allowance open for the zip to be inserted (**2**). Press the seams and central seam allowance open on the wrong side. Remove tacking.

■ Insert the **zip** into the opening with the wrong side of the fabric to the right side of the zip. The open section of the seam should cover the zip teeth. With the fabric right side up, tack and sew zip in place (**3**). Stitch as close to the teeth as possible and make sure the stitching is evenly spaced.

■ Press seam allowances around the zip. Open zip, making sure that the fabric does not catch and that the ends are stitched firmly (**4**). Leave zip open.

■ If a **piped** cord edging is required, place the covered cord on the right side of front fabric. Match the stitching line of the covered piping to the seam line (1.5cm in from edge), and align the raw edges of the piping fabric with the raw edges of the cover fabric. Pin in place. Unpick a few centimetres at each end of piping, join the fabric and cord ends and restitch the piping. Tack piping in place (**5**).

■ Place the cushion back to the cushion front with right sides facing and edges level. Pin, tack and machine stitch seam all round (**6**). If the edge is piped, use a zipper foot to stitch the edge keeping the stitching as close to the piping cord as possible. Press seam open on wrong side. If using a heavy-weight fabric, you may need to clip the corners of the fabric to minimize bulk.

Turn cushion cover right sides out through the zip opening. Press and insert cushion pad. Close zip.

· ROUND CUSHION ·

Calculating fabric amounts

Measure the diameter of the cushion pad; add 3cm seam allowance. You will need to cut a circular paper pattern of this diameter to be used directly for the front cover and as a basis for the back cover.

Frill: first decide the required finished depth of **frill**. For a **double frill** cut the fabric strips twice the required depth plus 3cm. For a **single frill**, cut the strips the required depth plus 2.5cm. For the frill length, measure around the cushion pattern 1.5cm in from the edge. For a **gathered** frill, allow 1½ to 2 times this length according to the amount of fullness required. For a **knife pleated** frill, as shown, allow 2 times the length around cushion. Divide the length of the frill by the width of the fabric to find how many strips are needed. Multiply the number of strips by the depth of the frill to work out the extra fabric needed.

You will need

- Fabric
- Matching sewing thread
- Cushion pad
- Zip fastener
- Frill (optional)

Frilled, piped, fringed, braided, ribboned – like square cushions, the basic round cushion shape can be enlivened in any number of different ways, most simply by the choice of beautiful fabrics for the outer covers. Round cushion pads are sold in various standard sizes. If you are using a smooth or shiny fabric, choose a firm cushion pad and make sure the cover fits closely, otherwise the edges will not stay crisp and any slight unevenness will be emphasized.

The circles for front and back of the cover are cut from squares of fabric – you can make a paper pattern as a cutting guide or draw directly on the fabric with a tailor's chalk pencil. The cover is fastened with a zip and it is easier to sew a zip across the back of a round cushion than to insert it in the edge, which tends to pucker and distort the seam. The zip is set in the upper segment of the back fabric, so it does not run across the full diameter, but the cushion pad can be easily manipulated through the zip opening.

Making up

■ Draw a circular paper pattern of the required diameter. Cut out the paper pattern and fabric circle for the front cover (**1**).

Using the same circular pattern, rule a straight line with a hard pencil across the pattern where the zip is to be placed in the back of the cover. The line should be 13cm longer than the length of the zip.

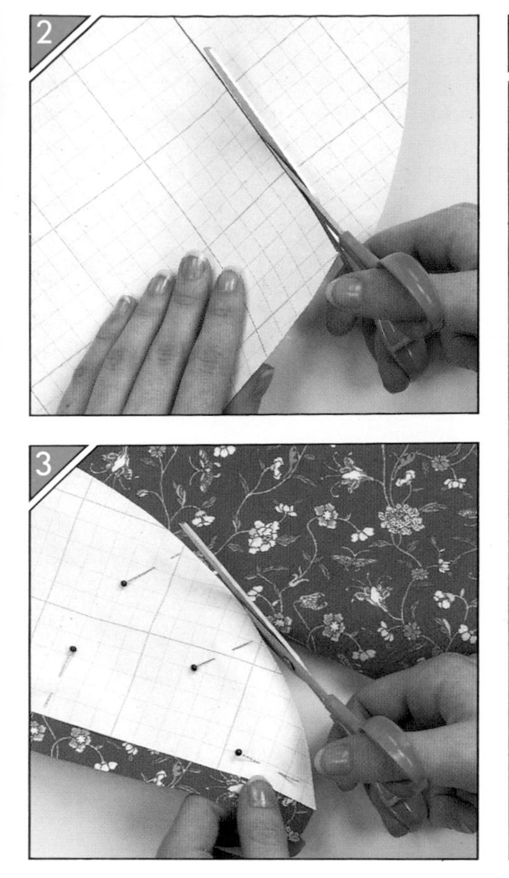

■ Cut the paper pattern along the line (**2**). Pin top section of back cover pattern to the fabric. Allowing 1.5cm for zip seam allowance on the straight edge, cut out the fabric (**3**).

■ Pin the bottom section of the paper pattern to the fabric, again allowing for the zip seam, and cut out fabric.

Right sides together and raw edges matching, pin and tack the straight edges of the back cover together. Sew 6.5cm from either end along the seam line (**4**). Press seam open on the wrong side. Remove tacking.

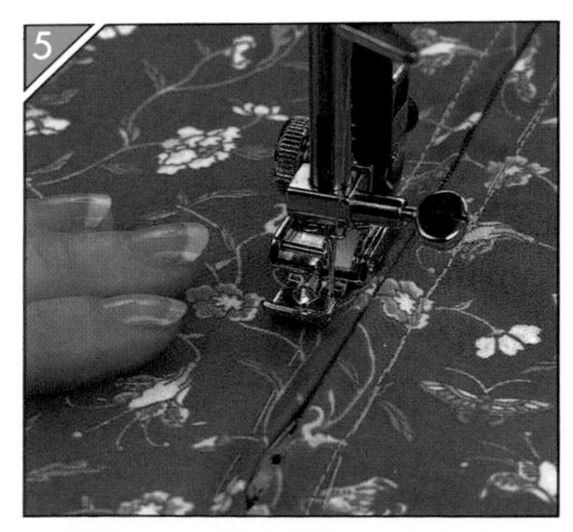

■ With the fabric right side up, insert the **zip** into the opening. The wrong side of the fabric should face the right side of the zip, and the open section of the seam should cover the zip teeth. Tack zip in place. Sew down both sides and across each end of the zip, keeping as close to the teeth as possible (**5**). Open zip.

■ Pin front and back circles together, right sides facing and raw edges matching, allowing for a 1.5cm seam. To add a **frill**, align raw edge of frill with raw edge of front cover, right sides together. Tack and sew frill in place. Pin and tack the right side of the back cover to the other right side of the frill, allowing for a 1.5cm seam all round (**6**).

■ Stitch the front and back covers together, sandwiching the frill in place if inserted (**7**). Notch the seam to minimize bulk inside the cushion.

Turn cover right sides out through zip opening and insert cushion pad. Close zip.

· BOXED CUSHION ·

Often made for a particular purpose – to fit a special chair or window seat – boxed cushions give a smart, crisp effect and are sturdy and practical in use. You can use a suitable cushion pad, or cut any shape your require from a thick foam block; this enables you to make regular geometric or irregularly shaped cushions, using the dimensions of the block to make a paper pattern before cutting out fabric. The cover is opened and closed with a zip in the side gusset and you can pipe the seams to make a neat, strong finish.

Covers for boxed cushions need to be firm and close-fitting. Medium weight cottons are highly practical, creating crisp lines and even seams. There is a wide choice of bold plain colours and patterns from traditionally pretty to powerfully abstract. The fabrics may have a matt or glazed surface, a textured weave or subtle figuring.

Calculating fabric amount

Measure the length and width of the top of the cushion pad; to each measurement add 3cm for seam allowances. Allow for two pieces of fabric this size, for top and bottom of the cushion cover.

The gusset is made from four strips of fabric. Measure the depth of the pad and the width on each side. For three sections of the gusset, add 3cm to length and width for 1.5cm seam allowances all round. For the back section which will enclose the zip, add seam allowances all round and add an extra 3cm to the depth for the zip opening.

You will need

- Fabric
- Matching sewing thread
- Zip approximately 10cm shorter than the width of the back gusset section

Round boxed cushion

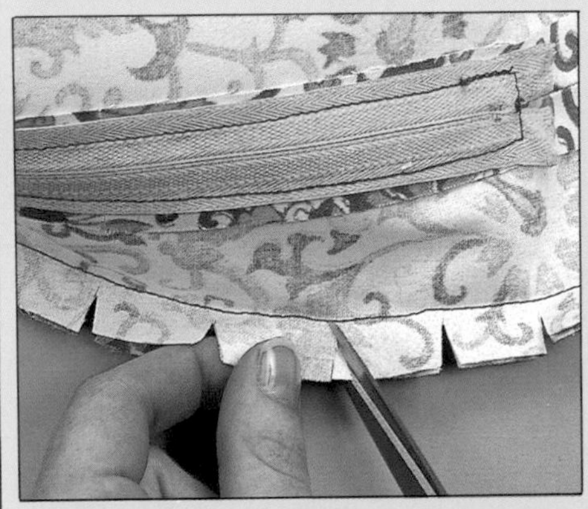

For a round cushion, the gusset is made from two seamed strips, one shorter section enclosing the zip. When attaching the gusset to the top and bottom cover pieces, ease the edge of the gusset onto the curve of the flat fabric, pin and tack to check the fit before machine stitching all around the cover. To ensure the seams do not pull when the cover is turned out to the right side, clip V-shaped notches in the seam allowances at regular intervals around the edge.

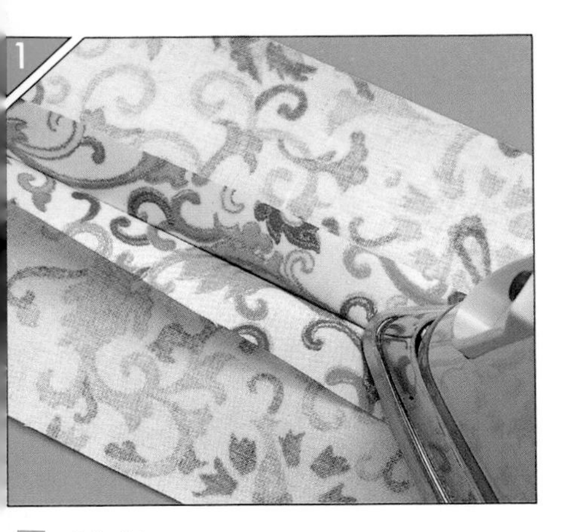

Making up

■ Cut back gusset piece in half lengthwise. Place the halves right sides together and tack a short seam on either side 1.5cm from the long raw edges. Each seam should be approximately 5cm, leaving a central opening for the zip. Press open the seam allowance (**1**).

■ Insert the **zip** in the back gusset. Pin and tack the zip to either side of the zip opening and machine stitch using a zip foot (**2**). Secure each end of the zip with a short line of vertical stitching.

■ Seam the four gusset pieces together at the short ends. Place them right sides together and stitch with 1.5cm seam allowance. Leave 1.5cm unstitched at top and bottom of each seam (**3**), but finish the stitching line securely. Press seams open.

■ With right sides facing, machine stitch the top edge of one section of the gusset along one edge of the top cover piece, taking a 1.5cm seam allowance. At the gusset seam, leave the needle in the fabric and raise the machine foot (**4**), turn the fabric and align the next section of gusset on the cover piece, lower the machine foot and continue stitching. Work all four sides in this way.

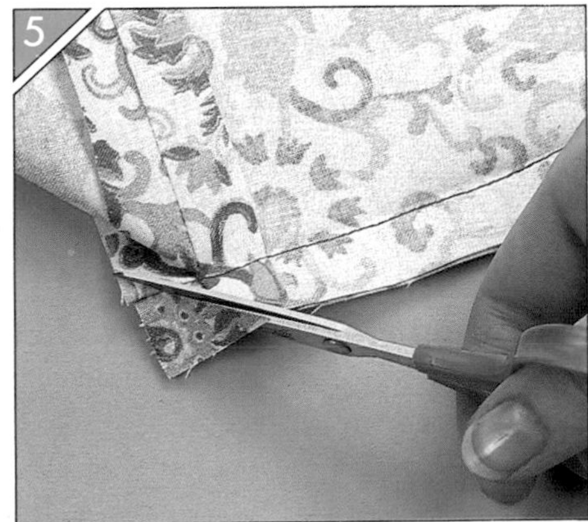

■ Clip the seam allowances diagonally across each corner close to the stitching (**5**), so the corners will ease out neatly when the cover is turned to the right side. Open the zip and then stitch the lower edges of the gusset to the botton section of the cover in the same way. Clip the corner seams and press all the seam allowances towards the gusset. Turn the cover out to the right side, through the open zip. Ease and straighten the seams between your fingers and push out the corners before inserting the cushion pad.

· BOLSTER ·

An elegant addition to a sofa, window seat or chaise longue, bolsters are a noticeable feature of the room that can be styled to create any mood. Your choice of fabric for the covers can make them roughly practical or luxuriously opulent, from matt-surfaced, textured weaves to shiny satin finished with silky cords and tassels.

There are three basic designs for bolster covers – fully fitted with flat ends; fitted with gathered ends; or a bag-like cover which pulls up with a drawstring at either end. The long, firm lines of a bolster lend themselves particularly well to directional designs such as stripes or trellises. If you choose a heavily patterned fabric, it is best made up in the fitted style with a zip closure, so the pattern is evenly stretched around the bolster shape. The gathered and drawstring versions can be informally styled in cottons and textured synthetic mixes, more formally finished in traditional chintzes or figured fabrics, or given a touch of glamour by a fabric with a definite surface sheen, which catches the light down the rounded length of the bolster and emphasizes the decorative effect of the gathers.

Calculating fabric amounts

The steps show a gathered bolster cover, which is made from a rectangle of fabric. Length: Measure the length of the cushion pad plus the diameter of the circular end. Add 3cm for the seam allowances.

Width: Measure around circumference of cushion pad; add 3cm for the seam allowances.

You will need

- Fabric
- Matching sewing thread
- 2 button moulds
- 2 tassels

Making up

■ Cut a rectangle of fabric for the body of the bolster. Fold it right sides together with long edges matched. Pin, tack and stitch long edges together making a **French seam** (**1**).

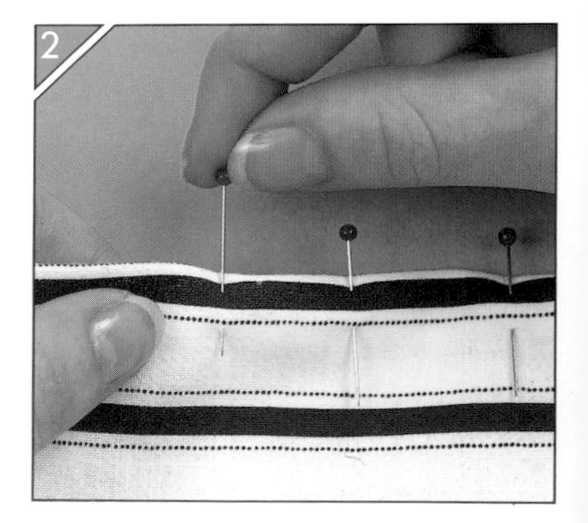

■ Turn the fabric tube right side out and press the seam. Turn under a 1.5cm hem at each end. Pin in place (**2**).

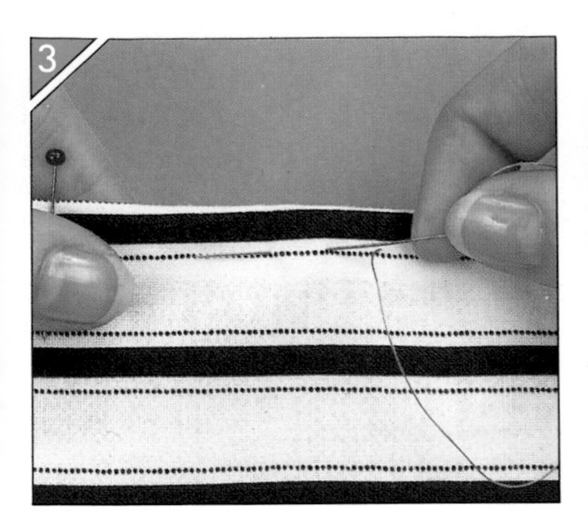

■ Tack each hem in place securely (**3**), using a contrast colour thread. Finish the tacking with a double stitch and remove the pins.

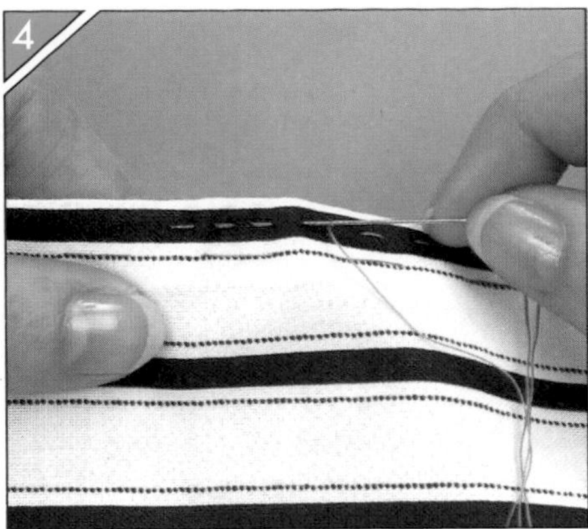

■ At each end of the bolster, hand sew a row of **gathering** stitches (**4**). Take care to position this stitching close to the fold and keep the stitches even.

Insert the bolster cushion pad into the tube of fabric. Make sure the cover fits snugly around the shape and is not loose along the body of the pad. Adjust it so the projecting ends of fabric are equal.

■ At each end of the cover, pull up the gathering threads to bring the edges of the cover in to the centre. Adjust the gathers to distribute them evenly from the centre. Make sure that the hole left at the centre will be covered by the button and fasten off the gathering threads with **backstitch** (5).

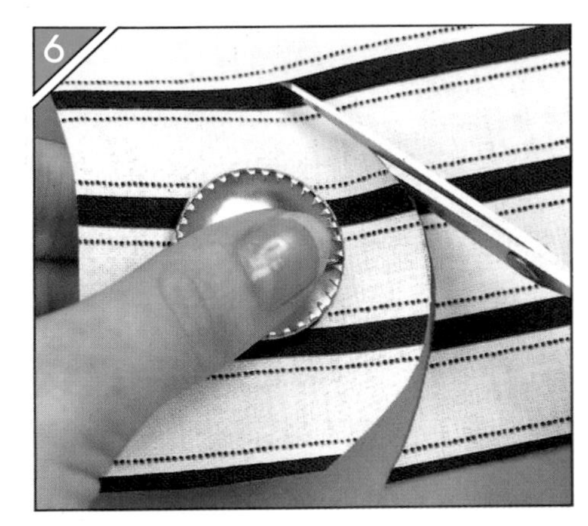

■ Cover both the button moulds with fabric. Cut a circle of fabric generously larger then the button (**6**). Fold it over the top section of the button and push the edges of the fabric inside the button top. Use your finger to push fabric onto the hooked spikes inside the button top; attach fabric first at two opposite edges, then again at the other two opposite edges. Finally work round the button hooking in the remaining fabric smoothly. Snap the lower part in place. The two sections are designed to fit securely, with tiny spikes inside to grip the fabric.

■ Using double thread, pass the needle through the bobble of the tassle so the thread end is hidden inside. Secure the thread with two small back stitches on top of each other. Take a small stitch through centre of button covering fabric, then one through top of tassle. Stitch securely and finish thread end. Stitch buttons at each end of the bolster (**7**), concealing the gathered edges behind the button.

· SHAPED CUSHION ·

Plain cushions don't have to be round or square – they can be triangles or diamonds, L-shaped or oval – or you can let your imagination wander into the range of slightly more complex shapes, such as hearts or fans. Any shape can be worked out as a paper pattern which can be used to make up your own cushion pad and a suitable cover. So once you've mastered the principle of cushion-making, you can consider decorative, unusual "fun" shapes based on flowers, fruits, animal motifs and so on, perhaps for a child's playroom or teenager's bedroom. As with the more conventional cushion shapes, as long as the pad is well-constructed and evenly filled, you can choose any type of fabric for the outer cover to suit the style of the design.

The simplest type of pattern consists of a front and back piece in the same shape, though not necessarily a regular shape. Otherwise, for a sturdier gusseted cushion, which can be designed to fit a particular alcove seat or chair, for example, you simply cut the front and back pieces and also strips of fabric long enough to go around the full contour of the cushion shape. Refer to the instructions for the boxed cushions shown on page 120 which explain how a gusset is sewn in.

Calculating fabric amounts

The amount of fabric needed depends on the design of your cushion. The steps show construction of a triangular cushion pad and cover. Draw up a paper pattern of the shape and make a second outline to allow for 1.5cm seams all around each piece. Measure the pattern across the widest and longest sections. If you are making the cover from fabric which just covers the width of the cushion, buy twice the length. If you can get two pattern pieces from the width, you need only the length of the cushion itself.

Use plain calico or downproof calico for the cushion pad, and any suitable fabric for the outer cover. If the fabric has a pronounced directional pattern or large motif, allow extra if you want both sides of the cushion to include the same area from the repeats of the fabric design. Add the necessary allowance for gusset strips if you are making a boxed shape.

You will need

- Fabric for the cushion pad
- Polyester filling
- Fabric for the cover
- Matching sewing thread

Making up the cover

■ Using the same pattern as for the pad, cut pieces of fabric for top and bottom of the cushion cover, but this time take a seam allowance of 1cm beyond the edges of the paper pattern (5). The outer cover needs to be just this much larger than the pad cover to give the extra margin needed for inserting the pad.

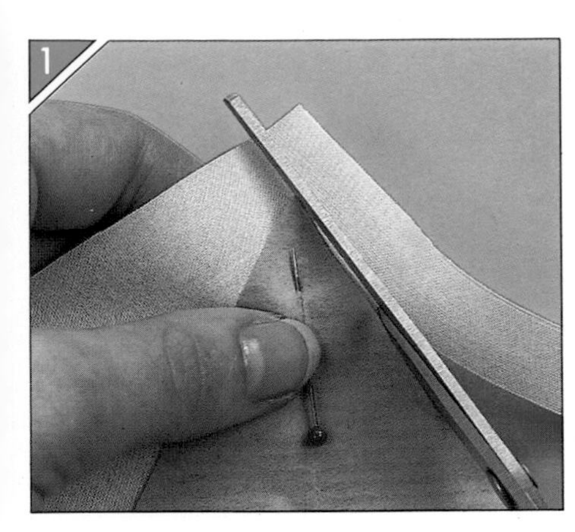

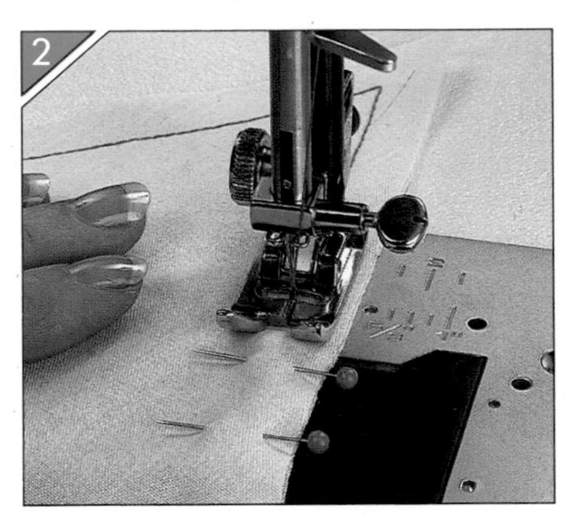

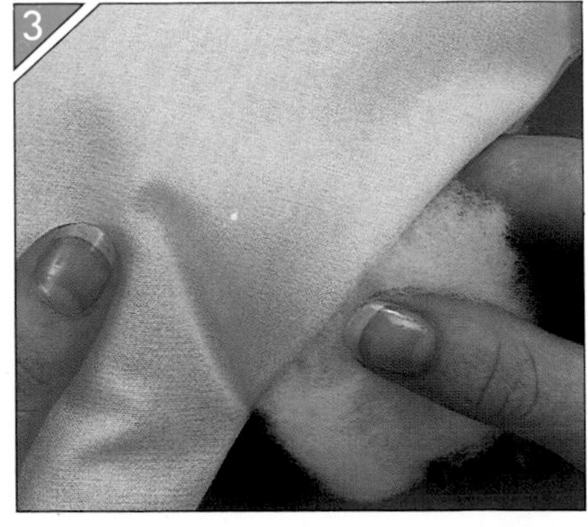

Making up the pad

■ Draw a paper pattern for the cushion shape and add on a 1.5cm seam allowance all around. If the shape is symmetrical, you can construct a pattern for half the shape and cut out on a fold of the fabric, cutting through both layers away from the folded edge. The shape is then perfectly symmetrical when the fabric is opened out.

Pin the paper pattern to the fabric and cut out the shape (**1**). Position the pattern separately for front and back pieces if the fabric has a definite design. For plain or miniprint fabrics you can cut through two layers of fabric placed right sides together, cutting front and back pieces at the same time.

■ Pin the two pieces of fabric right sides together and stitch around the edges taking a 1.5cm seam allowance (**2**), leaving an opening 15cm long for inserting the filling. If the shape has a distinct point or a sharply curved section, it is best to place the opening along a relatively straight part of the seam opposite the point. Then you can push the filling firmly into the shape and it will not be distorted when it comes to closing the opening in the pad cover. To give the seams extra strength, work a second row of stitching along the seamline on top of first row.

Insert the filling through the opening in the seam (**3**). Work it well into the contours of the shape and make sure it is distributed evenly so that the cushion pad is firmly filled out but not lumpy.

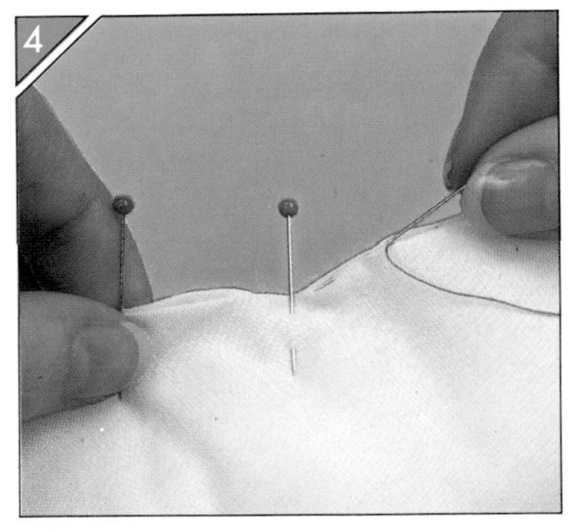

■ To close the opening in the seam, turn in the seam allowances neatly and pin the two sides of the gap together. **Slipstitch** by hand (**4**) as invisibly as possible.

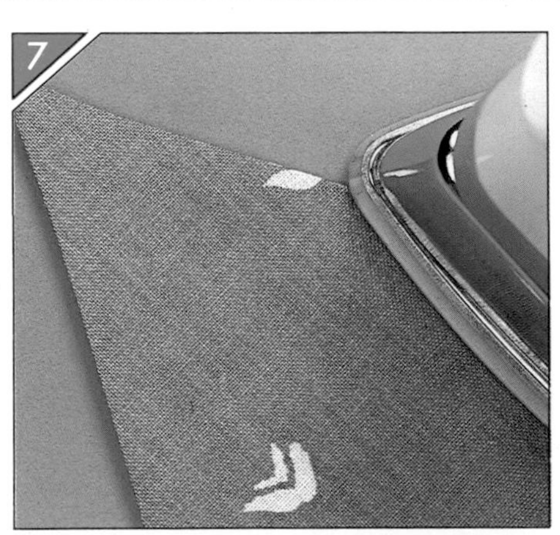

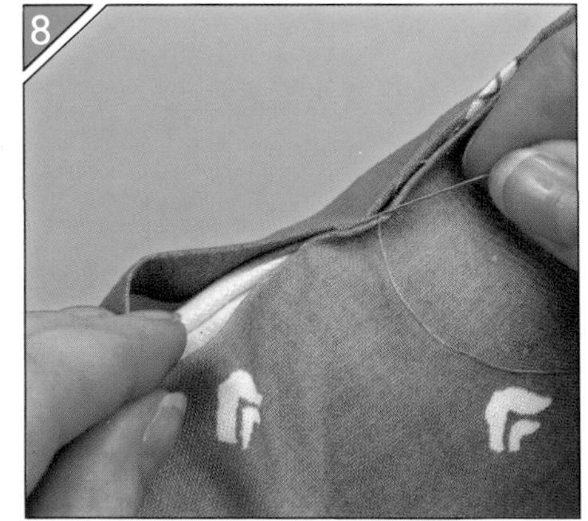

■ Put the pieces of fabric right sides together and pin. Stitch around the edge taking a 1.5cm seam allowance (**6**), leaving an opening in one side large enough for insertion of the pad. As with the pad cover, it is a good idea to make a second row of stitching to strengthen the seams.

■ Any decorative edging, such as **piping** or a **frill**, can be inserted in the seams, but stitched to one side of the cover only at the opening in the seam.

Turn the cushion pad out to the right side, pushing out the seams to achieve the correct shape. Press the cushion cover (**7**). Try to ensure that the seamlines are even along the contour of the shape.

■ Insert the cushion pad through the opening in the cover. Tuck in the raw edges neatly along the opening and **slipstitch** them together (**8**).

· DESIGN IDEAS ·

Your ideas for decorative features of cushions must be tailored to the kind of wear and tear they will be subject to, and the useful life you expect from them. A mass of scatter cushions is an exciting project for beginners and experienced sewers alike, because they are of manageable size and you can apply anything which can be stitched in place.

Ready-made edgings such as braids, cords, fringing and tassels are an obvious and attractive choice, easy to sew to the cushion cover and creating a smart finish providing the lines of the cushion are even.

A layered effect is unusual and adds an extra dimension to the design of the basic cushion. All-over lace on a satin base has a luxurious look, or a translucent sheer fabric over a plain-coloured opaque surface giving a subtle interplay of colours. You need not use only cut fabric pieces for making up the cushion cover; pretty handkerchiefs or scarves sewn together make an interesting finish, or you can convert favourite items, such as a lovely old embroidered traycloth or runner.

A very simple method of enlivening the basic rectangular cushion is to add a contrast edging stitched to the outer seams of the cover, or a heavy braid border sewn to the front of the cushion, aligned to the seam or with a self-coloured margin on the cusion edges. A self-fabric border can also be created by making up the cushion cover a little larger than the pad and stitching 4-5cm inside the seamlines all around. Lace makes an attractive appliqué design on the body of the cushion, and embroidery for borders and corners can also be appliquéd to the front section, particularly effective on a translucent fabric over a solid colour background. Pretty handkerchieves or scarves can be converted into cushion covers, stitched to a backing fabric in which the zip is inserted.

Decorative cushions can be made of any fabric, but boxed cushions and bolsters sometimes need to stand up to hard wear and should be covered in a firm, fairly heavy furnishing fabric. Lightly embossed and textured designs come in different colourways and reversible patterns offering a number of different ideas for a co-ordinated look. Plain-coloured piping creates a smart effect if the colour is chosen to make a link between variations in the fabric patterns.

Braids, cords, tassels and fringes add interesting texture to a cushion collection. Decorative trims may be plain or multicoloured, discreetly woven or heavily embossed. Handstitched to the outer edges of the cushion cover, they define the outline of the shape while disguising the seamlines.

CHAPTER SEVEN

· LOOSE COVERS ·

Whether to revitalize an old chair or change the colour scheme, loose covers are an attractive and inexpensive alternative to new furniture.

· LOOSE COVERS ·

Whether to give new life to an old chair or sofa, or to co-ordinate new furniture with other furnishings in the room, it can be well worth the time and effort to make your own loose covers rather than depend upon ready-made or custom-made items. Making the loose covers takes time and concentration and the cost of fabric has to be considered, but it can be an economical and satisfying solution to the problems of finding the right colour and pattern of fabric for such noticeable furnishings, which can set the tone of the room overall. Also, if you have a favourite chair or sofa which has seen better days, it is a pity to sacrifice its comfort and familiarity for the sake of a new look; but loose covers will revive a sound but old and shabby suite, giving it a totally new lease of life.

The exact styling and fitting of your loose covers obviously depends on the shape of the chair or sofa. If you are buying in new furniture with the intention of covering it yourself, boxy shapes are probably easiest for a beginner, but curved contours can be neatly managed with a little more care in the cutting and fitting of fabric. With methodical work and a conscientious approach to matching seams, pressing and neatening the pieces as they are fitted together, even a novice sewer can produce an immaculate, well-tailored loose cover.

CHOOSING FABRIC

Initial choice of the right kind of fabric will set you on the path to achieving a professional finish with minimum effort. Advice on suitable fabrics is usually available from a department store with a good selection of furnishing fabrics. Many of these, including highly glazed cottons, are really only suitable for seating which will be subject to light occasional use: for heavier daily duty, choose from the more robust and durable types, such as cotton/linen union, damask, heavy cottons, and others in the range of fabrics recommended for upholstery.

Select a fabric that is firm and closely woven, so that it will retain its shape. Ideally, it should also be shrink- and fade-resistant. Avoid very thick and heavily textured fabrics, as it is difficult to fit these to a specific shape and, where several layers are seamed or overlapped, they create too much bulk.

Plain-coloured fabrics and small overall patterns present no extra problems to the beginner. With plain colours, the weight and texture of the fabric are all-important, especially if you are fitting new covers to an old chair with well-worn lumps and bumps. The fabric must be firm enough to contain imperfections of shape, and remember that a light colour or shiny finish will tend to show up any undulations, whereas matt or slightly textured fabrics and deep colours will make them less noticeable.

A large print can look very impressive if the motifs are centred on the different sections of the chair or sofa and everything is symmetrical, but this can be wasteful of fabric and requires careful attention to pattern matching. If you haven't the time or the expertise to arrange the pattern perfectly, the final result will look disappointingly inexpert, however attractive or unusual the fabric.

The vast variety of fabrics available offer many exciting options in colour design and texture. There are smooth glazed cottons with modern abstract designs or traditional floral prints, hardwearing textured weaves and rich tapestry fabrics. Wherever possible borrow or purchase a good sized fabric sample to try on the chair in the room setting before deciding.

PIPING

This is a purely optional design feature, but it does have the advantage of strengthening seams and giving a crisp finish to the shape: conversely, however, nothing looks worse than a wavy line of piping that doesn't quite follow the contour of the chair. It can form an interesting contrast detail if made in a different colour from that of the main fabric, or it creates a smartly tailored finish when made up with self fabric bias strips. If you are using a contrasting fabric for the piping make sure that it is colourfast and preshrunk, and as durable as the main fabric.

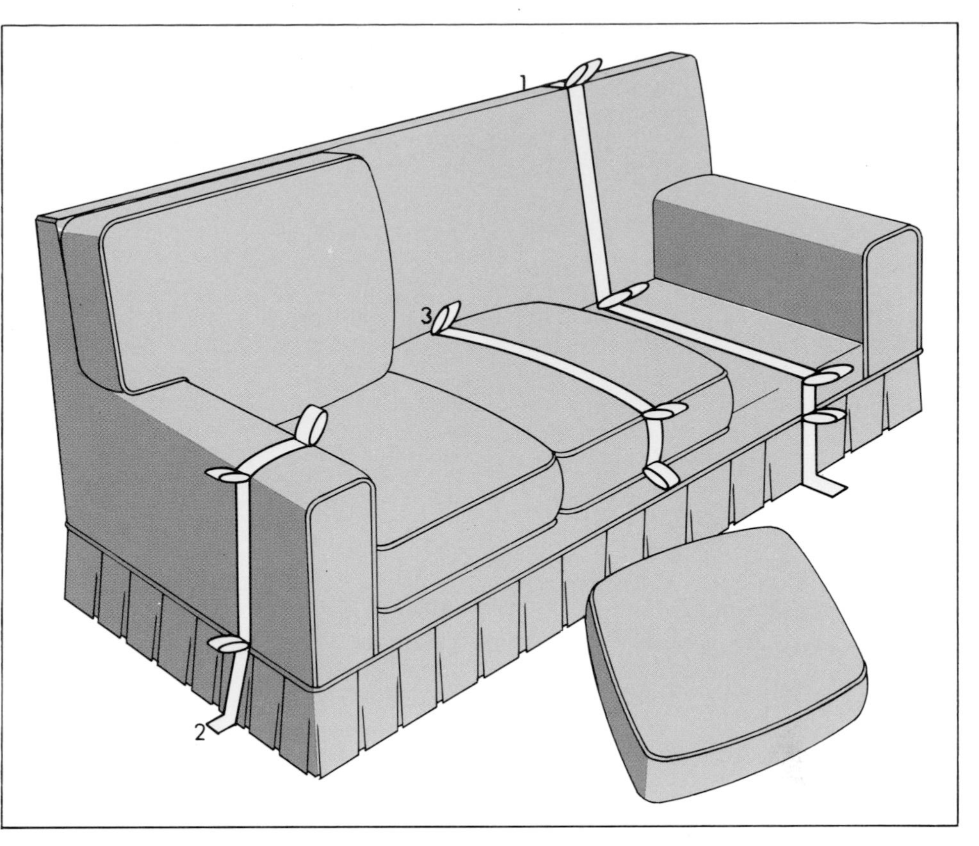

METHODS OF FITTING

It is best to fit the various sections of the cover onto the chair with the fabric right side out. This permits a fabric print to be positioned well and will allow for any irregularities in the chair's shape. Each section is smoothed and pinned, and repinned if necessary, until it fits perfectly. The cover is then removed section by section ready for stitching. An alternative method is to fit the cover with the fabric wrong side out. This will save a little time in repinning the seams ready for sewing, but will not allow for any unevenness in the chair's shape or pattern matching. If you are replacing an existing cover, unpick the old cover and use that as a pattern. When working with expensive fabric, or complicated print it is often worthwhile making a trial cover from a cheap muslin or calico to use as a pattern.

MEASURING UP AND ESTIMATING FABRIC

Although handling large amounts of heavy fabric can be cumbersome and awkward, cutting the fabric directly on the chair or sofa is the best way to arrive at accurate fitting. You must tailor the style of the cover to the shape of your chair making the necessary number of sections to ensure the fabric is not stretched or awkwardly draped around curves or corners on the back or arms. A chair or sofa will have a basic inner cover which can provide guidelines for where seams should be placed on loose covers. If you are removing existing, worn covers, look at them carefully to see how they are seamed.

Measuring up

You will need to take three main measurements to estimate the amount of fabric needed.

The front and back (**1**): measure up the back from the floor, across the top, down the front of the back, across the seat, and down the front apron and skirt to the floor. Add on 5cm for each seam crossed, 30cm for a tuck-in and an allowance for skirt hem. For a style without a skirt, measure to the bottom of the chair and add on 26cm for facings.

The side and arm (**2**): measure from the floor up the skirt and outer side arm, over the top arm and down the inner arm. Add on 5cm for each seam crossed, 15cm for the tuck-in and an allowance for skirt hem. For a style without a skirt, measure to the bottom of the chair and add on 13cm for a facing. Double the total amount for fabric length needed.

Cushions (**3**), measure the cushion from back to front plus its depth. Add on 5cm for each seam. Multiply the measurement by two and then by the number of cushions needed.

Calculating fabric

Once you have measured the lengths, check that the pieces can be cut from a single width of fabric; then add together the measurements to arrive at the full length of fabric needed. When measuring the width remember to allow an extra 6cm on back for a centre back opening, or 3cm on both side and back for a side back opening. Do not skimp on the amounts as insufficient width or length to include reasonable seam allowances will make it difficult to cut and fit the fabric on the chair; and you need to be able to ease and adjust the spread of the fabric over the shape. If you are making loose covers for a sofa it may be necessary to seam width of fabric together. Joining two widths along a single seam is the most economical, but if the pattern has a pronounced central motif, this should be centred on the sofa back with the seamed panels on either side making up the extra width. The sofa itself may have a panelled back, in which case follow the lines of its construction.

Extra fabric allowance must be made for pattern matching; if in doubt, buy a length of fabric which gives the full extent of the pattern and repeat. Use this to position the pattern motifs and plan the number of sections and their relationship to the length of fabric from the roll. Other allowances include fabric for bias strips to cover the piping cord, if you are using self-fabric piping, and for a gathered or continuously pleated skirt. For a gathered skirt allow twice the length for fullness, and for a continuously pleated skirt allow three times the length plus extra for joining at the seams.

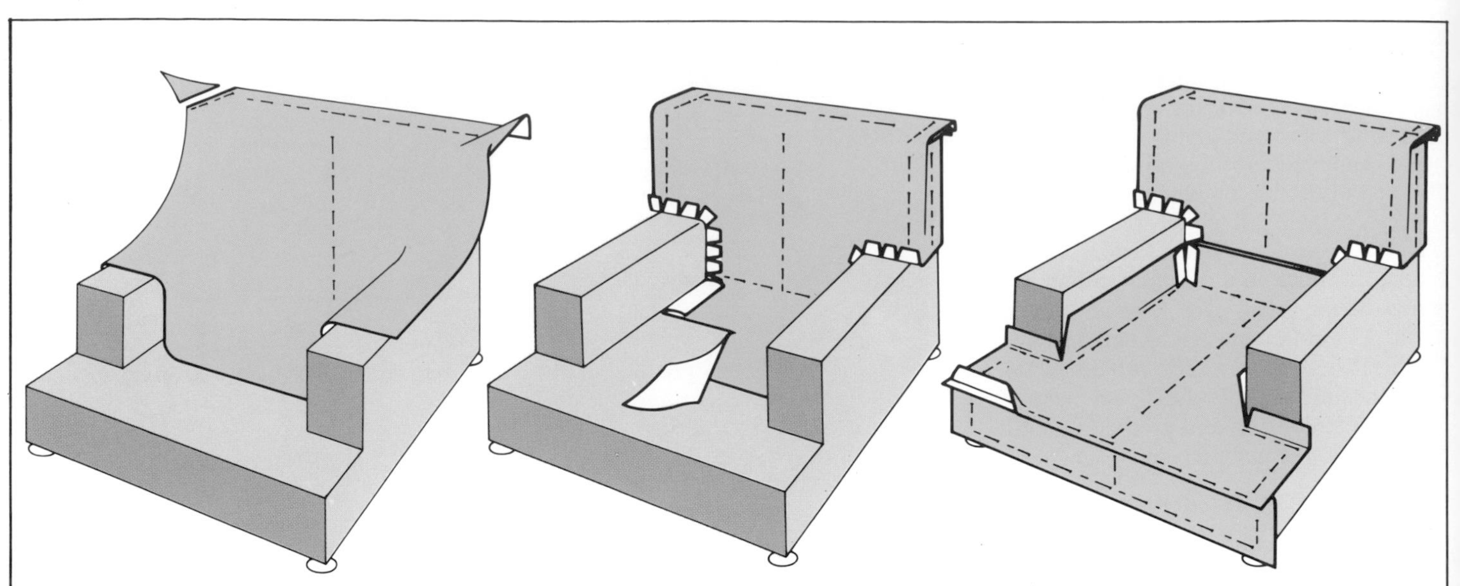

■ Place back section right side out on the chair. Arrange any large motif centrally and a little more than half way up. Allow 2.5cm to overlap the back edge of chair at top and sides. Pin the fabric centrally, then smooth it out to either side and pin the edges. Pin the side and top fabric together along the top corner of chair and trim away the excess fabric (**1**).

■ Work down the back fitting the fabric. If tuck ins are needed at the back arms, see steps 2 and 3 on the round back chair on page 134 . Otherwise fit the fabric in around the arm of the chair trimming away the excess and clipping the 2.5cm wide seam allowance so it fits smoothly. Allow 15cm for a tuck-in at the seat edge and trim away any excess fabric (**2**).

■ Arrange the seat section allowing 15cm tuck-ins at back and side edges and 2.5cm seam at front edge. Pin along the centre, smooth fabric out and pin at the edges. If the seat section needs to fit around any corners, clip the seam allowance at the corner. Arrange front apron allowing 5cm at lower edge and 2.5cm seams. Pin centre and edges, and top edge to seat (**3**).

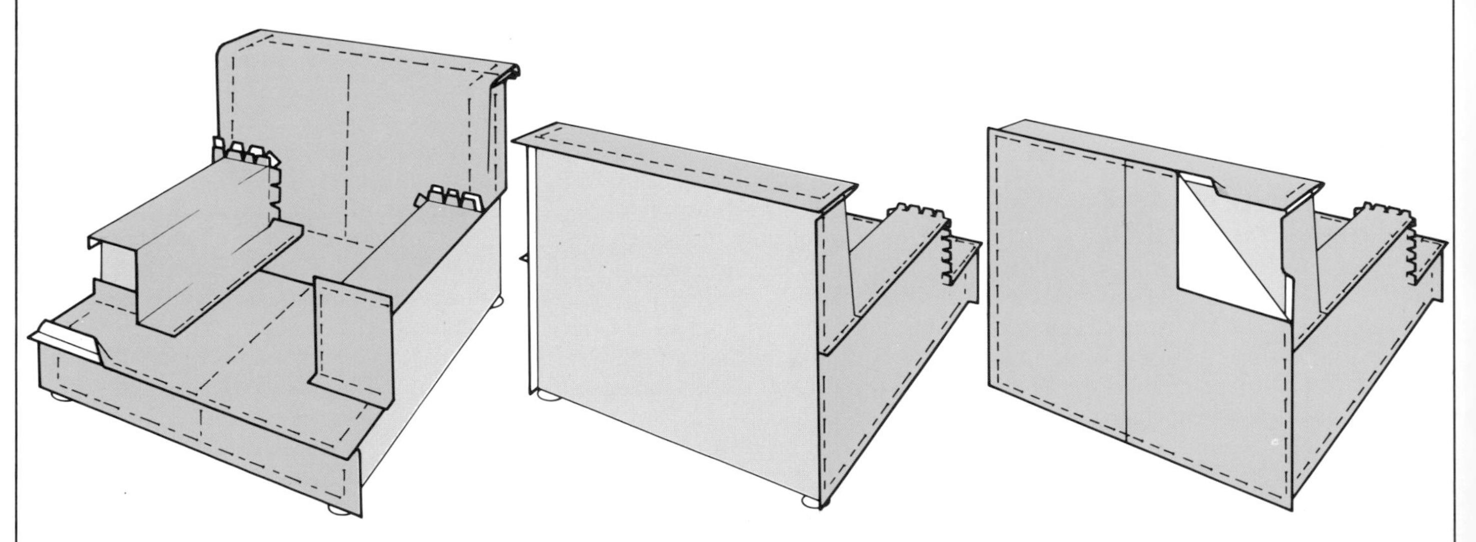

■ Place the inner arms over the arms allowing for a 15cm tuck-in at the seat edge and 2.5cm seams. Pin along the top arm, then down front edge. Clip the seam allowance at back edge and pin to the back. Place the front arm to inner arm and chair allowing 2.5cm all round for seams (**4**).

■ Place the outer arm section to the side edge of chair. Allow 2.5cm for seams and 5cm at the lower edge. This lower edge allowance, which will later be trimmed, is generous to ensure the cover will not fall short. Pin the side edge to edge of apron, seat and front, clipping at the corners. Pin the top edge to the inner arm and lower edge of side back (**5**).

■ Fold the back section in half lengthways and pin along 3cm from the fold for the opening allowance. Cut along the fold for opening. Pin the back section in place with 2.5cm wide seams at side and top edges and a 5cm allowance at the lower edge (**6**). Unpin the back seam for just as far as is needed to remove the cover. Mark the top of the opening.

FITTING LOOSE COVERS

Boxed chair

You will need to plan for at least seven separate sections of the chair: inside back, outside back, inside arm, outside arm, arm front panel, seat and front apron panel. When cutting sections for the arms you can use one arm as a template for the other, making sure fabrics are placed right side together. However if it is an old chair, which may not be perfectly symmetrical, these pieces should be cut individually. The seat section covers the chair base, a boxed cushion must be made up as a separate item (see page 120).

The fabric sections are pinned to the chair with the fabrics right side outside. This helps with the precise arrangement of the fabric pattern, and allows for any unevennss in the shape. The straight grain of the fabric, nap, and one way designs should run vertically down all sections. The pieces are pinned first at the centre then smoothed out to the edges and pinned there. Then as more sections are added the edges are pinned together. Allow 2.5cm seam allowances when cutting out to give room for adjustment, then trim them to 1.5cm when the fitting is complete and the seam lines marked. Tuck-ins are nearly always required around the edge of the chair seat. These are pockets of excess fabric which are pushed down into the crevice around the chair seat to allow the fabric some movement when the chair is sat upon. Some chairs also need tuck-ins where the arm joins the back, instructions for making these are given on page 134. Most covers will need an opening, this is simplest to make at the centre back, or if the back will be visible make the opening at a back corner. Allow 3cm turnings on each edge of opening.

There may be some variations on the number and shape of the sections needed. If the chair back is very deep or shaped at the side, separate panels may be needed for the side, or the side and top. Some arm tops may also need separate panels.

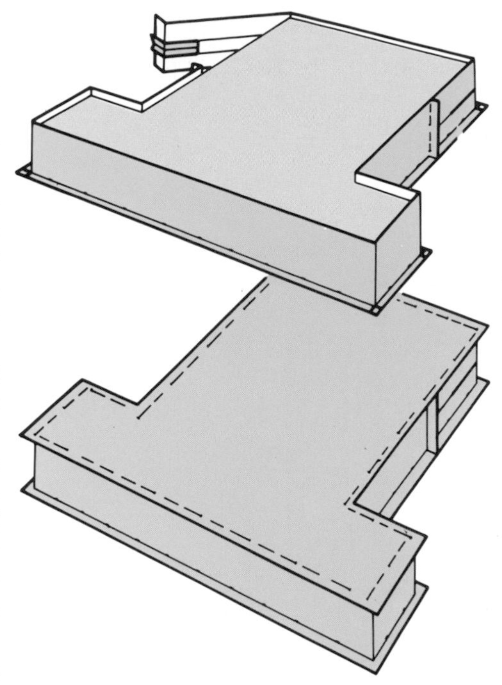

Covering the cushions

If you are using a fabric with a large motif, centre a motif on both main cushion sections so the cushion will be reversible. Position the side panel with the zip at the back of the cushion so it will not be visible. If the cushion shape is simple, it should be possible to measure and make the cushion with a normal 1.5cm seam allowance. On more complex shapes fit the cushion allowing 2.5cm seams in the same way as the cover. See page 120 for instructions on making a boxed cushion.

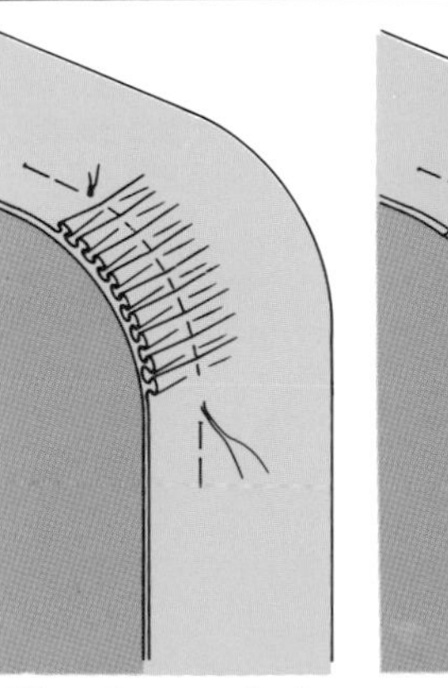

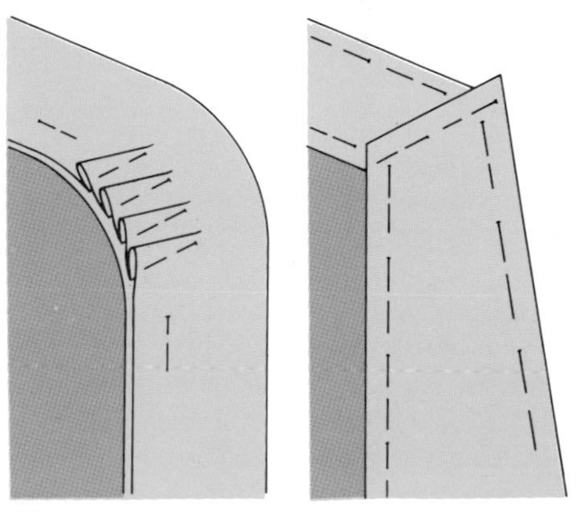

Shaping techniques

On chairs with rounded back corners, the fullness on the front section can be taken in with gathering, darts or tucks. These techniques may also be needed in other areas such as the end of arms. Chairs with shaped side backs will need the side back section cut separately as a boxed section.

Gathering

Pin the section in place for as far as it will fit smoothly. Stitch **hand gathering** along the seamline and pull up the gathering until the section fits. Fasten off the gathering and complete the seam.

Tucks

These can also be used to control fullness around a curve. Pin up to the curve, then, starting at the centre of the fullness, form equally sized tucks to take in the fullness. Tack tucks and complete seam.

Darts

Pin the section in place up to the point where there is excess fullness. Working from the centre, pin small darts to remove the fullness. Tack darts in place along seamline then complete the seam.

Boxed sections

When the side back is shaped other than a rectangle, it will need a separate section so the fabric straight grain can run vertically. Cut the section allowing 2.5cm for seams all round and pin in place.

Round-backed chair

The basic method for making the cover is very similar to the boxed chair method. The pieces are measured, seamed and the opening made in the same way as for a boxed chair, though the order of working is slightly different. The other main differences are the shaping on the rounded back and the addition of tuck-ins at the inner back arm seams.

When fitting the top of the back, there will be excess fullness on the front fabric which must be taken in by gathers, darts or tucks. When choosing which method to use, be guided by the previous cover, or test each method on a small section to see which looks best. The fullness may need taking in all round the back or just in two spaced sections.

The tuck-in on the back arm join, unlike seat tuck-ins, taper in depth along the tuck-in. The join starts as a normal fitted seam at the top of the inner back arm seam, then gradually extra fabric is allowed until it forms a full depth tuck in at the base of the join. Arm tucks-in are usually about 8cm deep.

Other shapes

Chairs and sofas are made in a great variety of forms and, while it is unlikely that shapes will match exactly, these methods can be adapted to suit most chairs. First see if you need tuck-ins by checking if the chair has crevices to push the tuck-ins into. Most chairs have these at the side and back of the seat base and some also have them between the arms and the back. Then look at the seaming on the old cover, or the base cover on the chair, to help decide which method or combination of methods is most suitable.

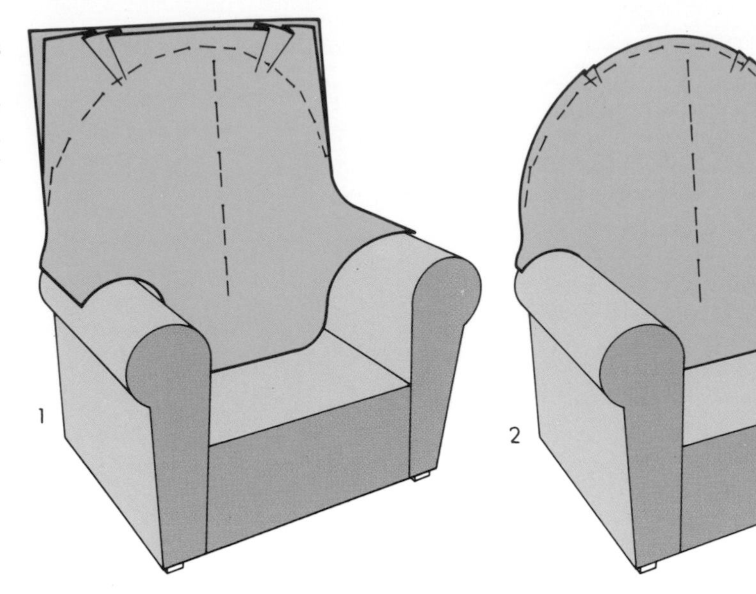

■ Make an allowance for back opening as shown in step 6 on page 132. Pin back and front sections centrally, allowing 5cm at lower edge of back and a 15cm tuck-in at seat edge of front. Pin front to the back taking in the fullness of front fabric with tucks, darts or **gathers**. Trim excess fabric allowing 2.5cm seams (**1**).

■ At the back arm edge of the back, trim the fabric to fit over the arm leaving a 2.5cm seam allowance at the top of the arm and tapering out the allowance to the full tuck-in allowance of 8cm at the base (**2**). If necessary, trim the seat tuck-in at lower edge of the back to 15cm.

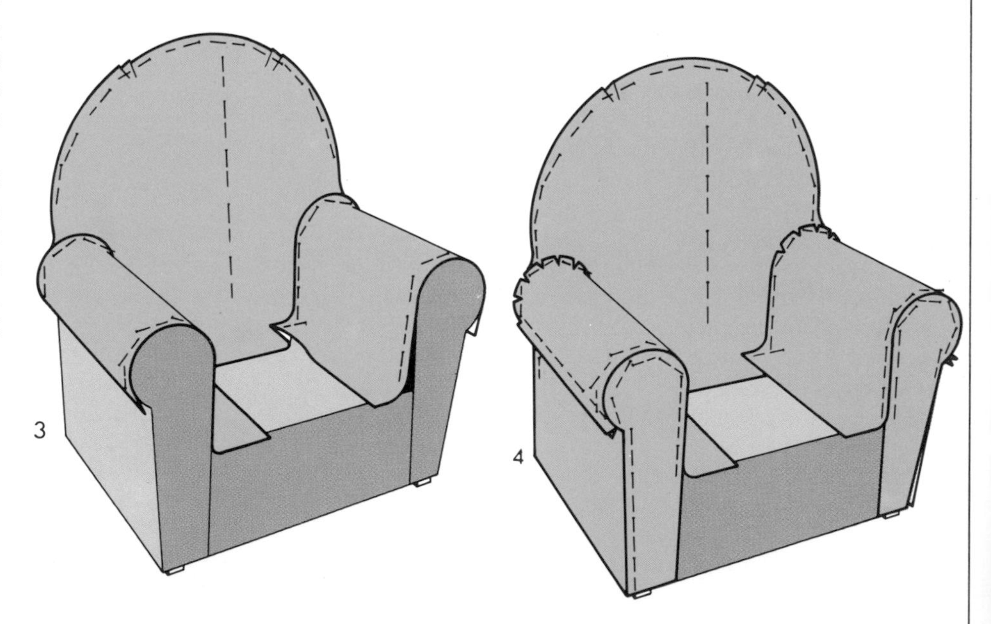

■ Pin the inner arms in place allowing 2.5cm for seams at outer and front edges and a 15cm tuck in at the seat edge. Trim the back edge of the arm allowing a 2.5cm seam allowance at the top and tapering out to the full tuck-in allowance of 8cm at the base. Pin the back edge of arm to the back 2.5cm in from the edge (**3**).

■ Pin outer arms in place taking 2.5cm seams, then pin the front arm to the outer and inner arm again with 2.5cm for seams. Clip the two seam turnings together around the top part of the back arm seam (**4**). Make sure these clips match when seaming the sections together. Complete remaining section in same way as the boxed chair.

Lower edge finishes

A skirt can be made plain with an inverted pleat effect at each corner, continuously pleated or gathered for a softer effect. The seam between the skirt and the cover can be piped or left plain. Alternatively the lower edge can be left completely plain or finished with piping and fastened to the chair with a facing.

First place the stitched cover on the chair to check the fit, then mark a level cutting line around the chair allowing 1.5cm seam below required stitching line for the seam. Skirts usually have a finished depth of about 18cm, add on the hem and 1.5cm top seam allowance to this.

The plain skirt with corner pleats is simplest when made in four separate sections with flap underlays placed behind at each corner. Cut four strips the length of each side adding 6cm for the opening and 10cm for turning back at the corners. Cut the corner flaps about 18cm wide.

For a continuously pleated frill, allow 3 times the required finished length. Measure the side and the front of the chair and establish a pleat width which will fit evenly into both measurements, so a pleat will fall at each corner. Press the pleats joining the fabric at the underfold of a pleat as you work.

For a gathered skirt allow about twice the required finished length for the fullness. Join the fabric section before gathering the skirt. The fullness should be distributed evenly around the skirt.

A plain or piped lower edge is finished with a facing. Cut the facing about 13cm deep, to fit along the four sides between the legs. Make hems along the two short and one long edge. Stitch the piping, then stitch the facing over the piping. The facing is fastened to the underside of the chair with touch-and-close tape or tacks.

Making skirts

Skirts can be made from single fabric with the lower edge finished by a double machine-stitched, or hand-stitched hem. Alternatively, where it will not make a gathered or pleated skirt too bulky, a lined skirt will give a better finish. For a gathered, or continuously pleated skirt, you will need to join a number of widths of fabric to make up the length. For a gathered skirt, join the lining and fabric widths separately, stitch them together at the lower edge and press the skirt with wrong sides together as shown in step 12 on page 142. Then treat the top edges as one fabric when gathering and stitching the skirt. For a continuously pleated skirt, join the lower edges first and press the pieces with wrong sides together. Then pleat and join the side edges treating the two layers as one fabric.

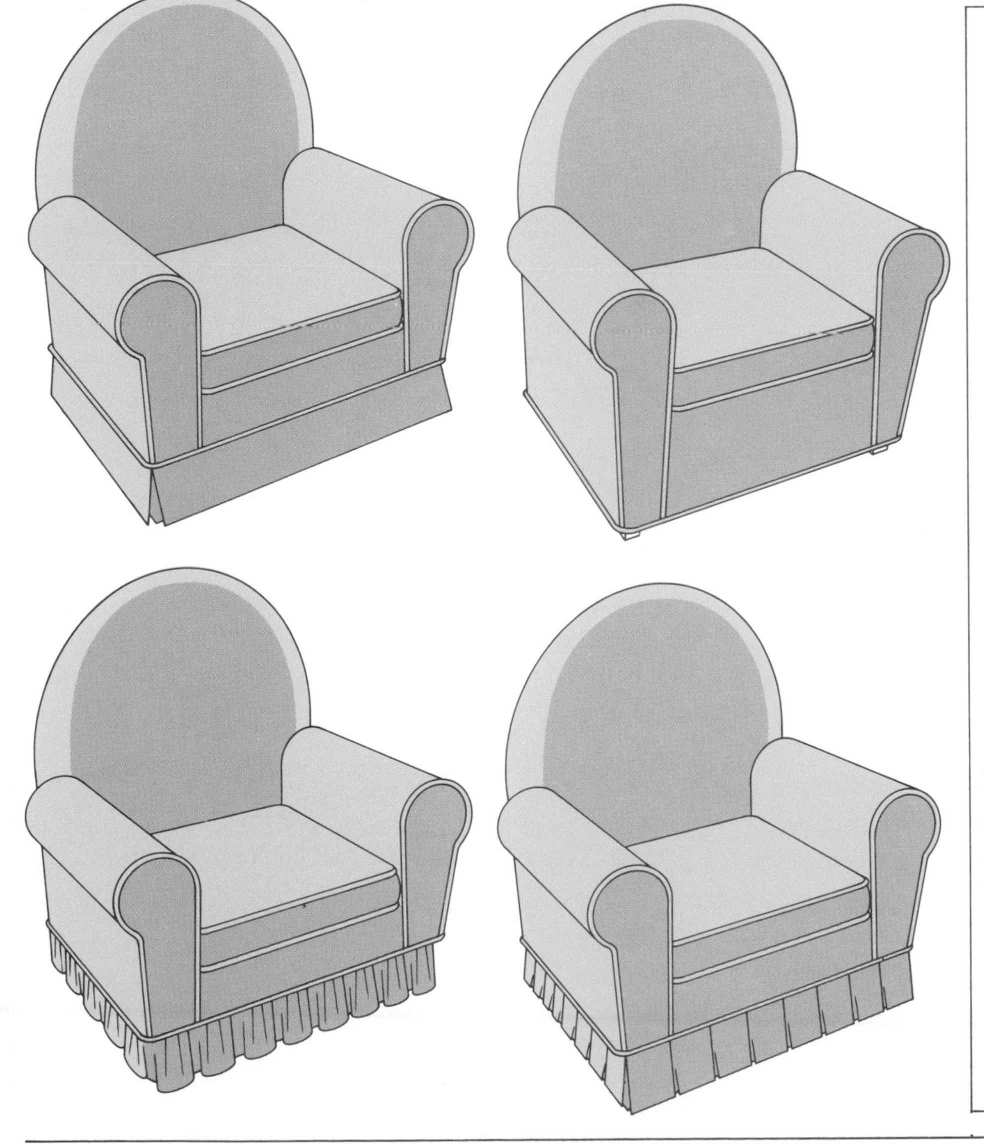

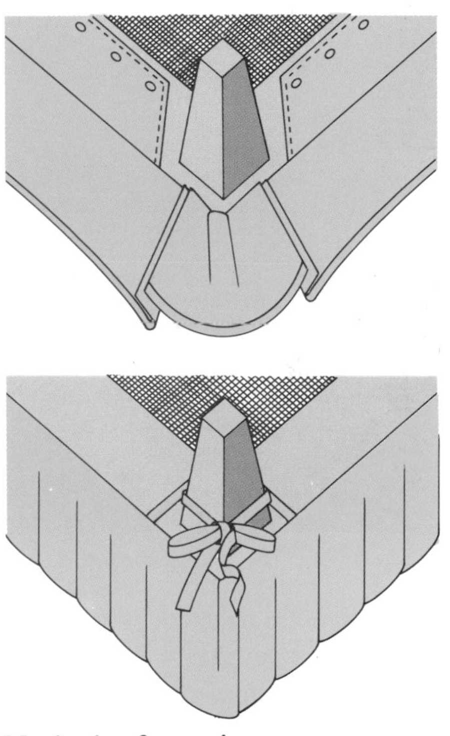

Methods of securing

The lower edges of loose covers can be fastened to the chair by a facing or ties. A facing is made from four separate strips, about 13cm wide, cut to fit between the chair legs or castors. Three sides are hemmed, and the other long edge is stitched to the underside of the skirt seam. The facing is fastened to the underside of the chair with touch-and-close tape or tacks. For ties, stitch 30cm lengths of tape to the skirt seam either side of the leg position.

· CHAIR COVER ·

Take the final measurements carefully and accurately before cutting out and it will save time at the fitting stage. Before you begin, measure the finished skirt depth up from the floor and draw a line around the chair at that level to measure down to. It is helpful to have a drawn outline plan of each piece to note down the revelant measurements of each piece as you go. Note the finished size required and then add on the amounts needed for the relevant number of seam allowances and tuck-ins. Mark the top or back edge of each piece on the plan, then, when you cut out, mark these edges with a couple of crossed pins. This is especially important on fabrics with a nap or one way design, but even on plain fabric it will save time sorting out which way up the pieces should go. If you have a number of pieces of a similar size it is also helpful to pin a note with the name of the piece to the fabric.

Calculating fabric amounts

Length: add on seam allowances and tuck-ins as you measure.
Measure from floor up back, across top, down the front of back, across seat and down front apron to floor.
Measure arms from floor up and over arm to seat. Multiply by 2.
Measure cushion from back to front and down depth. Multiply by 2.
Measure front arm and, if this will not fit beside another piece on the fabric, you will also need this length.
Add the amounts together and add on extra for corner flaps, piping, and matching the fabric design if necessary.
Width: The width of fabric should accommodate the widest piece.

You will need

- Fabric
- Matching sewing thread
- Lining for skirt
- Piping cord
- Touch-and-close fastening

Making up

■ Remove cushions before measuring. Measure across the front of the chair back continuing around the sides of the back to the back corners (**1**). Add on 5cm for a 2.5cm seam allowance at each of the back edges. If this is not the widest part of the chair, also measure the widest part again adding on 5cm for seams.

■ Measure the front of the chair back from the back edge of the top, down the front to the seat (**2**). Add on 2.5cm for the seam at the top back edge and 15cm for the tuck-in at the back seat edge. If the back is shaped measure down the longest part.

■ Measure the back of chair down its length to the skirt line, and across the width at widest point. Add 5cm to both these measurements for seams at edges, and another 6cm to width for the opening.

■ On the chair seat, first measure from the back of the seat to the front (**3**). Add on 15cm for the tuck-in at back edge and 2.5cm for the seam at the front edge. Then measure across the width of the seat between the lower edges of the chair arms. Add 30cm to this measurement to allow for a 15cm tuck-in at each side of the seat.

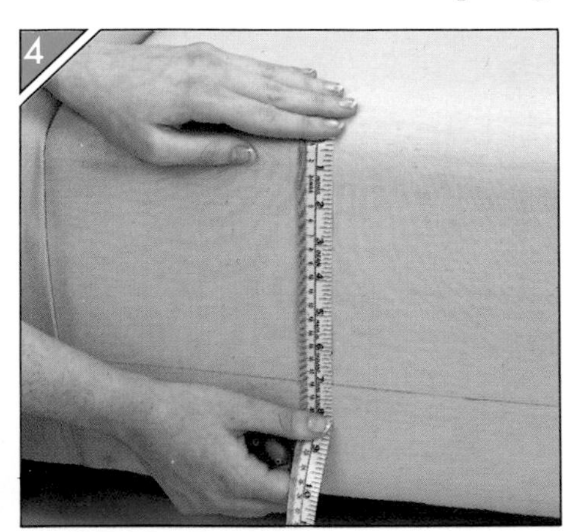

■ The front, vertical face of a chair is called the apron. Measure the apron from the front edge of the seat down to the line marked for the skirt (**4**). Add 5cm for a seam at each edge. Measure the width of the apron between the two arm front seams. Add on 5cm for seams.

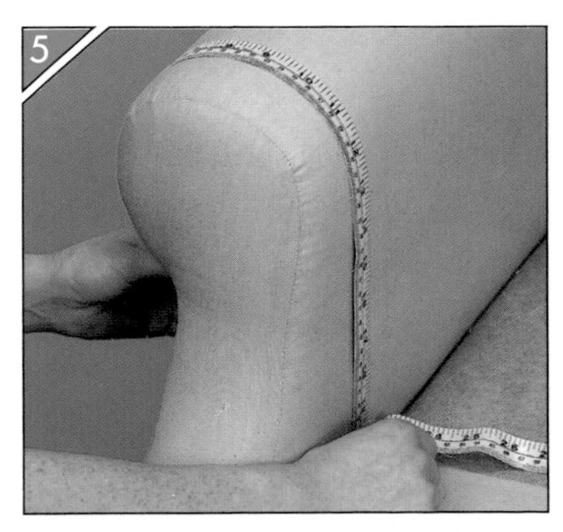

■ Measure the inner arm from the seat, up and over the arm to outer arm seam (**5**). Add 17.5cm for one tuck-in and one seam. Measure the outer arm from seam down to the skirt line. Measure the length of the arm at its longest point. Measure the front arm lengthways and widthways at its largest points. Add 5cm to each of these measurements for seams.

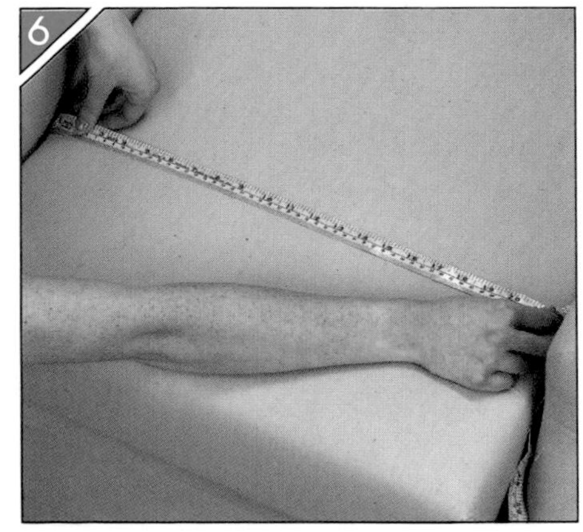

■ If the cushion is a simple shape, it is possible to measure accurately enough to cut the pieces to fit with normal 1.5cm seam allowances. Measure the cushion length and width (**6**). Add on two seam allowances to each measurement. Measure depth and length of cushion side, add on for seams, joins and zip opening, see boxed cushion on page 120.

CUTTING AND SEWING

Before you begin cutting out, decide if you would like a skirt around the lower edge of the chair. If so measure the required finished depth of the skirt up from the floor, and mark a line around the chair with tailor's chalk. The usual depth of a skirt is about 18cm.

Cutting out

There are two main methods of cutting out. The first is to cut the pieces with the fabric laid out flat. This method works well on plain fabric and fabric with all-over prints, which do not need matching at the seams or positioning in a certain place. The chair shape should be fairly simple, and the measuring done accurately with all the necessary allowances added on at the appropriate edges.

For the second method, the fabric is cut straight onto the chair. This may involve handling quite a large length of cloth which can be cumbersome, but it will allow the fabric pattern to be arranged precisely, and adjusted as you go along. This method is also useful when working on 'with nap' fabrics, such as velour, velvet or corduroy, where it is important that the nap runs in the correct direction on each piece. The nap, like a one way printed pattern, should run down the chair back and front, across the seat from back to front, and down the front apron. On the arm the nap should run over the top arm and down the inner arm to the seat, and down the outer and front arm pieces from top to bottom. Again remember to add on the appropriate allowances at each edge before cutting out.

Fitting the cover

T-pins, which are extra long pins with a straight bar instead of round head, or extra long glass headed pins are best to work with. The extra length makes pinning into the chair simpler, and the T-bars or large heads are easier to handle. Pin the centre of the first piece to the chair making sure the straight grain of the fabric is running vertically. Smooth the fabric out towards the edges, and pin the fabric to the chair at the edges. Pin the adjoining pieces in place in the same way, then, when they are fitted smoothly, pin the edges of fabric together and remove the pins fastening the edges to the chair. However when fitting the tuck-ins, leave the pins fastening the fabric to the chair in place until the fitting is completed.

When fitting allow for 2.5cm seams, so, if you need to adjust a piece and move it across a little, there is enough fabric to do so. You may need to work around the chair a few times adjusting the pins to make sure all the pieces are even and the seams are correctly placed exactly in line with the edges of the chair.

Marking the seamlines

When the fit is perfect, mark the seamlines. If you have fitted with the fabric right side out, open out the seams with your fingers, and mark along in the crease of the seam with tailor's chalk. This should mark the wrong side of both pieces of fabric where they meet. Also mark line across the seam turnings at intervals to serve as matching points when the seam is being repinned. If you feel you may become muddled as to which edge is which, use different coloured chalks on different edges.

On covers which have been fittedwith the wrong side out, mark the seamline on the wrong side over the pins. You will need to mark each side separately, and also mark some matching points. With this method you may only need to mark and unpin as much of the seam as is necessary to remove the cover ready for stitching.

When the seamlines are marked, remove the cover section by section, and trim the seam allowances to 1.5cm before stitching. Replace each section on the chair to check the fit as you work.

Making skirts

Skirts can be made from single fabric with the lower edge finished by a double machine-stitched, or hand-stitched hem. Alternatively, where it will not make a gathered or pleated skirt too bulky, a lined skirt will give a better finish. For a gathered, or continuously pleated skirt, you will need to join a number of widths of fabric to make up the length. For a gathered skirt, join the lining and fabric widths separately, stitch them together at the lower edge and press the skirt with wrong sides together as shown in step 12 on page 142. Then treat the top edges as one fabric when gathering and stitching the skirt. For a continuously pleated skirt, join the lower edges first and press the pieces with wrong sides together. Then pleat and join the side edges treating the two layers as one fabric.

■ Before taking the pinned cover off the chair, open out each seam with your fingers and run tailor's chalk along in the crease to mark the stitching line. Also mark lines across the seam at intervals and match these points when stitching (**1**). These matching points are particularly important on curves.

Remove the cover and unpin sections as you begin stitching. Trim the seam turnings to 1.5cm before stitching.

■ Arrange the fabric which will cover the top of the chair back and that which will cover the side edge of chair back level. Stitch across the top corner beginning the stitching 1.5cm in from the back edge (**2**).

Alternatively if you have separate sections for side back or top back, seam these sections together so the front, top and side of chair back is complete.

3

■ Stitch the front edge of the seat to the top edge of the apron. Zigzag stitch the edges together to prevent fraying (**3**). Press the seam downwards. Finish all seams in this way unless the instructions state otherwise.

Stitch the side arms to the inside arms, then begin joining the sections together. First join the back to the seat finishing the stitching 1.5cm in from the edges. Press this seam open and zigzag stitch the edges separately. This will make it easier to join this seam to the back corners of the arms in the next stage. Check the fit as you work.

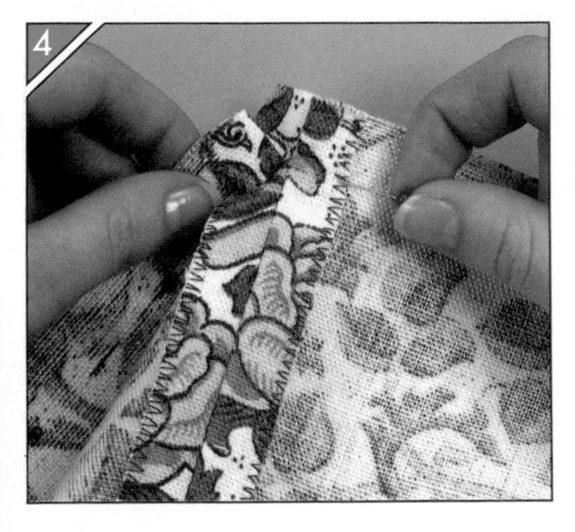
4

■ Join the side edge of the seat to the inner arms. At the back corners open out the back seat seam so it will fit around the corner (**4**). Then continue the seam, stitching the back edge of the arms to the side edge of the chair back.

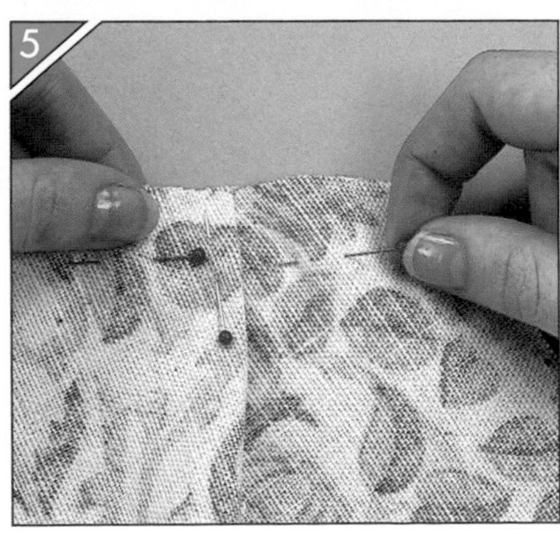
5

■ If the design of the chair is such that it has tuck-ins, you may find the edges do not exactly match where there is a little excess fabric on one edge. If so, take out this excess in a small tuck near to the back corner of the seat section (**5**).

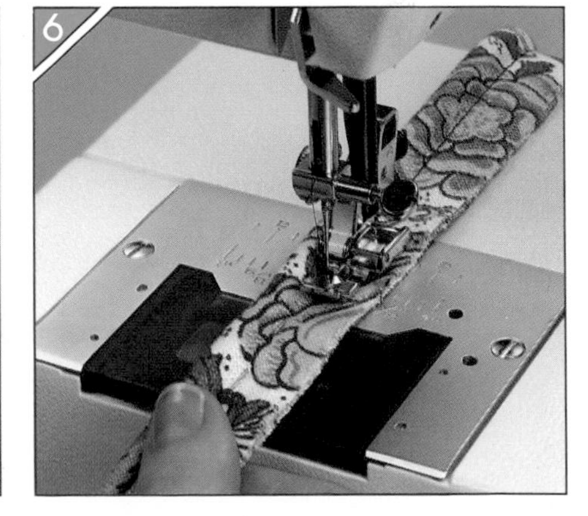
6

■ Cut **bias strips** for the **piping** allowing for a 1.5cm seam. Wrap the bias strip around the cord and, using a zipper foot, stitch along a fraction less than 1.5cm in from the raw edges (**6**). Use the lines on the feed plate as a guide for spacing the stitching. This machined method is quicker than tacking on large areas.

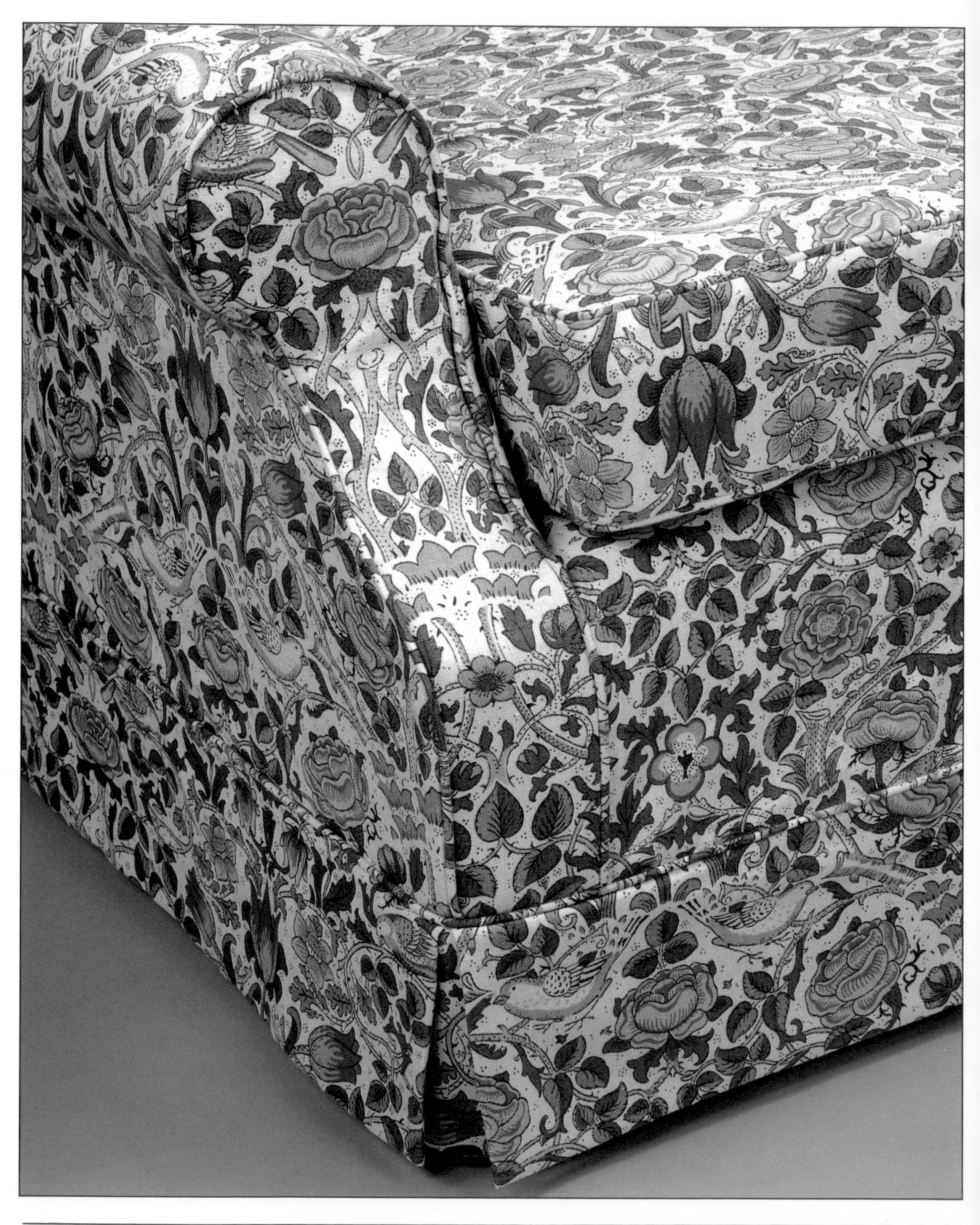

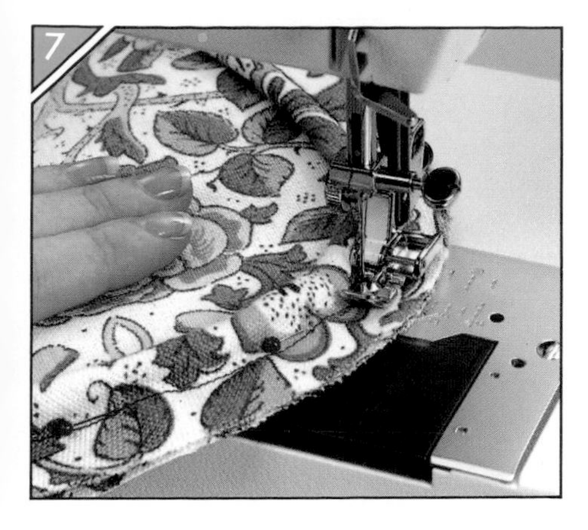

■ Arrange the piping around the front arm section. The bias grain of the piping fabric will allow it to ease smoothly around the curve. Take care not to stretch the piping around the curve. Pin the piping in place, then try the section on the chair arm to make sure it outlines the shape smoothly and accurately. Tack if you prefer, or remove pins as you stitch. Using a zipper foot, stitch the piping in place so the stitching is exactly on the piping stitching, or just inside the previous line of piping stitching (**7**).

■ Pin the front arm to the front edge of outer arm, inner arm and side edge of apron. Place the pins inside the previous line of piping stitching (**8**). Check the seam from both sides to make sure the edges are joined smoothly. If you are less experienced you may need to tack this seam. Using a zipper foot, stitch just inside the previous line of stitching so no stitching shows on the right side.

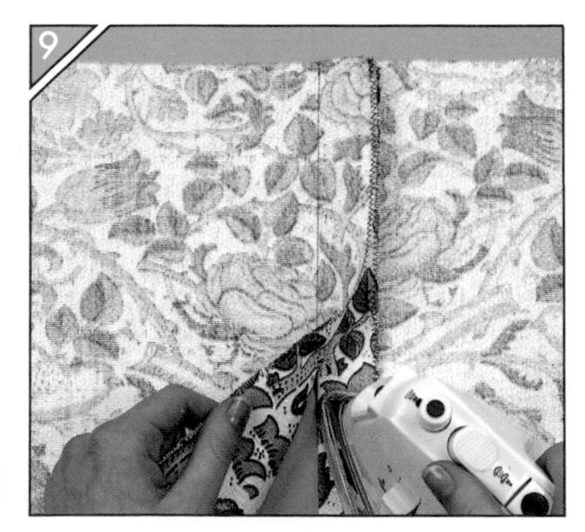

■ Stitch the back seam above the opening 3cm in from raw edges. Zigzag stitch the raw edges separately, continuing the stitching down edges of opening. Press seam to one side, and 3cm over to wrong side down under edge of opening (**9**).

Stitch the back to the cover around the side and top edge, opening out the top corner seam to fit around corners of back.

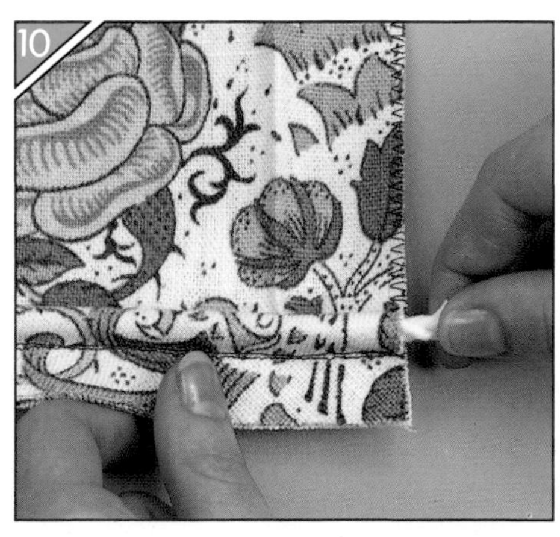

■ Unfold the pressed edge of the back opening for the next stage. Make piping cord in the same way as described previously arranging the position of any joins in the bias strip so they will be placed inconspicuously. Stitch the piping around the lower edge of the cover. Pull out the ends of the piping cord at the edges of the back opening (**10**).

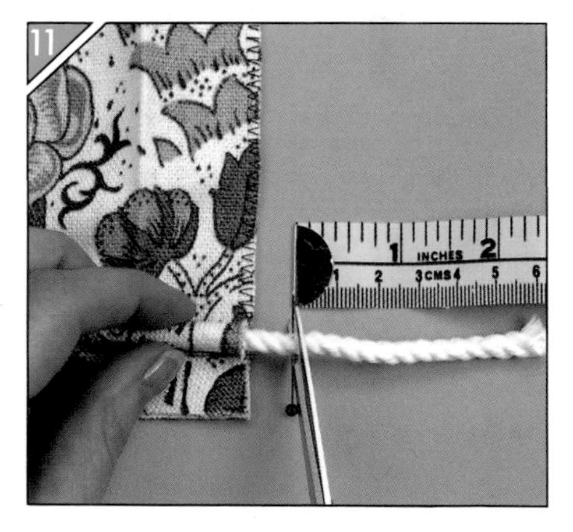

■ At the edge of the opening which has been previously pressed over to the wrong side, trim 6cm from the end of piping cord (**11**). At the other edge of the opening trim 4cm from the end of the cord. Pull the fabric flat so the ends of the cord finish 6cm and 4cm in from the edges of the opening. This will give a flat area where the fastening tape will later be stitched.

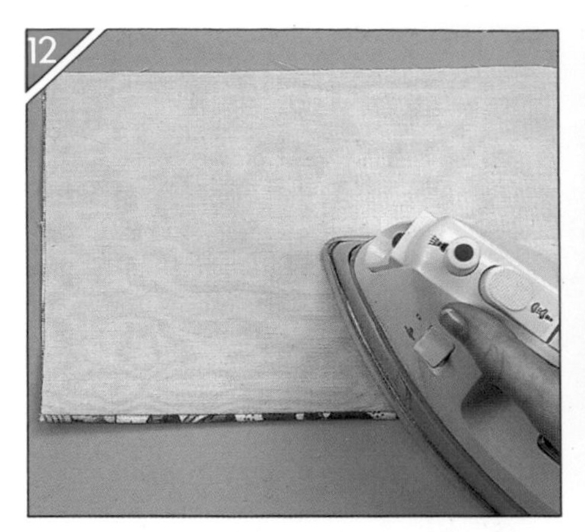

■ With right sides facing, stitch a skirt lining piece to a skirt section along the lower edge. Press the seam towards the lining, then fold the skirt so the wrong sides of lining and fabric are facing. Arrange the lower edge so about 5mm of skirt fabric is folded to the lining side and press (**12**). Trim top edge of lining level with top of fabric.

■ Make all the skirt sections as described in the previous step. Also make up the four skirt corner flaps in the same way. Zigzag stitch the side edges of lining and fabric together at both side edges of all the skirt sections and corner flaps (**13**).

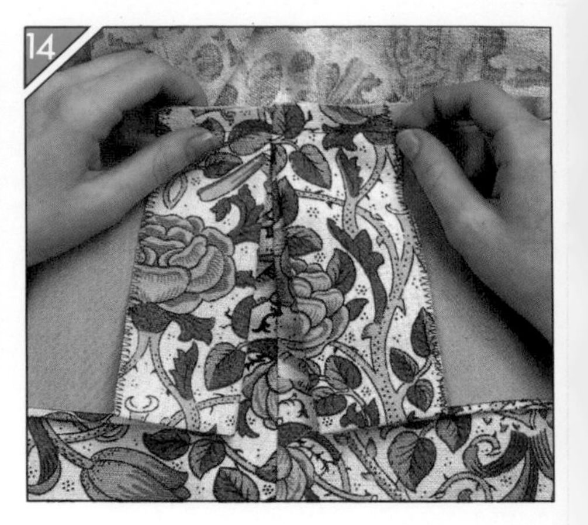

■ Arrange the skirt sections around the lower edge of the cover with right sides facing and raw edges level. At the corners fold back the side edges of the skirt for 5cm, so the folded edges meet in line with the corner seams of the cover. Also check the lower edges of skirt match. At the back opening plaçe the zigzag stitched edges of the skirt and opening level. Pin and tack in place just inside the piping stitching (**14**). Press in the folds at the corners of the skirt.

■ With wrong sides uppermost, place a skirt corner flap centrally over the folded-back edges of the skirt at each corner (**15**). Arrange the flap so the lower edges of the flap and skirt are level. Tack in place along the skirt seam at the top of flap. Using a zipper foot, stitch the skirt seam through all thicknesses just inside the previous piping stitching. Zigzag stitch all raw edges of the seam together and press it upwards.

Using touch-and-close fastening

Some chairs are shaped so the cover hangs loose where it should be held in close to the chair, such as under the outer arm on a chair with a scroll arm. This is remedied by stitching one half of touch-and-close to the inside of the cover and glueing the other half to the chair at the appropriate place. Then when the two halves are brought into contact they will hold the cover snuggly in place.

■ Touch-and-close tape is also a quick and simple way to fasten the cover's opening. Separate the two halves of the tape. Position one half on the underside of the overlapping edge of the opening, so the outer edge of tape is 5mm in from the edge, and the top end extends 3cm above the opening onto the back seam turnings. Stitch the tape in place along both long edges and across the ends.

Position the other half of the tape on the right side of the underlapping opening edge. Pin in place and check the two halves line up correctly when fastened, then stitch in place.

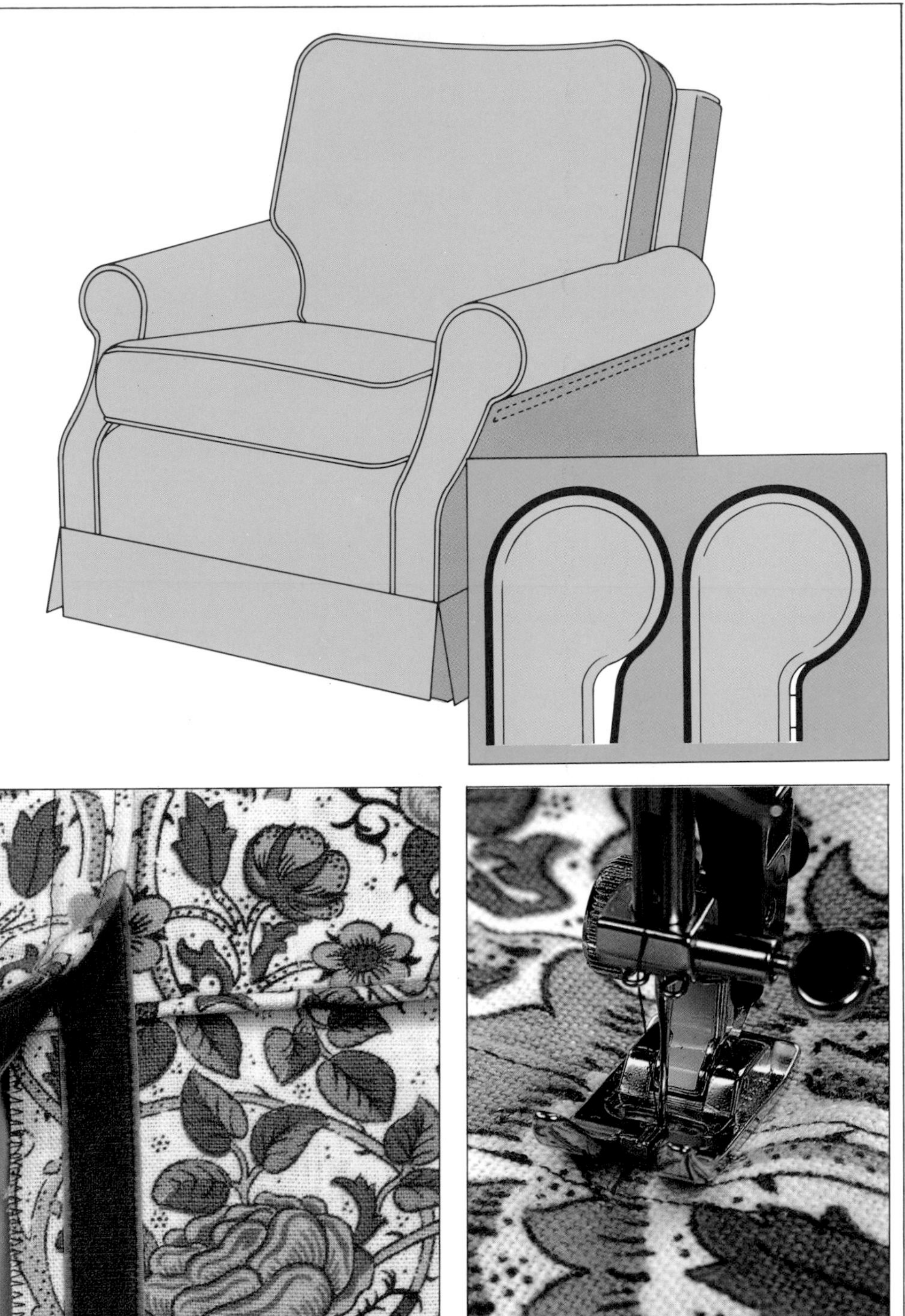

■ Finish the fastening by stitching across the opening at the lower end of the seam stitching. Work two rows of stitching on top of each and finish the ends securely.

Fabric samples

The great variety of furnishing fabrics offer a multitude of choices. There are plains, prints and fabrics with woven-in designs varying from small modern geometrics to large figurative scenes. Fabric textures also vary from closely-woven, smooth, fine cotton to crunchy, pebbly textures and chunky hardwearing weaves. While the appearance and feel of the fabric plays an important part in selection, its fabric content should also be considered. Cotton is a predominant fibre for many furnishing fabrics, but there are also many blends which combine two or more fibres. These blends are formed for a variety of reasons such as improving the texture, adding extra strength or increasing crease-resistance. The fabrics shown are:

Cotton: 1, 3, 4, 7, 8, 9, 10, 11, 17, 19, 21, 22, 23, 27, 29, 30, 31, 32, 34, 35, 39, 41, 42.
Polyester/cotton/viscose: 2, 6, 15.
Linen/cotton/nylon: 5, 16.
Cotton/viscose: 12, 14, 20, 24, 33, 43.
Polypropylene: 13.
Cotton/polypropylene/polyester: 18, 37.
Viscose/polyester: 25.
Cotton/acrylic: 26.
Cotton/viscose/polyester/polypropylene: 28.
Polyacrylic/cotton/polyester: 36.
Linen/cotton: 38.
Wool: 40.
Cotton/polyester: 44.

Clever choice of fabric will complement the chair's shape and help create the desired atmosphere. Left a muted floral design enhances a relaxed country setting. Centre, smart regency stripes suit a more formal chair shape in an elegant room. Below, a rich deep colour and surface texture add a warm cosy atmosphere capturing the mood of the exotic orient.

CHAPTER EIGHT

· DECORATIVE FINISHES ·

Ranging from simple patchwork to exotic embroidery, decorative finishes add a stylish and individual touch.

DECORATIVE FINISHES

Making your own soft furnishings is an opportunity to put your design skills to work, not only in the choice of fabric but in terms of the details which make the project representative of your personal style and taste. In addition to the sewing methods involved in making the main item, there are many techniques of decorative stitching and applied decoration which can extend the range of your ideas for soft furnishings.

If you enjoy fabrics and find it hard to settle for just one choice, patchwork and applique allow you to mix colours and patterns as freely as you wish on a small or large scale. Applied decoration such as ribbons and braids provide flashes of brilliant colour, while embroidery stitches and special techniques such as cutwork and drawn threadwork bring immense charm to linens. These pages illustrate the range of decorative finishes associated with soft furnishings projects.

Block patchwork (left) has a vibrant effect in a stepped pattern of bright pastels. Patchwork techniques can be adapted to regular shapes (above), if the edges are accurately matched.

Machine patchwork

The decorative effect of patchwork is always highly appreciated. It enables you to combine fabric colours and patterns to your own design to create an item with individual style. Machine stitched block patchwork can be made up quite quickly and is suitable for large projects such as bedcovers and tablecloths which would be infinitely laborious if the traditional hand-stitching technique were used. It lends itself to simple, regular shapes, such as squares, oblongs and triangles, and the key to a professional finish is to match the seams with absolute accuracy.

For beginners, it is advisable to limit the number of fabrics you use, until you get a feel for mixing colours and patterns together. A checkerboard effect using only two different fabrics can have remarkable impact, if you select the combination carefully. Colours can be highly contrasted or subtly moody; you can set off a discreet geometric pattern against a floral miniprint, with colour links between the two. Use fabrics of the same basic weight to avoid puckering at the seams. As you gain more confidence with this technique, you can develop the patchwork patterning more freely.

Handstitched patchwork

Traditional "pieced" patchwork requires a methodical approach and is best used for relatively small items such as tablemats, cushions and decorative panels. However, compared to machine patchwork, it is easier to work more complex designs, with diamonds, hexagons, stars and even curving fan shapes. You can plan out the colours and patterns before you begin, or let it grow piece by piece into the jewelled effect of mixed fabric patterns often seen in antique patchwork.

The fabric pieces are tacked to templates of paper or thin card with the edges turned on to the wrong side. With two pieces together, right sides facing, the edges are slipstitched to create a firm, neat seam. The templates can be removed when individual shapes are completely surrounded by others and stitched on all sides.

As with machine patchwork, fabrics should be of similar weight and if the finished item is to be washable, all must be shrink-resistant and colourfast. Printed cottons make beautiful patchwork and accommodate small shapes and intricate designs. Co-ordinated fabric ranges offer plenty of scope for patchwork designs, but there is great pleasure in selecting and combining fabrics from personal taste, and all sorts of scraps and offcuts can be given useful life in this way.

Quilting

In items such as tablemats and oven gloves, quilting provides the necessary thickness and an attractive finish for plain or patterned fabrics or patchwork pieces. Polyester wadding is sandwiched between two layers of fabric and the quilted pattern is machine stitched through all three layers. You can work the quilting and then bind the raw edges of fabric and wadding. Alternatively, treat the front piece of fabric and the wadding as one thickness, tacking them together, and seam them to the back section on three sides; then turn out to the right side and neaten the remaining seam.

Diagonal quilting adds interest to a plain fabric or simple geometric. Patchwork quilted along the lines of the template shapes has a very decorative, neat effect. A similar technique is used in quilting the outlines of a fabric design.

Appliqué

There is a special charm to appliqué and it is a technique which can be used for decoration of small or large items, from a placemat, cushion or pillowcase to a bedcover or curtains. It consists simply of applying one piece of fabric to another larger piece and there are several ways in which an appliqué motif can be stitched to the base fabric.

The motif may be a single piece of fabric, or constructed from any number of pieces which are tacked down in place to form the design and then secured with finished stitching. The stitching is worked around all the edges of the appliqué, whether they are raw edges or neatened with a narrow turn-in. Closely worked machine zigzag stitch secures an appliqué motif in place, so the fabric cannot fray or tear. If you use straight stitch, turn under the raw edges. Otherwise, the outlines of ...atly overstitched by ... any of a number of ...for a specially decora-

A motif cut from a printed fabric (above) instantly creates an attractively detailed applique design; the edges are finished with machine zigzag stitch. Embroidered appliqué (below) has a delicate appearance. Subtly graded colours suggest a softly three-dimensional effect with the embroidery extended into fine tendrils.

tive effect. The embroidery can also be used to develop the detail of the design and extend it more finely on the base fabric.

As with patchwork, it is necessary to select the fabrics carefully, matching them for weight to avoid straining or puckering, and compatibility for washing or dry cleaning. Appliqué designs worked in small pieces of plain-coloured fabrics have an attractive appearance particularly effective for borders and corners of sheets and pillowcases, but make sure the colours are fast or the first wash will ruin your work. Texture is another interesting element of appliqué; try a piqué or seersucker cotton on a plain weave ground, or with medium weight fabrics, a slubbed or figured weave for the appliqué shapes. Avoid loose weaves which will eventually fray, however carefully stitched to begin with.

A very simple but effective way for beginners to make the most of appliqué is to use a pattern motif cut from a printed fabric. You need only stitch the outlines, but it can look very pretty and intricate.

Combined techniques

Appliqué and patchwork are traditionally associated and there are many decorative possibilities in combining the techniques. Both use small offcuts of fabric with satisfying economy, yet the effects can be stylish or sumptuous, in designs with a particularly personal touch. Quilting can also be used with either or both of these techniques to add to the textural interest of a home sewing project. Bedcovers and cushions are well-suited to combined decoration of this type; the quilting supplies warmth and comfort. Pretty cot covers and children's quilts are less time consuming than a full-size item and you can elaborate the design as much as you wish on this small scale.

Try out different combinations of the techniques to see the range of effects. In block patchwork you can apply an appliqué motif to each piece before making up the patchwork, or work the appliqué as an extra layer over a finished section. A whole item can be quilted, following the lines of the patchwork or the appliqué, or you can quilt the appliqué motif itself: stitch around the fabric shape leaving a small gap and insert polyester wadding to pad it out before closing the gap neatly.

Fresh, bright colours and textural detail make a decorative cot cover pleasurable for a small child to see and touch. A simple block patchwork provides the background with a jolly clown motif appliquéd at the centre. Both the patchwork cover and the appliqué detail are padded; the clown's frilled collar and pompom hat add three-dimensional interest.

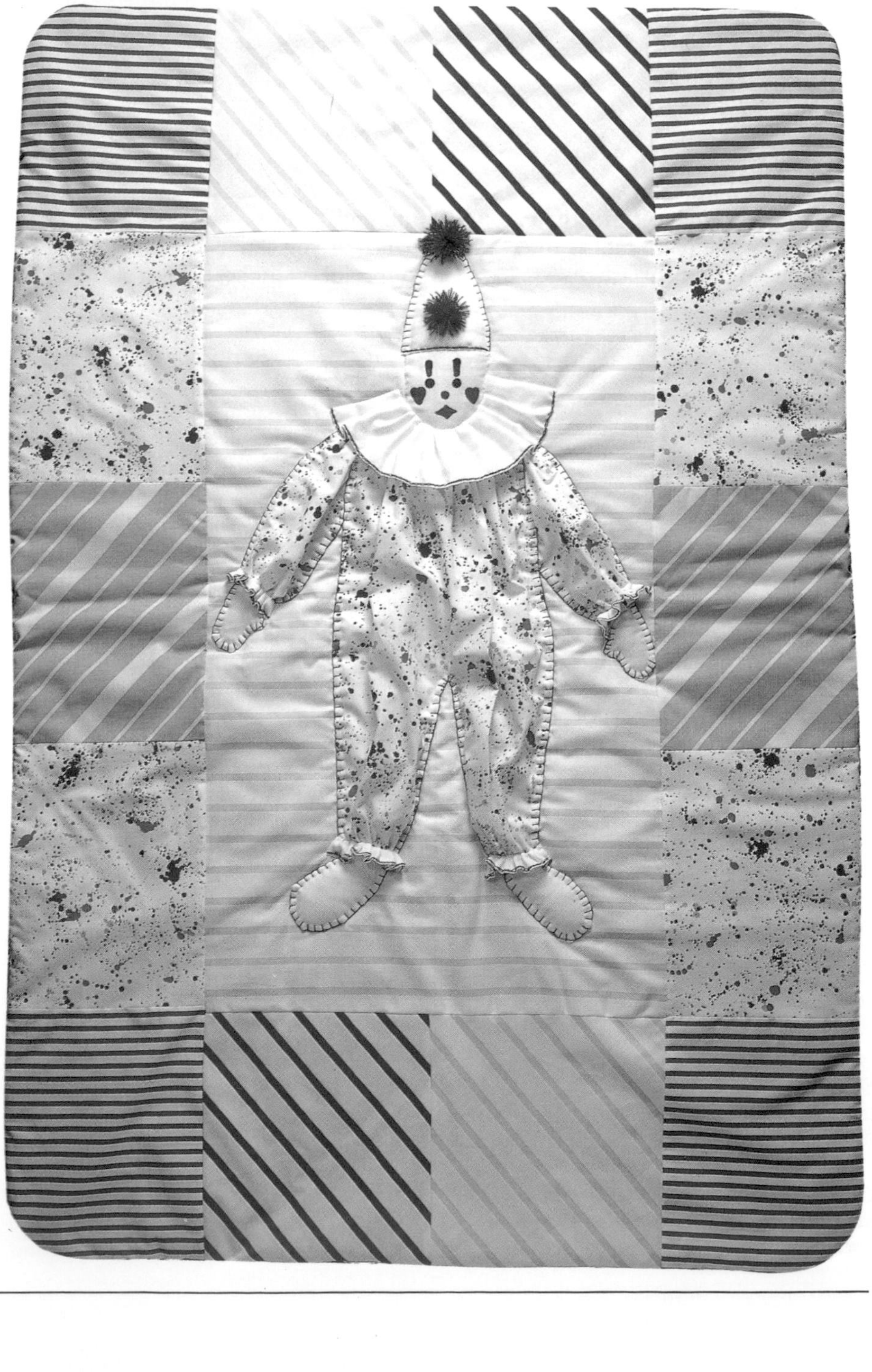

Ribbons and braids

Applied decoration takes little time but can be the perfect finishing touch for all sorts of soft furnishings. Department stores selling furnishing fabrics also stock a wide range of braids, ribbons, fringes, tassels and pompoms which you can quickly sew to a seam or hem to provide a contrast of colour and texture.

Plain ribbons make pretty edging for bedlinen, stitched across the short side of a pillowcase at the open end with matching borders across the sheet turn down. There are a number of other ways they can be used in large and small items around the home. Plaited ribbons make an inner border for curtains, cushions or placemats, while woven into a block, they form a colourful panel which can be inset in a cushion cover. Narrow satin ribbon can be threaded through the mesh of a net curtain or stitched to sheer fabric to cover the lines of seams and hems. Rich velvet ribbons make attractive trimming for more formal styles of curtaining in medium weight fabrics.

A slightly more complex effect is achieved using richly decorative braids, with woven-in or embroidered motifs and patterns. These are available in silky finishes or heavier woollen-type fibres. The colours range from the brightest pure hues to rich moody tones and clear pastels. When considering decoration of this kind, match the weight of the braid to the fabric weight, or you will get a puckered and distorted effect. This is especially important with curtains as a too-heavy trimming will disturb the hang of lighter weight fabric, while fine braids are inappropriate to heavier fabrics such as velvet or damask.

If you are machine stitching ribbons to a flat piece of fabric, start at the same end when you machine down each side, otherwise there is a tension between the lines of stitching which pulls the ribbon out of shape and causes unsightly puckering. For curved edges, it is sometimes easier to stitch by hand so that you can ease the line of the braid or ribbon around the curve.

Heavy cords and braids suitable for curtain weight fabrics or loose covers offer a range of patterns and textures, usually in more subdued colours than the lighter ribbon trims. These are designed to team with traditional chintzes, silks and damasks in more formal furnishing styles. As well as textured and pique-edged trims, there are fringes and knotted tassels particularly useful for edging a curtain valance or pelmet.

While an attractive trim will enliven plain coloured fabric, don't be afraid to mix and match patterns and try your more ambitious ideas. If possible, try to get small samples of different types of trimming to see the various effects when they are set against your fabric choice. As well as providing the finishing touch for newly made soft furnishings, they may give you useful ideas for refurbishing other items.

A small selection of braids, ribbons and furnishing trims suggests the range of possibilities for supplying additional colour, texture and pattern with simple applied decoration.

Narrow satin ribbons make lightweight, pretty decoration for sheer curtains (right), as a hem border or in a line of eye-catching bows. The extra touch of solid colour enhances the subtly translucent effect.
An embroidered braid carefully matched to the colours of crewel embroidery adds to the horizontal emphasis of the design (below). A decorative plain-coloured ric-rac braid is also used, secured by embroidery stitches.

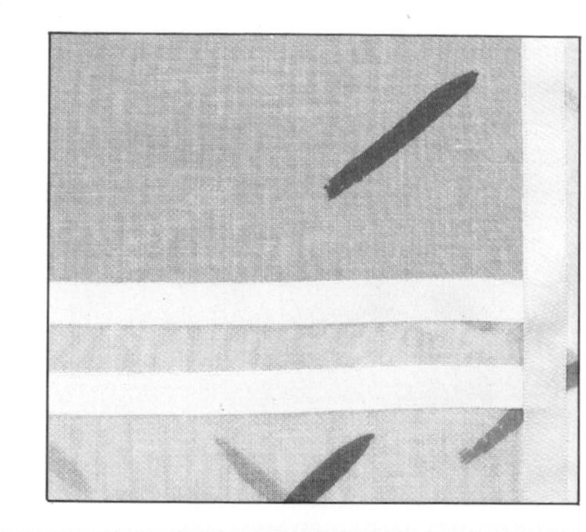

Embroidery

A craft long associated with home sewing, embroidery adds delicate detail to beautiful tablelinen and bedlinen, fine curtains and luxurious cushion covers. There are literally hundreds of different embroidery stitches that can be used singly or combined to build up pretty edging, intricate corner motifs, deep borders and scattered colour detail. Outline and filling stitches, cutwork embroidery, cross stitch and drawn threadwork offer a range of decorative possibilities for application to a variety of fabrics. Embroidery requires patience and skill – a good effect depends upon neat, even stitching – but it is a rewarding craft and embroidered items often become treasured family heirlooms.

To make a design for embroidery, you can use commercially available transfers which are ironed on to the fabric or traced over using dressmaker's transfer paper to leave a faint colour outline on the fabric. Alternatively, draw up your own designs or trace attractive motifs from books or magazines, or even from the pattern of a favourite fabric. Sheets and pillowcases embroidered with a motif echoing the printed fabric of the bedcover have a stylish and well co-ordinated effect. Flower patterns, small animal motifs and abstract symbols such as Greek keys or linked circles are traditionally popular embroidery motifs, but with a little invention you can adapt any type of form or symbol to a line drawing which forms the basis of a stitched motif.

Embroidery threads are available in glowing colours and subtly graded tones; stranded thread allows you to vary the thickness of the stitch and creates a smooth, silky finish, while the heavier cotton perlê yarn has a lightly textured sheen suitable for medium-weight fabrics. Woollen yarns have traditionally been used for heavy crewelwork embroidery which has a striking character all its own, but the fabric weight must give firm support and this technique is best suited to cushions or curtains made from a sturdy fabric. Yarns of a wool and synthetic mix are practical materials. Lightweight embroidery detail on sheer fabrics has a lovely effect when seen against the light, making pretty curtains for daytime use; ends of thread at the back of the work need to be very neatly finished to avoid spoiling the clarity of the design.

Satin stitch is one of the most common filling stitches in embroidery, for small blocks of colour. The stitches should be even, closely spaced and not too long and the finished effect is a flat colour area with attractive surface sheen. The stitching is worked across the shape, rather like shading in a drawing. Crewel-type stitches radiate from the centre of the motif outwards, again filling the shape solidly. Long stitches tend to pucker and distort the fabric, so judge the direction of the stitching carefully.

Outline stitches range from simple running stitch or back stitch, to fancy linear effects such as chain stitch or feather stitch. Subtle colouring sometimes needs some outline detail to make the pattern more distinct. Embroidered edgings give a well-finished look when interior detail is also embroidered. Bold outlines and strong colours match up to modern styles of furnishing; though there is a special charm to traditional embroidery designs, it is an adaptable craft which need never look old-fashioned.

An embroidered corner motif is attractively framed in a scalloped and pointed edging. Clear colours and the fresh contrast of pink and yellow against green on a natural linen background create an informal but eye-catching design. Discreet self-coloured stitching secures the edges of the fabric.

***Anchor** threads are ideal for embroidery and are available in a wide range of colours.*

Cutwork embroidery

The intricacy and delicacy of cutwork embroidery makes it appear quite a complex technique, but it depends upon a basic type of stitching and careful organization of the design. It requires the patience to stitch evenly and closely and the dexterity to clip out the cutwork detail without leaving any snippets of fabric or fraying threads which will spoil the final effect.

The design in cutwork consists of outlines which are worked solidly with close blanket stitch. The inner sections are then cut away using an extremely sharp pair of scissors. The design must be carefully worked out so that no element becomes detached from its neighbours when the open areas are cut.

The cut areas should be kept fairly small, or the fabric is weakened and does not retain a crisp finish. Interwoven shapes provide the complexity and floral designs have always been a particularly effective vehicle for cutwork. Interior detail such as leaf veins and flower stamens can be worked with fancy embroidery stitches, but the main character of the design depends upon the balance between open and solid areas. Cutwork is especially suited to tablelinen and bedlinen: the fabric should be firmly woven and not too heavy, but not so lightweight that the stitching can cause distortion.

Cutwork makes beautiful edging and corner detail for table linen. The colours of the embroidery against the fabric are all important and a change of colourways can create quite different emphasis in the design. This type of embroidery also looks highly effective in white on white or beige on cream, making a subtle textural contrast.

Cross stitch

A remarkably simple but versatile technique, cross stitch provides a range of decorative effects from single motifs and narrow edgings to deep, complex borders or even embroidered pictures.

Cross stitch involves working one stitch over another as a diagonal cross which effectively fills a tiny square. The stitches build into lines and blocks of colour; any design for cross stitch can be worked out on graph paper using the small divisions to represent single stitches. It is essential to use a base fabric in which threads can be counted to regulate the stitching, such as even-weave linen or heavy cotton. Special fabrics are also available with a grid-like weave of tiny holes, or you can follow the woven pattern of a finely checked fabric.

Drawn threadwork

Like cutwork embroidery, drawn threadwork introduces an extra dimension to the finished effect of an embroidered item. The openwork areas are created by clipping and drawing out a certain number of warp or weft threads, depending on the direction of the fabric grain and the position of the pattern, and working the embroidery stitches to gather the remaining threads into knots or ladders, forming a regular pattern of holes in the design. Using different embroidery stitches, the holes may be square or rectangular, rounded, or triangular forming a zigzag or herringbone pattern in the fabric weave.

To obtain the correct framework for the embroidery, an even-weave, medium weight fabric must be used which enables you to count the threads and cut them cleanly so they can be drawn out without damage to the threads running in the opposite direction. The dependence on the fabric grain enables you to position the design accurately and keep it even and straight-running, in alignment with the edge of the fabric piece.

Drawn threadwork is used to create borders or blocks of pattern. A good effect of subtle texturing is obtained using an embroidery thread in a colour close to that of the fabric. A busier appearance comes from the use of a definite contrast between thread and fabric colours, and you can combine different threads in alternate or complex stitching, but it is as well to limit the number of colours or the overall shape of the design becomes confused.

The single-direction threads can be grouped vertically or diagonally and secured with hemstitch or heavier overcasting along each edge of the border, stitched to create distinct bars in the design, or herringbone stitched which forms an undulating diamond pattern. Knots centred on each group of threads pull them into delicate star shapes.

Frills and gathers

Fancy edgings are a quick and easy way to add a special finishing touch to plain or elaborate soft furnishings. There are many types available ready-made, which need only to be hand or machine stitched to a seamline or hem.

Lace frills can be obtained in different widths and small, delicate patterns or loosely structured, chunky designs, made of natural or synthetic fibres which can be matched to the different types of main fabric used. Broderie Anglaise is enduringly popular and a pretty edging of eyelet embroidery gives new life to a plain pillowcase or sheet. It looks particularly attractive teamed with embroidered fabric, framing a corner motif or delicate border, for example. Pretty embroidered frilling is also available with different colours – soft pastels or bright primaries – on a white base. You may prefer a very discreet edging, just to give a small touch of colour and texture to a fine piece of fabric. Narrow lace or tatted or crocheted edgings can be attached to a hemline fold.

These decorative trims are made with a firm binding along one edge which you can hand stitch to a finished item, or attach by machine stitching while making up. A frill need not be confined to the edge of a cover, sheet or tablecloth, however. Sewn across the front panel of a cushion or at the top of a curtain border, they put fresh interest and lively texture into the central expanse of the main fabric.

You may prefer to make up your own frills and edgings, from the same fabric as the basic design, or in a contrasting colour or pattern. A double frill or the extra fullness of a circular frill (see page 169) makes a good alternative to the simpler gathered version. Add these to round or shaped cushions, plump pillows or for a wonderfully frivolous effect, to the softly swagged drapes of an Austrian or festoon blind. Make sure the fabric or ready-made edging is practical for washing or cleaning in the same way as the main fabric.

Gathers are not only for making outer frills and flounces. In any item made up from panels of fabric, whether large or small, you can gather the fabric across the width or length of one section to make a richly textured surface. This technique can be applied to small pieces for cushion covers, sections of patchwork, or a broad area such as the lined main panel of a fitted bedcover. Make sure the gathering is evenly distributed and secured at the seams. Keep it fairly tight and firm but not too full, unless it is cushion decoration when it can be more adventurous without becoming impractical.

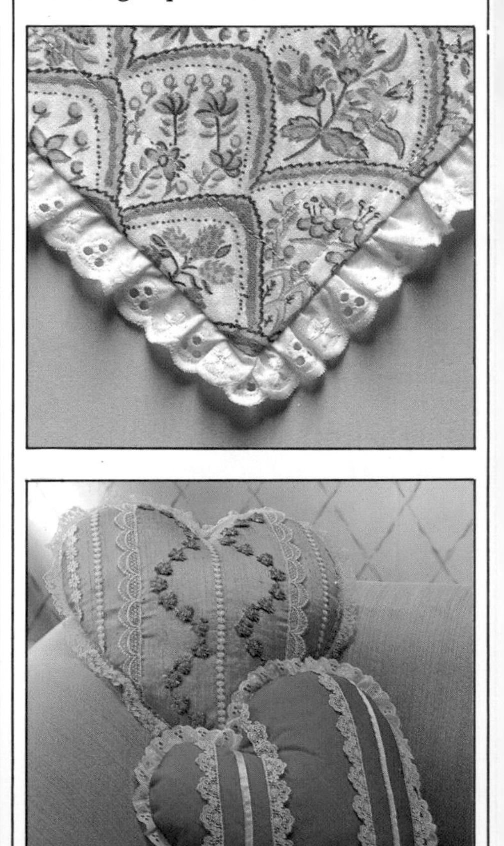

Ready-made frills and embroidered edgings are a quick way to liven up the design of pillowcases and cushions. Add them to the edge of a cover or across the width of a pretty, shaped cushion.

Lacy edging in cool pink makes an attractively restrained finish for white linen (left). For tablelinen, this adds a touch of colour to offset fine china or gleaming glass and silverware. Gathered fabric gives a sumptuous effect used here to cover luxurious padded hangers (below) which brighten up the wardrobe and keep clothes in good shape. Strong colours and fabric with a surface sheen enhance the decorative effect of the gathering.

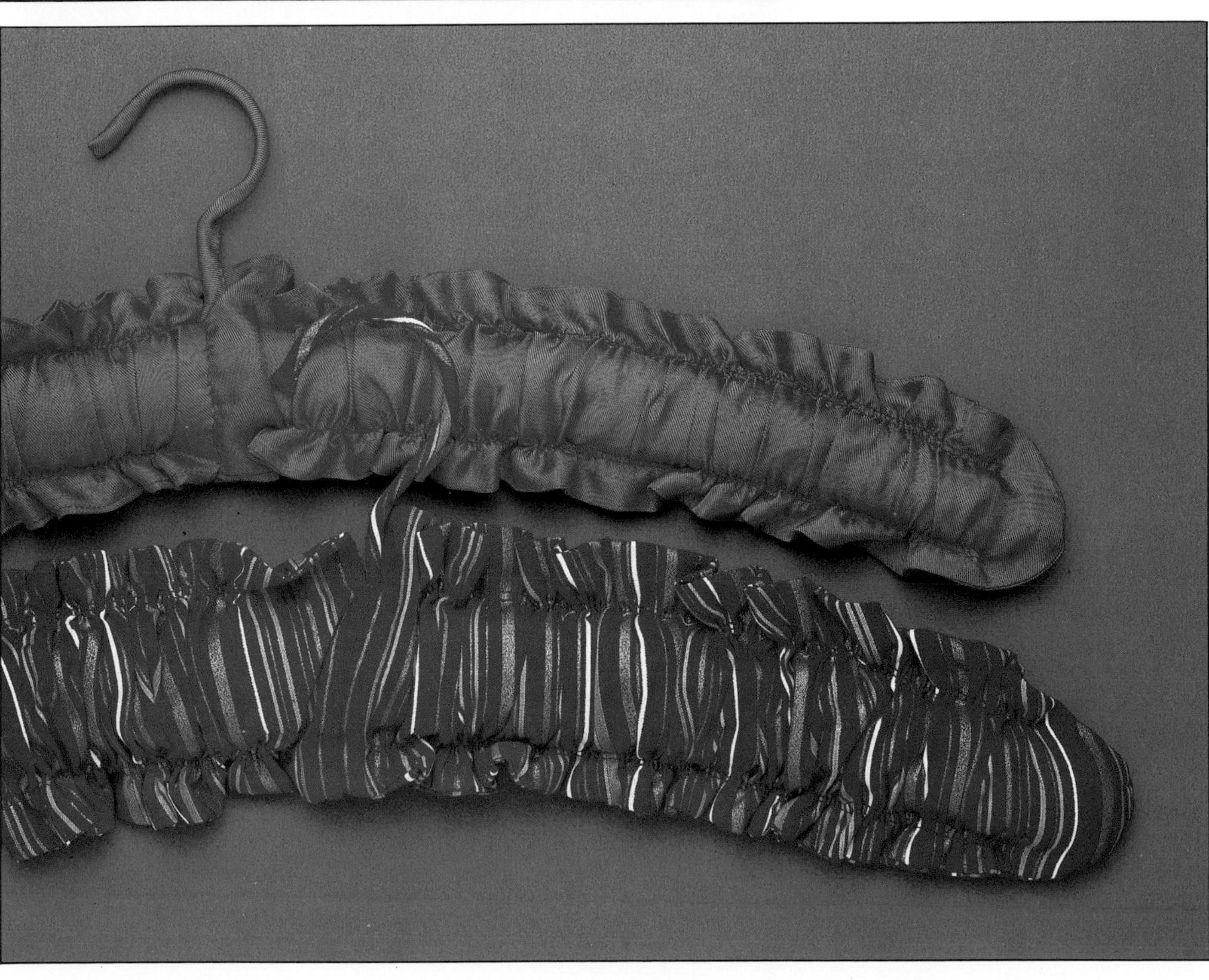

CHAPTER NINE

· TECHNIQUES ·

Once mastered, these basic sewing techniques will produce professional results time after time.

Coats
super sheen
Mercerised Cotton
100yd
91m
40

· HAND STITCHES ·

Even when items are made using a sewing machine, there will be times when some hand stitching is necessary. This may be temporary stitching which just holds the fabric in place while it is being machine stitched, and is then removed; or final stitching, when neater hand stitching is preferable to machine stitching. Other hand stitches serve a special purpose where machine stitching is not suitable.

Always use a suitable weight thread for the fabric and a fine needle which will not leave unsightly puncture holes in the fabric. Begin and finish the stitching securely. Temporary stitching can be started by knotting the thread. For permanent stitching, two tiny back stitches worked one on top of the other will look neater and be more secure. Finish the stitching in the same way positioning the back stitches where they are least noticeable, such as the folded-up part of a hem rather than the main fabric. Pull the stitches through firmly but not too tightly as this will pucker the fabric. Hemming stitches are best left a little loose so they do not show on the right side.

Alternatives to hand stitching

There may be occasions when you need to use a non-sew alternative to hand stitching. This may be for sheer speed, when you need to finish an item quickly and do not have time to hand stitch the hem, or as a temporary measure, which will later be replaced with stitching.

Fusible bonding is a web like strip of adhesive, which is placed between the two fabric layers of a hem. The hem is then pressed to activate the adhesive which glues the hem in place. The bonding strip is about 2.5cm wide, when used at that width it will fasten the hem securely, but may also stiffen the hem. To avoid the stiffening effect, cut the bonding into 5mm wide strips and use these near the top of the hem allowance. This may not be quite as secure as the full width bonding when the item is laundered, but it will lessen the stiffening effect. Always make a test hem on spare fabric to check the finish which may vary on different fabrics.

Tacking tape is a very narrow sticky tape which has adhesive on both sides. This is purely a temporary measure, used to hold fabric in place before stitching. It can be very convenient if you wish to hang curtains to test the length before stitching the hem. The tape can be used to hold the trial hem in place, this can then be adjusted to correct the hem level while the curtains are hanging. Tacking tape can also be used as an alternative to tacking where two wrong sides need holding together.

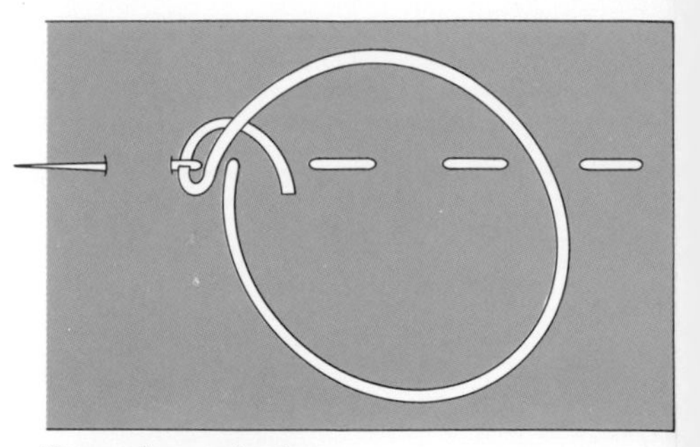

Running stitch
This is a small stitch used mainly for hand-stitched gathering. It is worked by passing the needle in and out of the fabric forming a stitch of equal length on both sides of the fabric. Begin the stitching securely with two small back stitches on top of each other.

Tacking stitch
Used to hold fabric in place while it is being permanently stitched, this should be done in a contrasting colour thread so it can be removed easily. Tacking stitch is formed like running stitch but with longer stitches on the working side and smaller stitches on the other side.

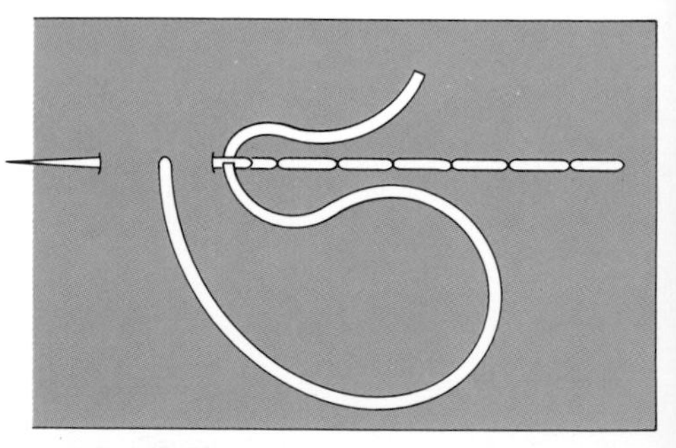

Back stitch
A small strong stitch which can be used in place of machine stitching on small tricky areas. Take a stitch backwards and in at the end of previous stitch then bring the needle out an equal distance in front of the thread. Two back stitches worked on top of each other can also be used to finish thread ends.

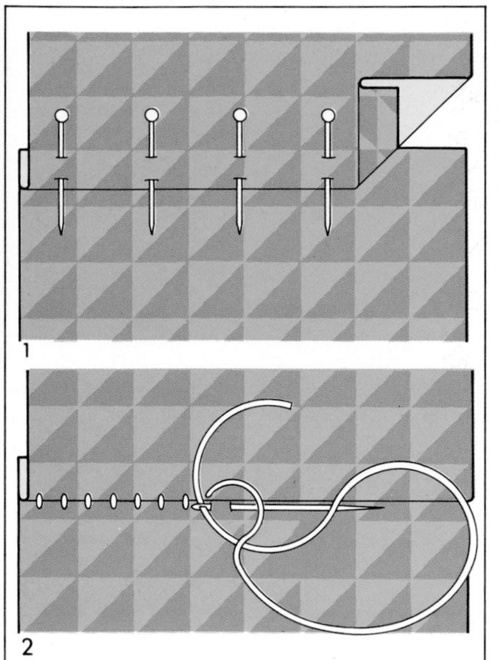

Ladder stitch

This is used when the pattern on the fabric needs to be matched exactly. Press the seam turning to the wrong side on one of the edges. Lap this edge over the other edge so raw edges are level and the pattern matches. Pin in place (**1**).

Slip the needle along inside the fold of the upper layer, then take a small stitch through the under layer next to the fold. On small areas, use a small ladder stitch as the final stitching. On larger areas use the stitch as a tacking stitch before stitching a flat seam (**2**).

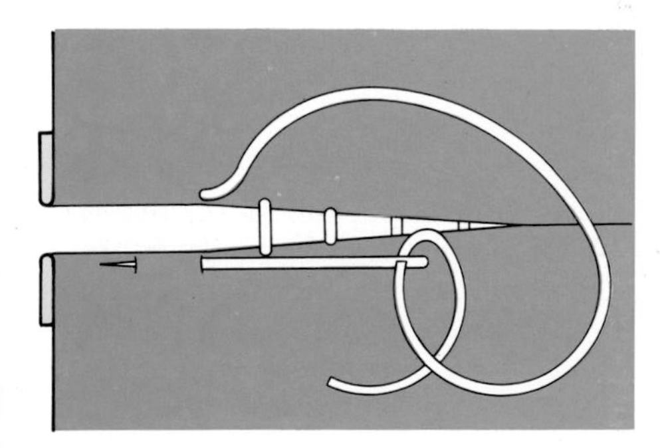

Slipstitch

This is used to hold folded edges of fabric together, such as on a mitred corner. First press the turnings to wrong side along edges. Slip the needle along inside the fold of one edge, take the needle across to the other edge and slip along inside that fold. Pull the thread to close the edges together.

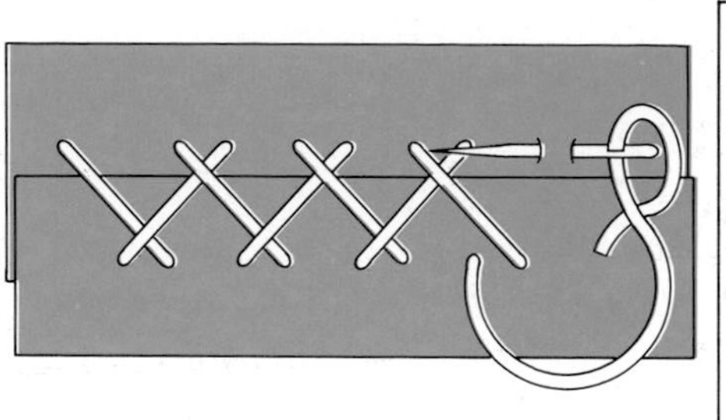

Herringbone stitch

A flat stitch used to stitch a raw hem edge, and also for joining two overlapping edges of wadding. Take a small stitch from right to left, then take the needle diagonally up to the right ready to begin the next stitch.

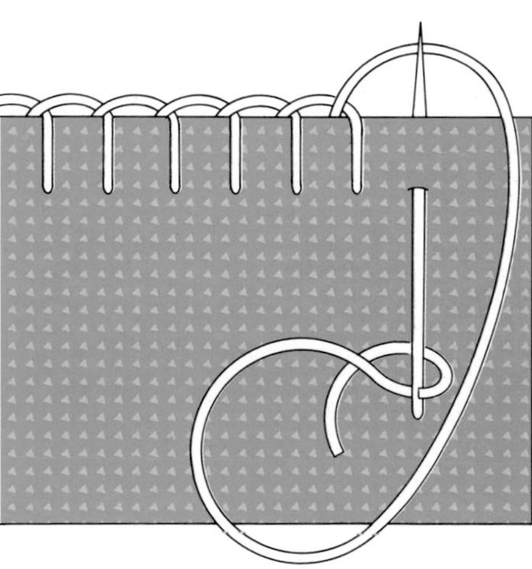

Blanket stitch

This can be worked over a raw edge to neaten it, or closely over strands of thread for a thread eye. Take a stitch through the fabric, loop the thread behind the needle before pulling through.

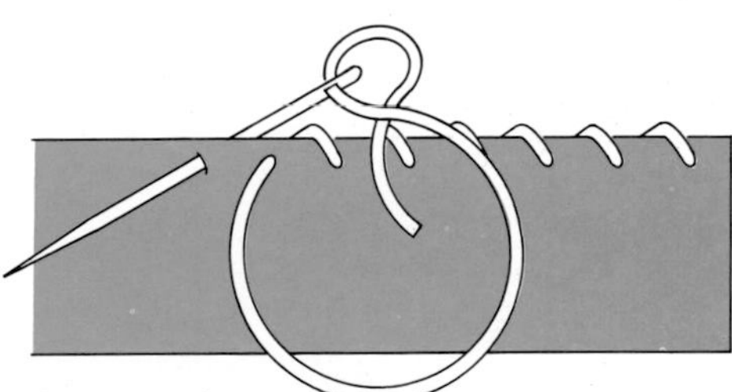

Overcasting

A hand-stitched alternative to machine zigzag stitch for neatening the raw edges of seams or hems. Work the stitches diagonally over the edge working from right to left. Avoid pulling the stitches too tightly as this will roll the edge of the fabric over into a lumpy ridge.

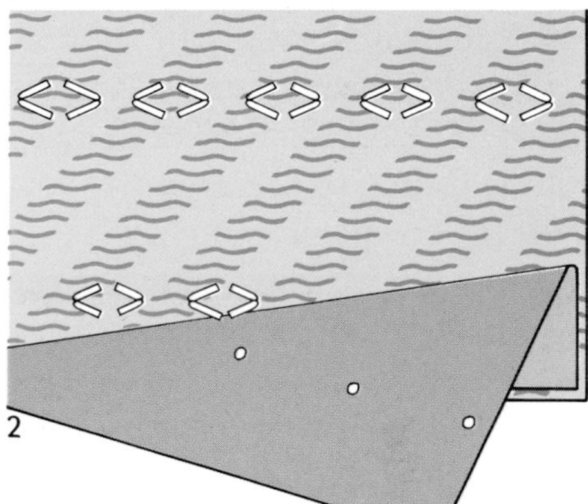

Tailor's tacks

These are used to transfer pattern markings from a paper pattern onto the fabric. Using double thread in a contrasting colour, take loose running stitches through both the pattern and fabric. For single markings make a single stitch through the marking (**1**).

Snip the centre of the stitches where they pass over the pattern. Gently lift the pattern away from the fabric. This will leave tufts of thread marking the line on the fabric (**2**).

· SEAMS & SEAM FINISHES ·

Seams are used to join pieces of fabric together and form the basic structure of any item. A flat seam is the most common type of seam used. As the raw edges of the seam are visible on the wrong side, flat seams are best used when the wrong side is hidden by lining or inside the item. An overlock seam is self-neatening with the raw edges hidden inside the finished seam. This is most successful on finer fabric and is particularly suitable for joining a gathered edge onto a flat edge.
A lapped seam is worked from the right side of the fabric which makes it easier to match the fabric pattern on difficult designs; two rows of stitching will show on the right side of the finished seam.

A flat fell seam is a sturdy seam which encloses the raw edges in the seam. The first row of stitching can be worked with the wrong sides of fabric facing, so there are two rows of stitching on the finished right side as shown; alternatively if the first row is stitched with the right sides of fabric facing, only one row of stitching will show on the finished right side. French seams are also strong seams which enclose all raw edges, no stitching shows on the right side.

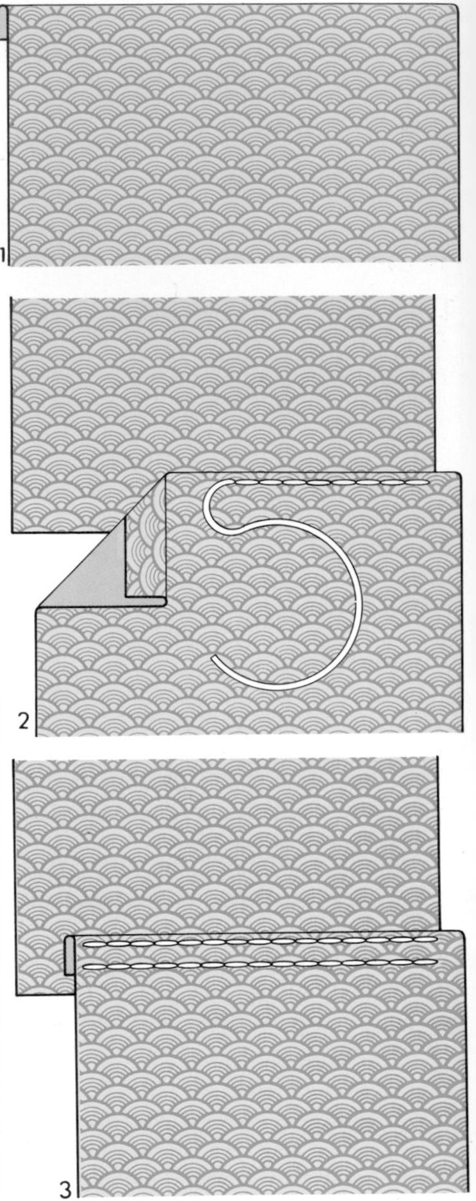

Overlock
Overlocking is a way of enclosing the raw edges of a seam, thus hiding any fraying ends. It works best on lightweight fabrics that do not fray too easily. Pin the two pieces of fabric together, right sides facing and raw edges matching. Stitch a flat seam and press. Trim the top seam allowance to 3mm (1). Turn the edge of the other seam allowance under 3mm and press (**2**). Turn it again, bringing the folded edge to the seamline, so that the trimmed edge of the top seam allowance is enclosed, and press again. Handstitch the folded seam allowance to the fabric, as close as possible to the first line of stitching (**3**).

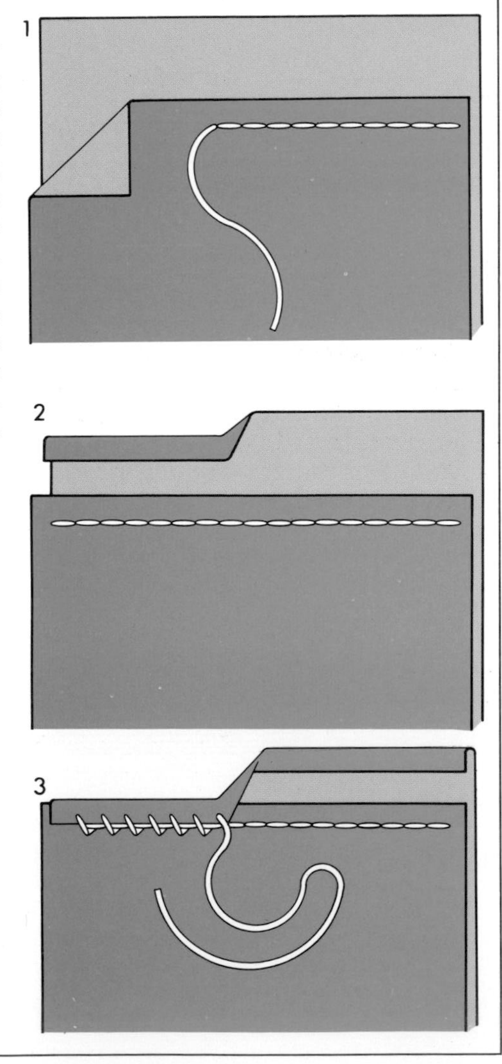

Lapped seam
This seam is very useful if you want to make sure that patterns on the fabric match exactly. It looks similar to the flat fell seam but it differs in that the first line of stitching is sewn from the right side of the fabric. First, turn under 5mm of the raw edge of the fabric and press it flat to make a neat fold (**1**).

With right sides facing upwards, pin and tack this folded edge to the other piece of fabric, matching any patterns. Stitch the seam from the right side (**2**). Press.

Stitch a second row of machine stitching 6mm away from the first working through all the thicknesses (**3**).

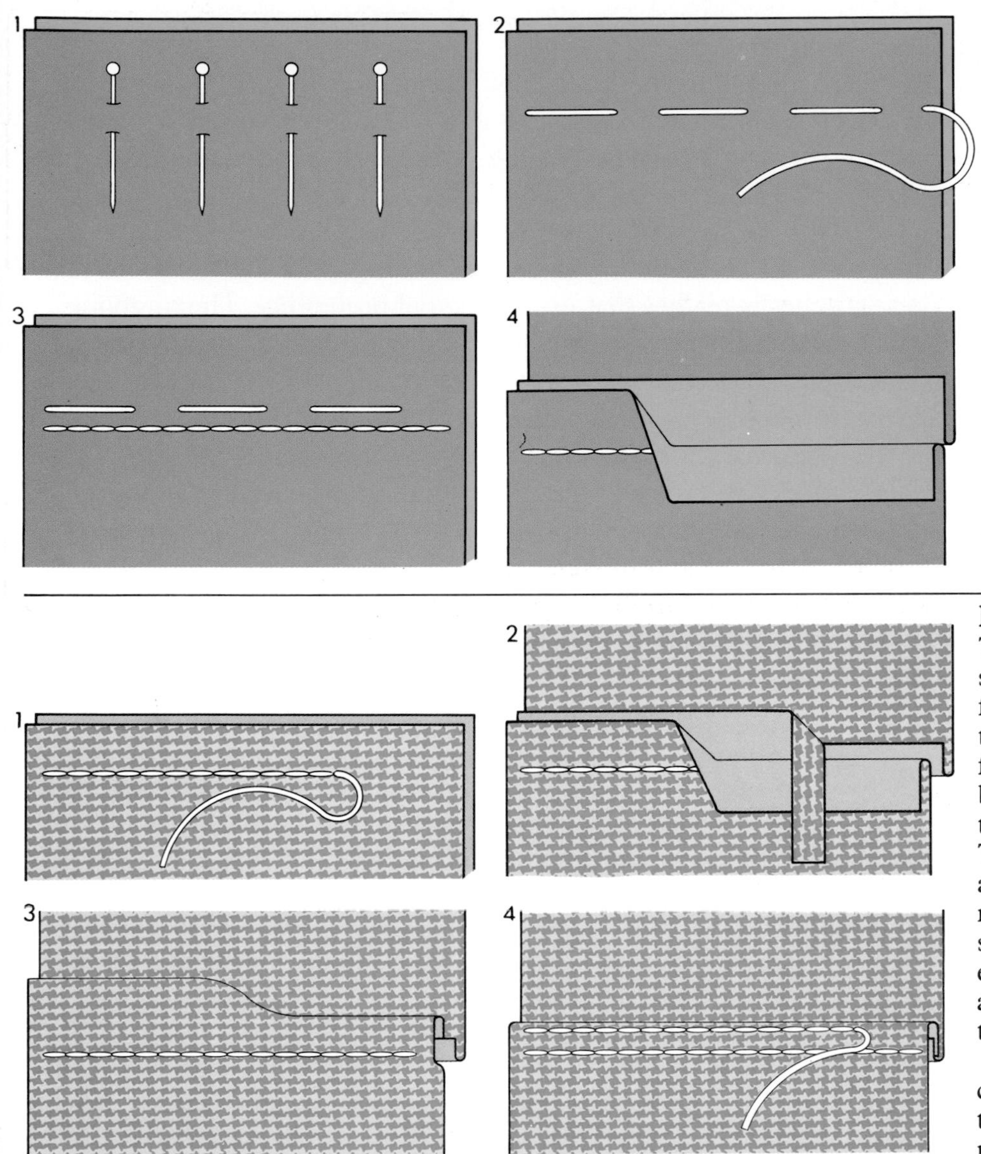

Flat seam

This is the seam most commonly used in home sewing, and is very simple to do. With right sides of the fabric together, and raw edges matching, pin the two layers together, placing pins at right angles to the raw edges down the line of the seam (**1**). Tack down the length of the seamline, 1.5cm from the edge, and remove the pins (**2**). Stich by the side of the tacking, not over it, making a few reverse stitches at the beginning and end of the seam to give a firm finish (**3**). Remove tacking, open the seam and press it flat (**4**). If the fabric edges are selvedges, clip every 10cm along the selvedge to prevent the fabric from puckering after cleaning.

Flat fell seam

This seam gives a flat finish but two rows of stitching will show on the right side of the fabric. With wrong sides of the fabric together, and raw edges matching, stitch a flat seam 1.5cm from the edges (**1**). Press both seam allowances to one side. Trim the under seam allowance to 3mm (**2**). Turn under 5mm of the upper seam allowance and press down over the trimmed seam allowance (**3**). Stitch the top seam allowance to the fabric, close to the edge of the fold, so that the trimmed seam allowance is enclosed in the fold (**4**). Press the seam flat.

Alternatively the first row of stitching can be worked with right side together so there is one row of stitching on finished right side.

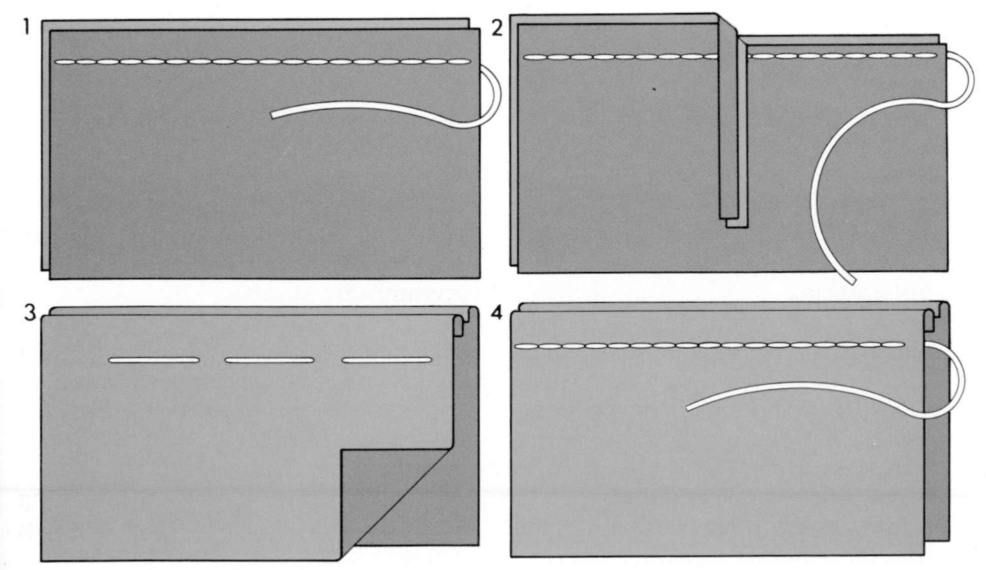

French seam

This seam gives a very neat finish with no stitching line showing on the right side of the fabric. With the wrong sides of the fabric together, and raw edges matching, stitch a flat seam 5mm from the fabric edge (**1**). Trim edges to 3mm (**2**) and press. Turn the fabric back on itself so that the right sides are facing and the seam is on the fold, and tack the two layers together (**3**). Stitch another seam 1cm down from the first seam, enclosing the raw edges (**4**). Remove tacking, press and turn the seam to the wrong side.

· HEMS & MITRING ·

Hems are used to finish the edge of fabric. The depth of the hem can vary between 5mm and 15cm and should relate to the size of the item, a narrow hem on a large item will give an oddly unfinished look, while a too deep hem on a small item will look very clumsy.

Hems can be stitched by hand or machine. Hand stitches include blind hem stitch, hemming and sliphemming, and the choice between these stitches is really a matter of personal preference. Herringbone stitch is worked over the raw edge of a single hem on lined curtains, and is especially useful on thick fabrics. Straight stitch machined hems are quick to make, especially on large areas. Machine blind hem is most suitable for thick pile fabric where the stitches do not show. Zigzag stitch is a strong hem used for the decorative effect of the stitch.

Mitring is a neat way to finish deep hems at corners. The method shown here is for hems of an equal depth, an alternative method for mitring hems of different depths is shown on page 36.

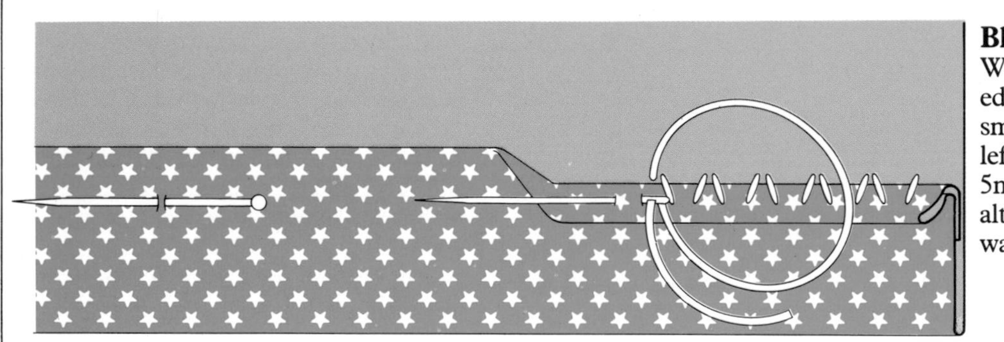

Blind hem stitch
Work from right to left. Fold back the hem edge and fasten the thread inside it. Sew a small stitch in the fabric about 5mm to the left. Then sew a small stitch in the hem, 5mm to the left again. Repeat the stitches, alternating between fabric and hem, all the way along.

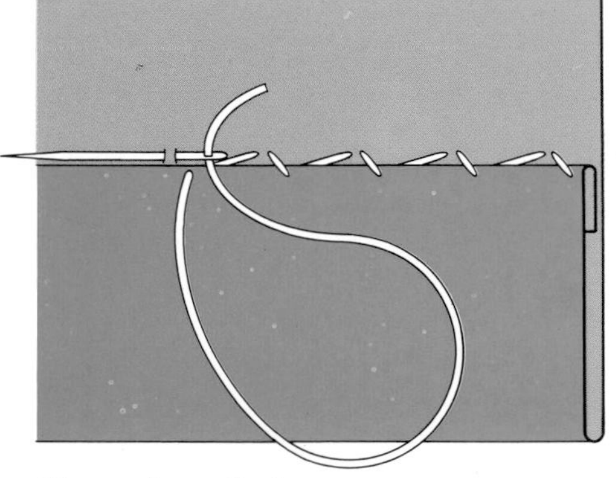

Hemming stitch
Work from right to left if right-handed, with the turned-under edge towards you. Make two stitches on top of each other on the folded fabric to secure the thread. Just above the folded edge pick up a couple of threads of flat fabric. Insert the needle slightly to the left into the two layers of fabric close to the fold and draw the thread through. Repeat stitch to complete hem.

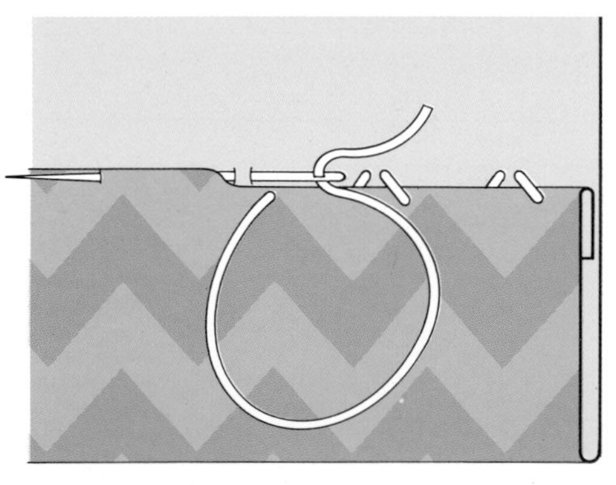

Sliphemming
Beginning at the right (if you are right-handed), make a couple of stitches in the folded fabric to secure the thread. Catch the flat fabric and then insert the needle inside the folded edge, sliding it along for about 5mm. Bring the needle out of the fold and catch a couple of threads from the flat fabric immediately opposite the point where the needle emerged.

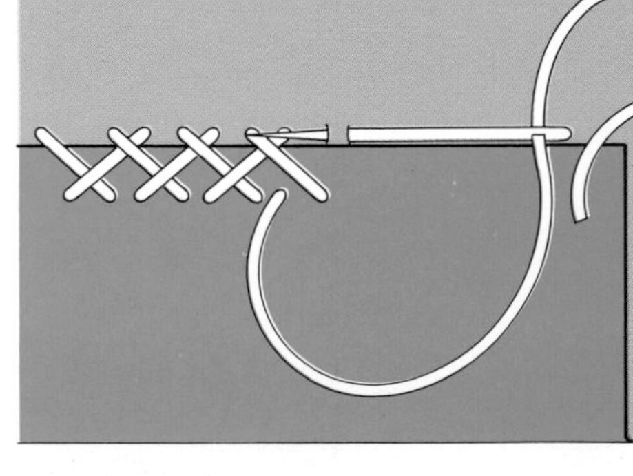

Herringbone stitch
Work from left to right if you are right-handed. Secure the thread in the folded fabric. Pick up a couple of threads from the flat fabric with the needle pointing from right to left. Pull the thread through. Position the needle further to the right, still pointing it to the left, and take a horizontal stitch through the folded fabric.

MACHINE STITCHES FOR HEMS

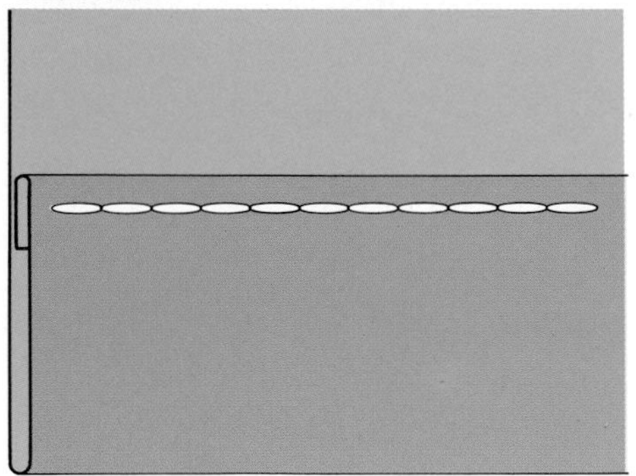

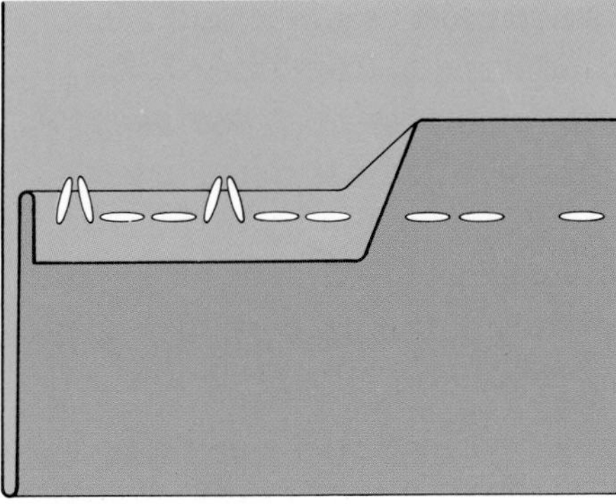

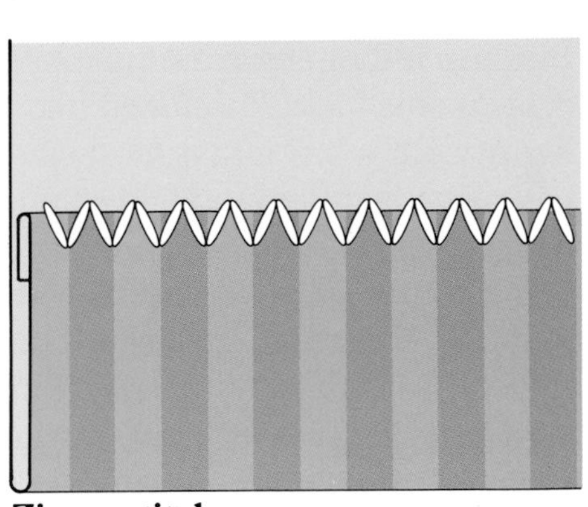

Straight stitch
The simplest way to fasten a hem is to use a machine straight stitch. Position the foot at the edge of the fold so that the needle enters the folded fabric 5mm away from the fold and stitch across the width of the hem. Reverse stitch at ends.

Blind hem stitch
A combination of straight stitch and zigzag stitch, blind hem stitch is best on thicker fabrics where the stitches do not show. The straight stitches are made above the fold and the zigzag stitch catches the folded edge to secure the hem.

Zigzag stitch
An extremely secure overcasting stitch, zigzag stitch can range from short and narrow to long and wide. Position the fabric so that the bulk of the zigzag is on the folded fabric and only the tops of the stitches form above the edge.

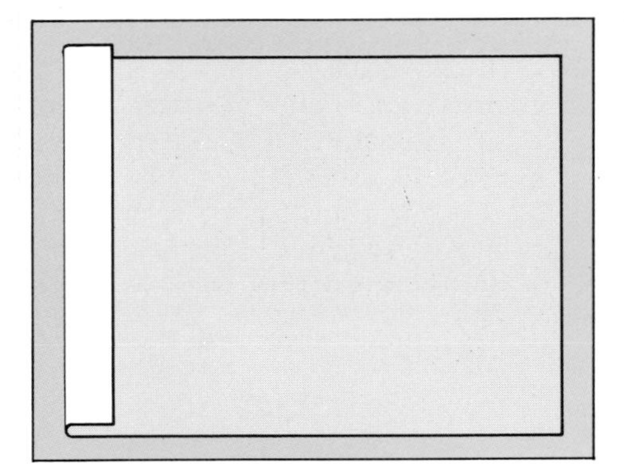

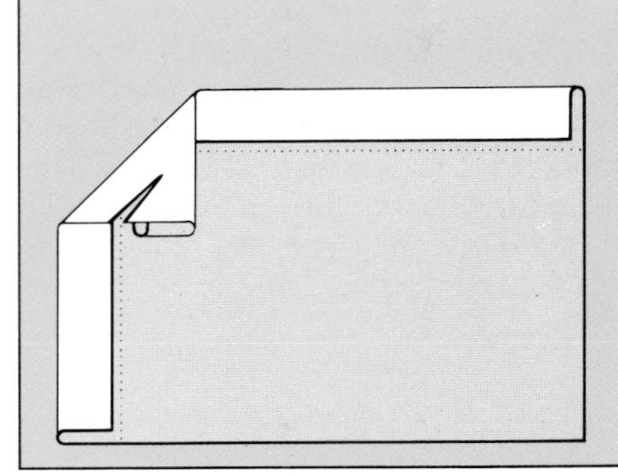

MITRING CORNERS

Mitring the corners of a piece of fabric that is being hemmed reduces bulk and results in a much neater corner. Turn under first fold of hem on one edge (**1**).

Turn under first fold of hem at the other edge (**2**). Press edges in place. Fold the material along the hemlines. Press and unfold the hems.

Press the corner over, so the diagonal fold passes exactly through the corner of hemline crease. Leaving a 5mm seam allowance, cut off the corner (**3**).

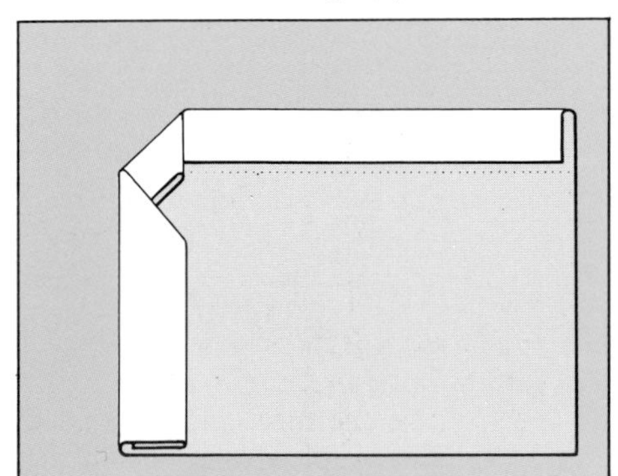

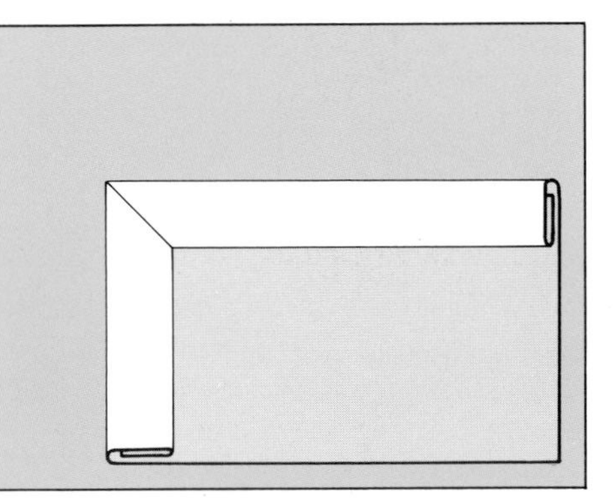

Turn in one hem along the hemline line crease, making sure the corner is folded very accurately (**4**). Press and pin in place.

Turn in the other hem along the hemline. Pin and stitch in place. slipstitch the diagonal seam to secure (**5**).

· BINDING & PIPING ·

Binding and piping are simple but effective finishes which add a professional look. Purchased bias binding is made from fairly lightweight fabric and is most suitable for edging smaller items such as tablemats, napkins and tablecloths. For larger items and heavier fabric, bias strips made from fabric of a similar weight to the item being bound will give a much better finish.

Piping is made by covering a purchased piping cord with bias strips, this is then stitched into a flat seam to give a smart tailored finish. The cord is available in different thicknesses for large and small items. Piping is most commonly used to outline the seaming around cushions and loose covers, but it will also form an attractive edging on duvet covers and pillowcases, and in the seaming of bedcovers.

Both binding and piping can be made from matching or contrasting fabric, and, as the strips are cut diagonally on the fabric, striped and checked fabric can be used for special effect.

Finding the bias

Bias binding is used to strengthen raw edges and to add a decorative finishing touch. Because it is cut on the bias, it has more give than binding cut on the straight grain. To find the bias of a piece of fabric, fold a straight raw edge in diagonally so it is parallel to the selvedge of the fabric. This fold line is the bias line.

Mark out 4cm strips parallel to the bias line (**1**) and cut them out. To join the strips, place two with right sides together and at right angles to each other.

The raw edges will be parallel and there will be two triangular corners. Pin and stitch the seam 5mm from the raw edges (**2**). Open the seam out flat and press. Trim the corners (**3**).

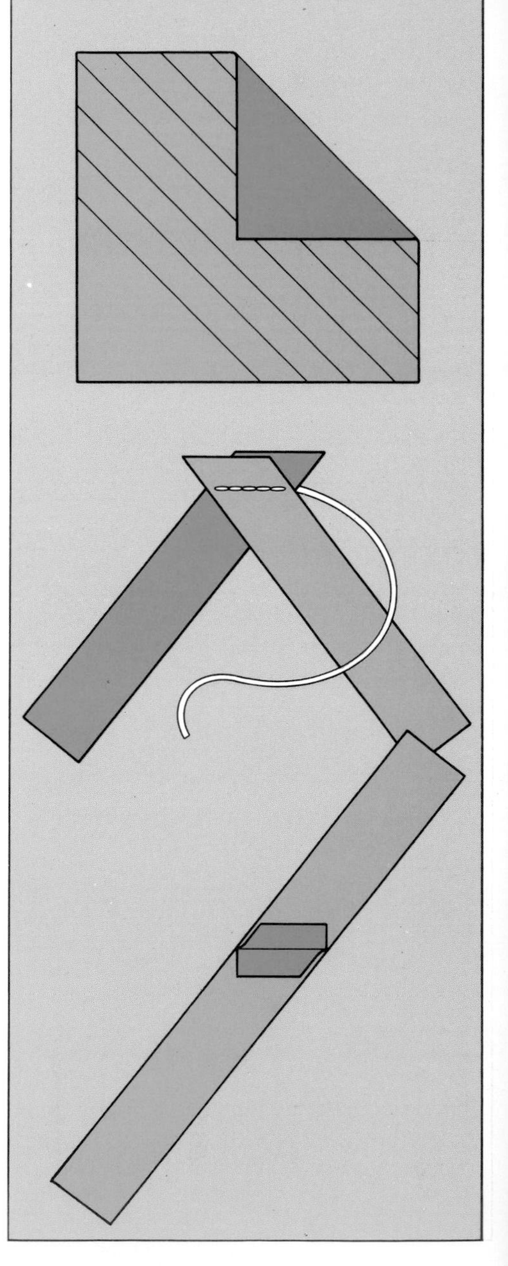

Applying binding with machine

Fold the bias binding, wrong side down, over the raw edge of the fabric to be bound and press. Tack in place and then machine stitch through the fabric and the two folds of binding, close to the edge of the binding. Remove tacking.

Binding by hand

Open one folded edge of the bias binding and match this edge to the raw edge of the fabric to be bound, right sides together. Pin and stitch them together down the fold line of the binding (**1**).

Refold the binding and turn it over to the wrong side of the fabric being bound, enclosing the raw edge of the fabric. Pin in place and sliphem the second folded edge of the binding to the fabric along the first line of stitching (**2**).

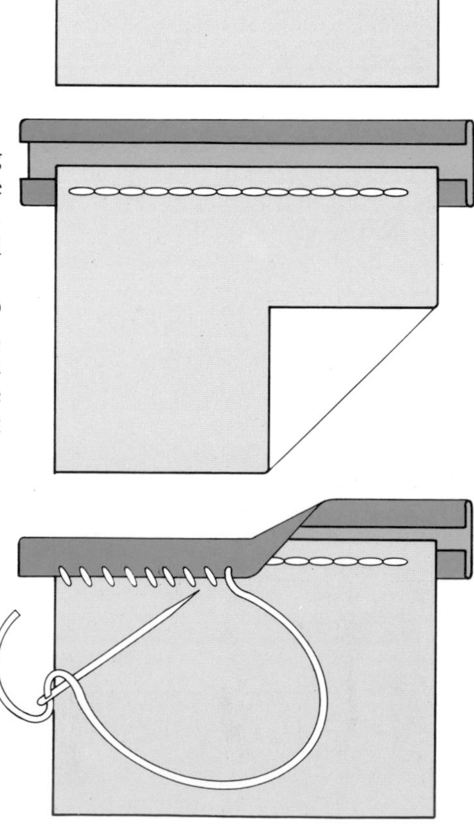

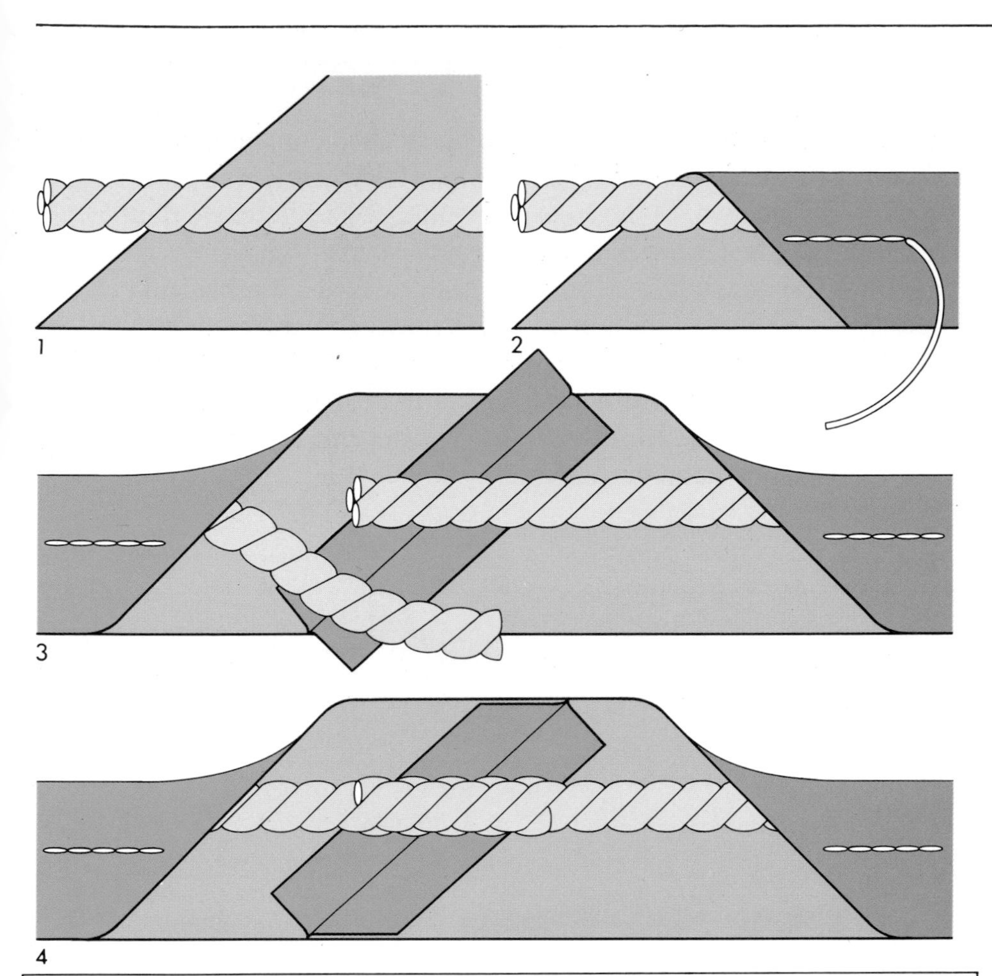

Covering piping cord

For a professional look, piping cord can be inserted in a seam. It is available in a range of thicknesses so you can decide how prominent you want it to be. Piping cord first has to be covered with bias binding; you will need enough binding to wrap round the cord and to allow 1.5cm on each edge for seam allowances. Press the bias binding strip flat, right side down, and place the piping cord in the middle (**1**). Wrap the binding round the cord, wrong sides facing, and tack the front and back wraps together, enclosing the cord. Using a zipper foot, stitch as close to the piping cord as possible. Remove the tacking (**2**). To join two pieces of cord, first join the bias binding strips with a flat seam along the grain (**3**). Trim the binding edges. Unravel the two ends of piping cord and trim the strands to different lengths. Then overlap the ends by 2.5cm. Intertwine the strands to make a smooth join (**4**). Wrap the binding round the piping cord as before and complete stitching the cord.

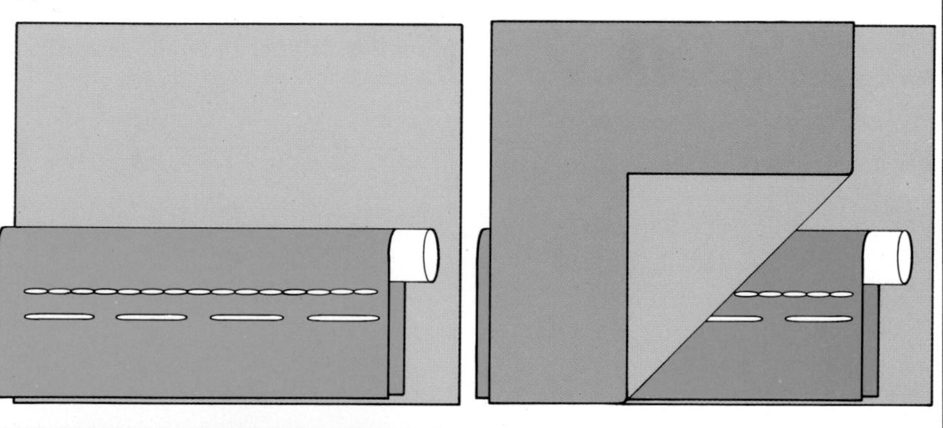

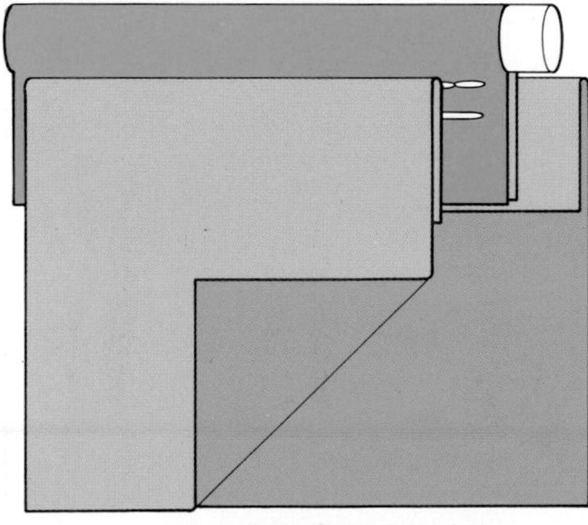

Inserting the piping

The piping cord is sewn into the seam as you stitch the main seamline. Place one piece of fabric wrong side down. Lay the piping cord on top so that the raw edges of the binding face outwards and match the raw edges of the fabric. Tack in place (**1**). Place the other piece of fabric right side down over the top, with raw edges matching. Using a zipper foot stitch the four layers together on the seamline (**2**). Remove tacking. When you turn the material right side out, the piping cord makes a decorative edging along the seam (**3**).

· FRILLS & GATHERS ·

Frills give an attractive finish to the edge of cushions, bedlinen and other soft furnishings. A single frill, made from one layer of fabric, has a narrow double hem at the edge and is more delicate than a double frill. A double frill is quick to make from a strip of fabric folded in half. The right side of the fabric shows on both sides of a double frill making it particularly suitable for fabrics with a noticeably different wrong side. Both types of frills can be pleated or gathered in to fit the edge. Pleats, which give a more tailored look, can be formed side by side or spaced apart. A gathered frill will give a softer finish, and the gathering can be worked by hand or machine.

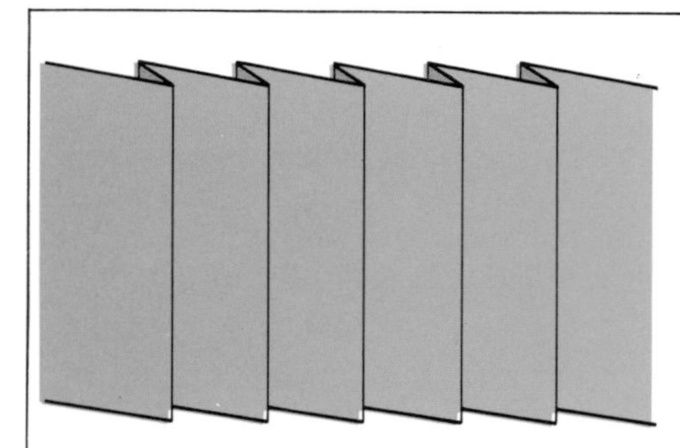

Knife pleats
Each pleat has one fold which is aligned with another line. All the pleats face in the same direction.

Box pleats
Each pleat has two folds which are turned away from each other. Back folds are facing and may meet on one line.

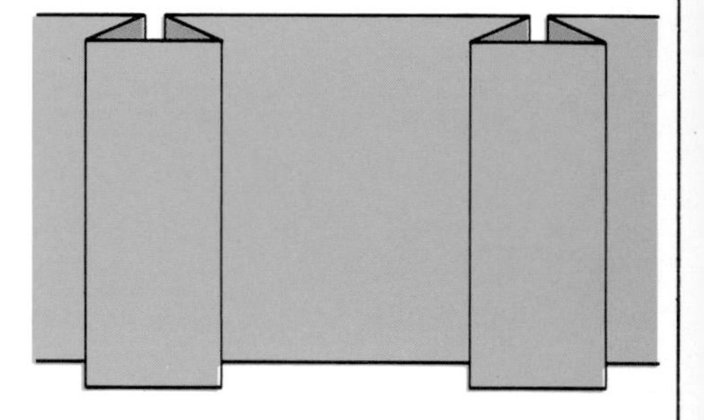

Inverted pleats
Each pleat has two folds which are turned towards each other and meet on one line. Back folds face away from each other.

Hand gathering
Using tiny backstitches, fasten the thread securely in the fabric. Sew a line of small running stitches along the gathering line of the fabric. At the end, gently pull the thread, spacing the gathers along the length of fabric until you achieve the required fullness.

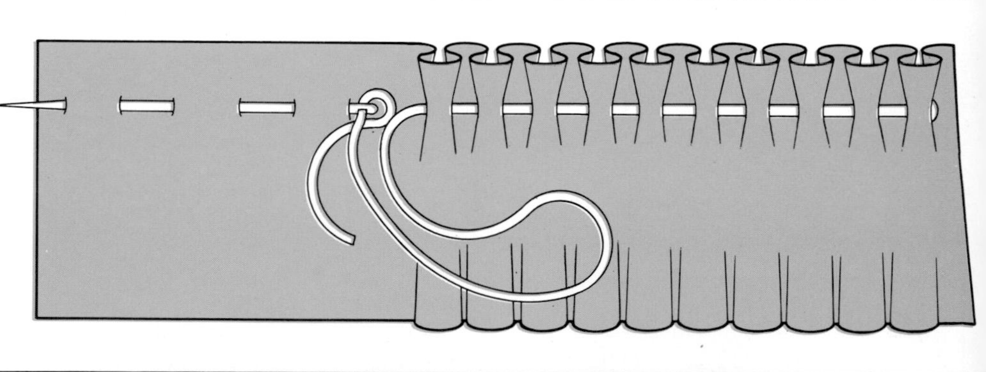

Machine gathering
This is the quickest method of gathering fabric. First, adjust the machine to the longest stitch and machine two rows of stitches along the fabric edge (**1**). Gently pull the top threads, spacing the gathers along the fabric until you achieve the required fullness (**2**).

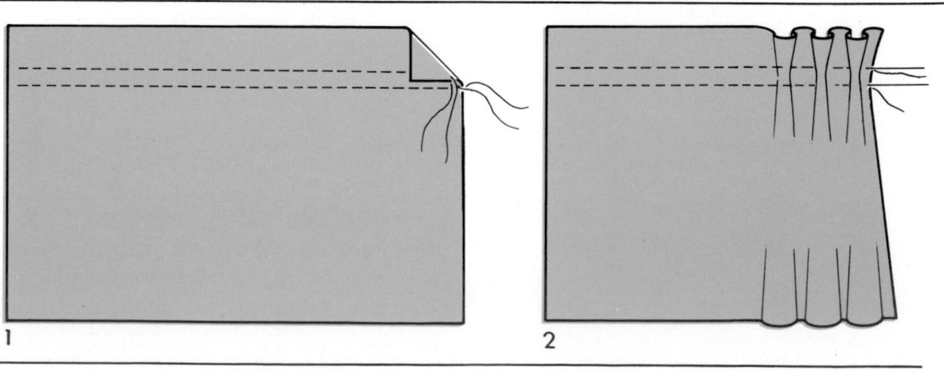

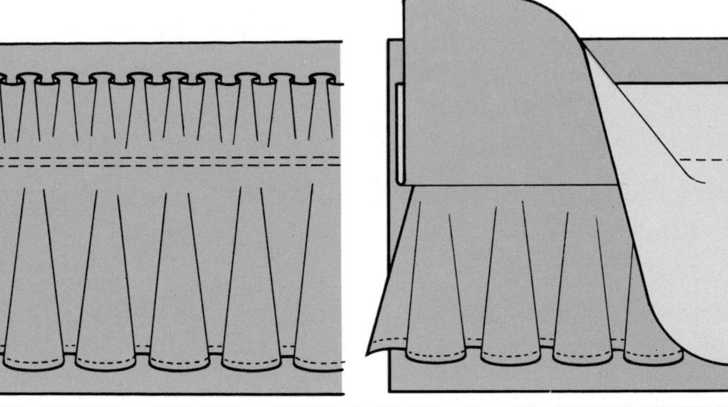

Frill applied to seam

With right sides facing upwards, pin the frill to one of the pieces of fabric to be joined in the seam, matching the seamlines. Adjust the fullness of the frill to make the gathers even and then tack in place. With right sides together, pin the second piece of fabric over the frill, matching the seamlines. Stitch the seam, and press.

Double frill

This is formed from a strip of fabric folded in half. To finish the frill end, fold in half with right sides facing, stitch across and turn right side out. For a joined frill, join the ends with a flat seam before folding the frill in half. Fold the frill in half lengthways and press. Gather and stitch the frill in the same way as a single frill.

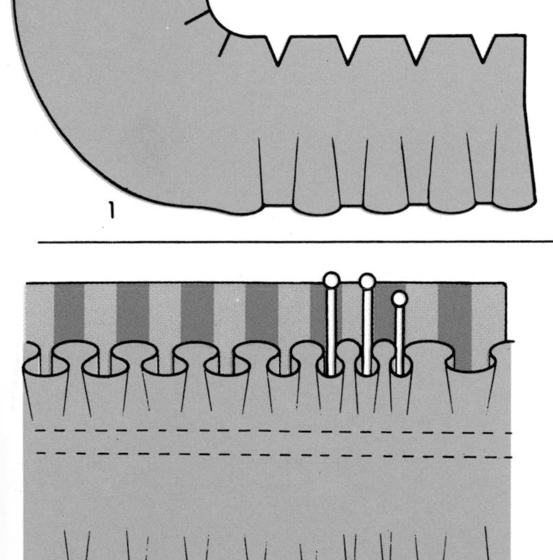

Circular frill

To make a circular frill, cut out a circle of fabric, and then cut out a smaller circle from its centre. Clip round the inner edge of the circle. Cut through from the outer edge to the inner edge and flatten the inner edge in a straight line, so producing fullness on the outer, longer edge (**1**). Staystitch (small machine stitch) the inner edge of the frill. With right sides facing, pin and tack the inner clipped edge of the frill to the fabric. Stitch along the seamline and then turn back the frill so the stitching is hidden (**2**).

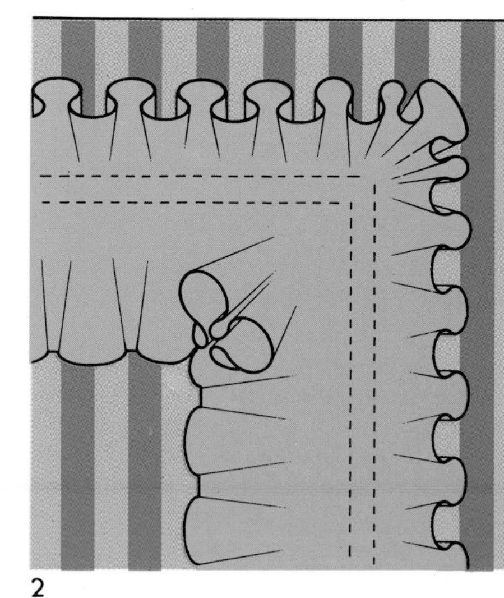

Turning a corner

With right sides together, pin the gathered frill along one edge of the fabric, finishing 1.5cm in from corner (**1**). Arrange extra fullness at the corner so the frill will fit around when the frill is turned right side out. Pin the rest of the frill along the edge of the fabric (**2**). When stitching, stitch to 1.5cm from edge of corner. Leave needle down and pivot work to continue along other edge.

· FASTENINGS ·

Fastenings are mainly used on items such as duvet and cushion covers which must be removed for laundering or cleaning. There are many types of fastening available and the choice is often a matter of personal preference. For duvet covers there are two main choices, a strip fastening or single fasteners. Strip fasteners include press stud tape, which comes with the press studs ready fastened to a tape; and touch-and-close tape, which is just pressed together to fasten. Single fasteners include sew-on press studs, circles of touch-and-close fastening and non-sew press studs which just clip through the fabric. For cushions where the opening needs to be firmly and neatly fastened a zip is the best choice.

Touch and close fastenings

These are available in the form of circular spots, rectangles and strips. One half of the fastening has fluffy loops and the other tiny hooks which adhere to the loops. The fastenings are available with an adhesive backing or to sew on.

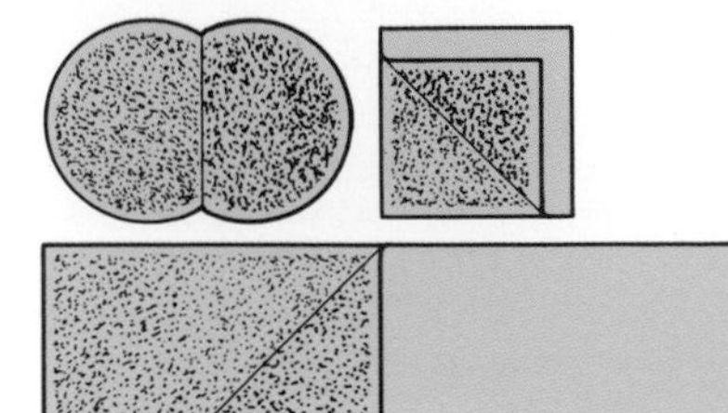

Press studs and poppers

Metal press studs come in a range of sizes and in a black or silver coloured finish. Small square white or clear plastic studs are also available, these are less sturdy than metal poppers but handy where a small flat fastening is needed. Poppers are non-sew press studs. Each half of the popper has a backing section which clips through the fabric to fasten the popper in place.

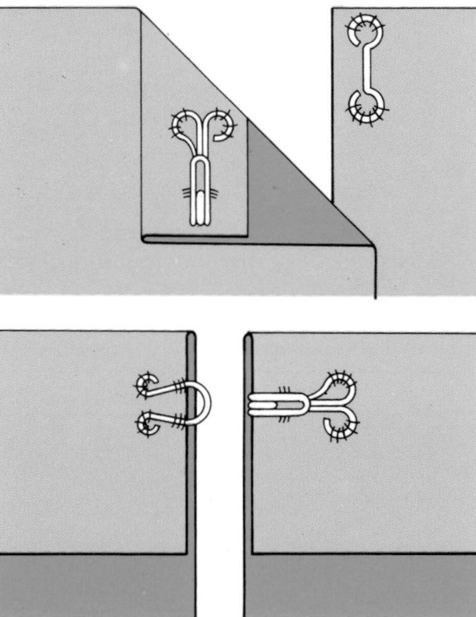

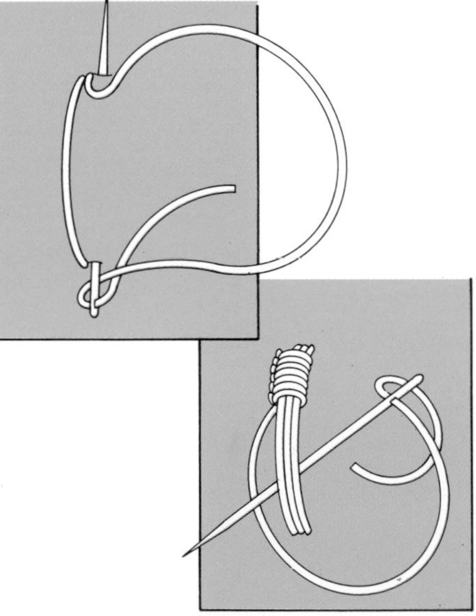

Fastening tapes

Touch-and-close tape and press stud tape are ideal for fastening a duvet cover opening. Separate the two halves of tape and stitch half to each edge of the opening along the long edges. Use a zipper foot on press stud tape to pass by the studs. The ends of tape are usually finished into the end of opening and stitched across.

Lapped and abutted hooks

For overlapping edges, sew the hook on the inside of the overlapping edge of the fabric and the bar on the outside underlapping edge. For abutting edges, sew both the hook and eye on the inside of the fabric. The eye should extend slightly over the edge.

Making a thread eye

A thread eye provides a decorative alternative to a metal eye, but is not as strong. Mark the two points where the eye should start and finish and sew a few long stitches from one point to the other, keeping them fairly loose. Secure the ends. Then sew closely spaced blanket stitches over the strands of thread to form the eye.

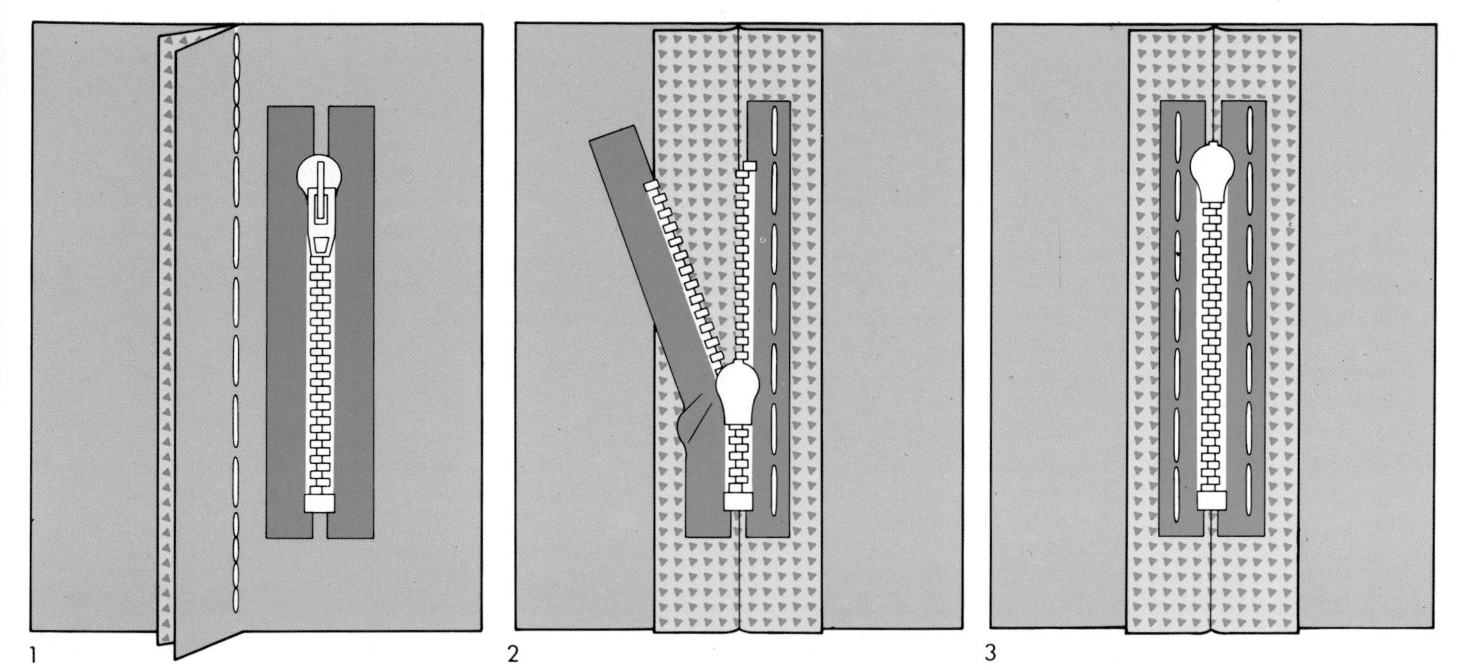

1

2

3

Inserting a zip

Measure and mark the length of the opening to the length of zip teeth plus 5mm. Stitch a flat seam in the fabric, leaving a gap at the centre for the zip. Tack the opening in the seam so that the fabric does not slip. (**1**).

Press the seam open. With the zip open, centre the zip face down over the seam. Pin and tack one side of the tape in place through both layers of fabric positioning the lines of stitching 3mm from the teeth of the zip (**2**).

Close the zip and keep the tab pulled up. Pin and tack the other side of the zip tape 3mm from the teeth of the zip (**3**). Check that the zip is positioned correctly and that there are no gaps in the seam.

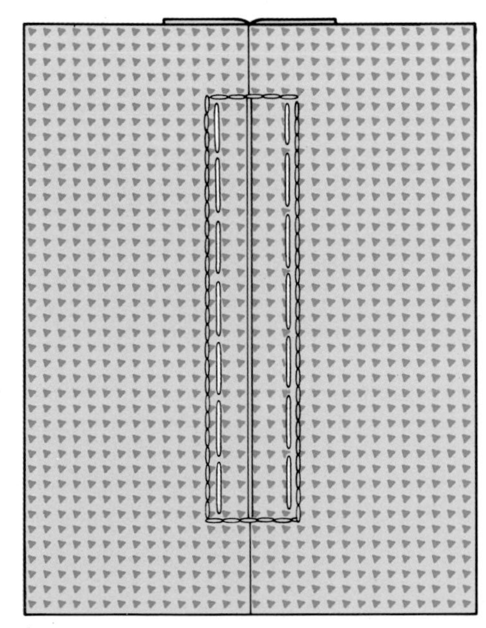

4

Turn the fabric right side up and, using the zip foot attachment of the machine, topstitch through all the layers of fabric, seam allowance and tape. Stitch just outside tacking and across ends as close as possible to the ends of the zip (**4**). Remove the tacking.

1

Inserting a zip offset

A zip is inserted offset so that it is more concealed from view. Leave an opening as described in step 1. Position the zip over the seam opening so that the teeth of the zip are in the centre of the right seam allowance. Pin and tack one side of the tape in position 3mm from the teeth of the zip (**1**). Close the zip and tack the other side of the tape through the other seam allowance near the opening. Turn the fabric right side up and, using the zip foot attachment, topstitch through all layers of material, seam allowance and tape. Stitch as close as possible to the ends of the zip (**2**). Remove the tacking.

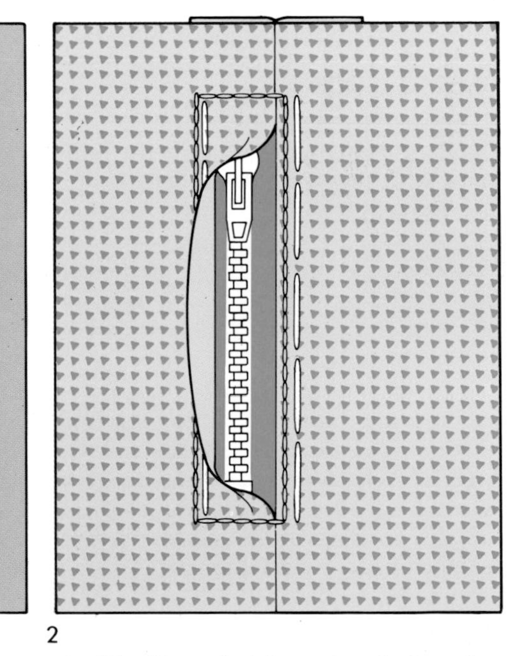

2

· GLOSSARY ·

Abstract designs are those in which the pattern does not represent specific shapes or objects.

Acorns are the pullers which are threaded onto the end of the cord by which shades are operated.

Appliqué is a form of decorative work where cut-out pieces of fabric are stitched onto a background fabric.

Ball point needles and pins have special rounded points designed for working with synthetic jerseys. They will pierce this type of fabric more easily than ordinary needles and will help prevent skipped machine stitches.

Basting is a long stitch used to hold fabric in place prior to the final stitching. Another name for tacking.

Battens are lengths of wood by which the top edges of Roman shades are fixed to the wall or window.

Bias strips are lengths of fabric cut diagonally across the warp and weft threads of the fabric. They are used to bind edges and cover piping cord.

Brackets are supports, forming a right angle, which hold up the underside of a shelf or cornice board.

Buckram is a strong, coarse cotton or linen cloth, impregnated with gum or other stiffening agents, which is used to stiffen fabric cornices.

Casings are fabric channels through which wire, tape or elastic can be threaded. When the casing is at the edge of an item it is made in the same way as a hem but with openings at the ends or a gap in the stitching to thread through.

Colorways are the color or combination of colors used in a fabric. Most fabrics have the same design produced in a number of different colorways.

Cornices are fitted across the top of windows to cover the top edge of curtains. They can be made from wood or stiffened fabric mounted onto a cornice board.

Cornice stiffening is used to stiffen fabric cornices. The various types include buckram, non-woven cornice stiffening and a special type with an adhesive backing.

Counted threadwork is a general term for any of the various types of embroidery where the stitches are worked over a counted number of threads, such as cross stitch, or drawn threadwork.

Curtain poles are decorative fitments for suspending curtains. The curtains are suspended below the pole so it is visible when the curtains are closed.

Curtain track is the plastic or metal bar from which curtains are suspended by means of hooks and sliders. The track is usually hidden by the curtain heading when the curtains are closed.

Curtain wire is a tightly wound coil of wire covered in plastic which is threaded through the top casing of net curtains. The wire is pliable and will fit around curved shapes.

Cutwork is a decorative technique in which a motif or pattern is outlined in close blanket stitch and the fabric is then cut out in various sections of the design.

Drawn threadwork is a type of counted thread embroidery in which a thread, or threads, are drawn from the fabric and the spaces left are then filled or edged with different stitches.

Dress fabrics are those produced for the purpose of making clothing. Many are less durable than furnishing fabrics and are not fade-resistant.

Dressing is a substance applied to a fabric to improve its feel or appearance. When used to enhance fabric of an inferior quality, the dressing may rub off or be removed in laundering.

Dressmaker's carbon is special carbon paper made for marking fabric. When placed between a paper pattern and fabric, lines or designs can be marked through onto the fabric beneath.

Edgings are decorative trims which are applied to the edge of an item. They may be made from fabric such as a frill, or purchased such as lace or eyelet. Edgings have one finished edge and one raw edge by which it is attached to the item.

Even-weave fabric has warp and weft threads that are identical in thickness and provide the same number of threads over a given area, enabling stitches to be worked by counting the threads.

Facings are used to finish edges in places where hems are unsuitable, such as a scalloped edge. The facing is made from a separate piece of fabric, cut to the same shape as the edge to be finished.

Figurative designs are those which include life-like shapes within the pattern. The figures may represent birds, trees, flowers or scenery.

Figured weaves are those which have figurative designs woven into the fabric. The different areas of the design may be woven in different colors or with a contrasting texture.

Geometric designs and prints are repeated patterns of evenly spaced and shaped squares, triangles, diamonds or other regularly shaped motifs. The pattern may be printed or woven in.

Headings are the various types of finishes used at the top edge of curtains or shades. The heading may be finished with a casing, facing or heading tape.

Heading tapes are used to draw in the fullness at the top edge of curtains and shades. The fullness may be arranged in pencil pleats, cartridge pleats, triple pinch pleats or gathers depending upon the type of tape chosen.

Hems are used to finish the raw edge of the fabric to prevent it fraying. They are made by folding over the raw edge of the fabric and stitching on the wrong side of the fabric. For a single hem the raw edge is folded over once, and for a double hem the edge is folded over twice so the raw edge is completely hidden.

Interlining is a fabric which is placed

between the main fabric and the lining to strengthen or stiffen the fabric, or to give it extra body. On fabric cornices and tie-backs the interlining is placed between the fabric and the buckram stiffening to mask the coarse weave of the buckram and give a softer more pleasing feel to the fabric.

Lathes are thin strips of wood which are inserted into the casings at the lower edges of Roman shades to keep the fabric stiff and straight.

Lining is a backing fabric stitched to the wrong side of the main fabric to hide the raw edges, prevent fraying, and add extra body. Furnishing linings are weft-faced, piece-dyed, cotton sateen fabric.

Locked-in linings are a method of lining curtains where the lining fabric is stitched to the wrong side of the curtain fabric at intervals across the width of the curtain. This method, involving much hand stitching, is used on expensive and heavy-weight fabric.

Man-made fabrics are formed from fibers which are made by man. These include synthetic fabrics which are made by chemical processes, and fabrics made from regenerated fibers which use natural substances to make the fibers.

Mercerized fabric or threads have been treated under tension with caustic soda which causes the fibers to swell. This method of treating cotton and other cellulose fibers gives the fabric, or thread, extra luster and a soft handle.

Miniprints are small, all-over, printed fabric designs. When seen close to the individual pattern motifs are clear and when seen from a distance they merge into an overall effect.

Miters are a way of finishing the corners of hems to give a very neat finish.

Monochrome refers to designs or room color schemes which contain shades of one color only.

Motifs are small complete designs, or a section of a larger fabric design which is repeated at intervals across the width or down the length of the fabric.

Natural fabrics are made from fibers derived from natural sources, which fall into two main groups: vegetable fibers derived from plants and trees, and animal fibers from the hair or fleece of animals.

Patchwork is a decorative technique which joins together small pieces of fabric to make a larger piece of fabric. The shape of the fabric pieces and the combination of colors and prints form the design of the larger fabric.

Pattern repeats are the places where exactly the same motif is repeated again in the same position further down the fabric. The length of a pattern repeat is the distance between these places.

Pinking is a method of preventing fabric from fraying. The raw edge is trimmed with pinking shears which are specially shaped to cut a zigzag edge.

Piping is a cord with a projecting flat strip of fabric which is inserted in a seam leaving the cord part exposed at the seam edge. It can be purchased ready made, or formed by covering piping cord with bias strips of fabric.

Quilting is the process by which a layer of batting is sandwiched between two layers of fabric. All three layers are stitched together in a pattern of straight lines, squares or diamonds to form a quilted fabric.

Returns are the side edges of a cornice between the front edge of the cornice and the window or wall.

Scallops are a series of curves along the edge of the item. A edge cut into scallops is called a scalloped edge.

Screw eyes are round metal eyes attached on a screw. They can be used alone or to fasten into matching screw hooks.

Seams are a basic process by which two pieces of fabric are stitched together. There are various methods of making seams suitable for different items.

Self fabric is the same fabric that has been used for the main part of the item.

Selvages are the finished-off edges of fabric which run down both sides of a length of fabric.

Skirts are the pleated or gathered strips of fabric which may be fitted around the lower edge of a loose chair cover. The term also refers to the side parts of a fitted bedspread which hang between the top of the bed and the floor.

Straight grain of fabric is along the warp threads which are parallel to the selvages.

Stretch stitch is a machine stitch, which will automatically stitch two straight stitches forwards then one backwards in a continuous line so each stitch is stitched twice making a very strong seam.

Swing needle machines have the facility to stitch side to side as well as forwards and backwards. They are also known as zigzag machines.

Synthetic fabrics are man-made entirely from chemicals.

Tailor's chalk is a triangular-shaped block of fabric-marking chalk wich will rub off when used lightly. It is also available in pencil form.

Tube-lined curtains are made by a method in which the lining is stitched to the fabric down both side edges forming a tube open at top and bottom. The tube is then turned right side out before finishing the top and bottom edges.

Tuck-ins are flaps of excess fabric formed around the seat of a loose chair cover. They tuck into the crevices of the chair to allow the fabric some movement.

Twin-needles are two machine needles joined together at the top. The two needles stitch simultaneously side by side using two different top threads both of which link into the same bobbin thread.

Warp threads are those which run lengthways, parallel to the selvages, in woven fabric.

Weft threads are those which weave under and over the warp threads and run across the fabric between the selvages.

· INDEX ·

Page numbers in bold refer to captions & illustrations

· CREDITS ·

Dorling Kindersley would like to thank the following for their help in the production of this book. Stylist – Sue Duffy; hand model – Fiona Chilcott; project assistant – Gavin Fry; makers – Beryl Miller, Imogen Forkner, Liz Mundle, Fiona Chilcott and Enid Watton; curtain makers – Rufflette; paste-up – Steve Gardner and John Simmonds.
Carpets – Tintawn; furniture – Wesley Barrell, Bevan Funnell and Estia; cane furniture and cutlery – Candlelight; wallpaper and bed linen – Coloroll; wallpaper – Next, Laura Ashley and Sanderson; fabrics – Warners, Sanderson and Liberty; hand-printed fabrics – Rushton Aust and Jon Lys Turner; bedside table and vases – The Futon Shop; kimonos and Japanese sandals – Neal Street East; duvet – Slumberdown; curtain track and poles – Swish; lamps, vases and accessories – The Reject Shop; sewing machines and overlocker – Toyota; haberdashery – Coats.

Photographic credits
All photographs specially commissioned for this book by Steve Tanner, with the exception of pages 2/3, 12/13, 16/17, 56, 112, 128, 146, 152/3, 154/5, 156/7 and 158/9 by Mark French; pages 45, bottom left on 98, 99 and 111 from Elizabeth Whiting & Associates; and pages 130 and 144/5 from Wesley Barrell
Jacket photograph – wallpapers and fabrics from the Sanderson Celebration collection.

Filmsetting
Text Filmsetters Ltd

Lithographic reproduction
Universal Colour Scanning Ltd